Writing Ourselves Whole

Using the Power of Your Own Creativity
to Recover and Heal from Sexual Trauma

Jen Cross

Published by Mango Publishing Group, a division of Mango Media Inc.

Cover Design: Laura Mejía

Layout & Design: Morgane Leoni

For permission requests, please contact the publisher at:

Mango Publishing Group

2850 Douglas Road, 3rd Floor

Coral Gables, FL 33134 USA

info@mango.bz

For special orders, quantity sales, course adoptions and corporate sales, please email the publisher at sales@mango.bz. For trade and wholesale sales, please contact Ingram Publisher Services at customer.service@ingramcontent.com or +1.800.509.4887.

WRITING OURSELVES WHOLE: Using the Power of Your Own Creativity to Recover and Heal from Sexual Trauma

Library of Congress Cataloging-in-Publication number: 2017911416

ISBN: (paperback) 978-1-63353-619-7 , (ebook) 978-1-63353-620-3

BISAC SEL001000 SELF-HELP / Abuse / Self-Esteem

Printed in the United States of America

*For all the survivor-writers
who've risked uncapping their pens
and pouring onto the page
the stories that were never meant to be told.*

*You broke that isolation open,
and created change in the world*

*And for Sarah,
who is my heart*

Praise

Writing Ourselves Whole is rich, intelligent, passionate, intimate, honest and encouraging. Jen Cross draws from her personal experience, her many years of facilitating writing groups with survivors of sexual abuse, and the wisdom of a variety of teachers and writers, to provide guidance for writing—and for life—that's both sensible and inspiring. This book is a treasure trove!
- Ellen Bass, poet and co-author of the ground-breaking The Courage to Heal

Writing Ourselves Whole is a raw, powerful, necessary, wise and practiced guidebook to the revolutionary practice of finding the words, language and voice to transform suffering. It is chock full of insights, exercises, experience and the kind of fierce love and teaching that transforms pain into power. Jen Cross is a brave and brilliant transmitter of the deepest healing and healing practices. To anyone who has experienced abuse, violation and trauma, this book is a way out of the darkness.
— Eve Ensler, playwright, performer, and activist, author of the Vagina Monologues, founder of the One Billion Rising campaign

This is the most essential book on writing practice I know.
— from the Foreword by Pat Schneider, poet, author, and librettist, founder of the Amherst Writers & Artists writing workshop method

If only my mother had picked up a pen and trusted herself to let the maelstrom of her inner emotions out. If only she could time-travel and step into Jen's living room, begin the work of letting her secret self be articulated.
— from the Afterword by Carol Queen, author, sexologist, and activist, founder of the Center for Sex and Culture

Writing Ourselves Whole is a profound book of lessons. It teaches the power of taking up space with the most singular of stories (your own), and the power of bearing witness collectively. Jen Cross offers a pathway to find your own truth in writing, and unites us in the transformative power of storytelling.
— Amy Scholder

Contents

foreword

writing ourselves whole
Pat Schneider

This is the most essential book on writing practice I know. It goes, at great depth and length, into territory that other books, including my own, have treated as important but not as fully-developed methodologies. Those of us who have written about writing, and have included writing as a healing practice, have been waiting for this book. Jen Cross is the perfect author to have created it. Although the central focus here grows out of her own profound experience of sexual abuse, there is little in her content that does not apply to other kinds of trauma. She expands upon the definition of trauma in the *Diagnostic and Statistical Manual of Mental Disorders* ("exposure to actual or threatened death, serious injury or sexual violence.") She writes: *"Trauma is a site of shock in the body and/or psyche. It's a rupture, a bifurcation, a disassembly. Trauma marks the moment when what was ended, and something new emerged."* Then she asks, *"But what was the moment of trauma?"*

This book is about the search for and the uncovering of, that moment: its actuality; its lingering images; its effects in the life of the person who experienced it; and a proven healing methodology: writing. Every writing teacher, writing coach, writing workshop or group leader—and every person with a history of any kind of trauma needs this book. The teachers and guides need it because in every group, class or workshop they lead there will be trauma survivors. Survivors need it because it is a methodology that can be used, as Jen makes clear, alone or in tandem with therapy, counseling, and/or medical interventions.

She suggests that almost everyone has suffered some trauma. *We may take trauma into our bodies and lives through our parents' physical violence ... It may be an assault by a stranger, someone who took us by surprise on the street or in our home ... It may be living under racism, and/or other forms of oppression. It may be living or fighting in a warzone.*

I have had in my workshops, and now in my deeply personal friendship, a man who was a survivor of trauma during his youthful years as a medic in the Vietnam war. Our first contact was when he called me to ask if he could join my writing workshop. The leader of the workshop he had been attending asked him not to come any more, because the other members of the workshop "could not take" what he was writing about.

That silencing, and that silence, is at the heart of Jen Cross' book. She brilliantly and explicitly makes clear the mechanisms of silencing at work in sexual predation, as the predator threatens his or her prey in order to protect the predator. But she never forgets the silencing that goes on in relation to other kinds of trauma – the reluctance to *hear* the almost unbearable truths of human cruelty, human suffering.

Yet deeper even than that silencing is the silence of the self, the inability to remember, the unwillingness to revisit old trauma, the fear of what might happen to self or to others if voice was give to old wounds, old pain. Writing alone and/ or in a supportive group of peers, Jen makes clear, can be a safe way to open images that had been locked in inner and/or outer silence.

She gives careful attention to the fears of writing that plague most people who try to put pencil to paper, fears that inhibit and often fully prevent artistic creation. In her sections of journaling for her own healing, and in her suggestions, prompts, and helps for her readers, she stresses the crucial importance of what Peter Elbow termed "free writing." *To write is to enter the mess, is to spill out all your syllables, is to devil the precious eggs everyone else treads so carefully upon. Writing opens the wound, lets in oxygen and releases pus, helps me breathe again, I mean, breathe with gills & webbed toes, breathe against the tide that's coming in, breathe through the mountains of fear I live within. . . . This is what writing does.*

Writing Ourselves Whole is a book of many treasures: that lyrical beauty of language; a practical, measured trove of specific helps both for an individual seeker and for a person wanting to create a supportive group for trauma survivors like the ones Jen so clearly describes; and somewhat unexpectedly, pages of what Jen calls "delicious body stories"—accounts of workshops dedicated to erotic writing. Through all of this quietly, rather subtly, Jen's own story emerges from the beginnings of the abuse she suffered until the dramatic end of it and through her own recovery of self through her writing practice. Sprinkled throughout and condensed near the book's end are writing prompts and suggestions for confronting, understanding, and surviving the various stages of recovery.

I deliberately stress the word "survive" in relation to the stages of recovery. For me, personally, the greatest "Ah-HA!" of the book came in the section where Jen, walking on a beach alone, deals with the possibility that she, herself, is *not broken,* as she has defined herself throughout her healing practice. "*Not* broken or unbroken: *rather, intact and imperfect. Wounded, sore, struggling, scared, funny, hopeful.*" There, at that point in the reading of her book manuscript, I felt myself thinking, *I need to write. I need to write how it might feel if I imagine myself* not broken *where I was hurt, where I have no memory, but lingering effect of something bad happening. I need to write.* I would be surprised to learn that anyone could read though this book and not be stopped, surprised, and finding him or herself thinking: *I need to write.*

Nowhere does Jen imply or state that recovery through writing will be easy. But the essential initial act of courage, she makes very clear, is to break silence. And the first effective step toward recovery may in fact be breaking one's own inner silence, privately by writing, or openly by writing and reading aloud in a supportive group.

No writer before Jen Cross, I believe, has made that fact so irrefutably clear. And no writer before her has translated their own deep experience of trauma and recovery more passionately, more beautifully, more richly with quotations from other writers, medical professionals, philosophers, and poets.

Writing Ourselves Whole is cause for celebration. Its time has come. It will be an invaluable training and tool for both professionals dealing with trauma survivors, and for survivors looking for a private and/or beginning revelation of their own stories.

Amherst, MA
May 2017

introduction

how to restory

To write is to enter the mess, is to spill out all your syllables, is to devil the precious eggs everyone else treads so carefully upon. Writing opens the wound, lets in oxygen and releases pus, helps me breathe again, I mean, breathe with gills & webbed toes, breathe against the tide that's coming in, breathe through the mountains of fear I live within. To write is to enter the fuse, electricity on my lips, close the circuits, let sparks fly—to write is to see what I forgot I was thinking, is to be unstable, grammatically incorrect, metaphorically questionable. To write is to pass the words forward, to dance around old truth, to hunger with pen and ink, to kill him over and over, that he who is only saved by the unmentionings, the unsaying, the not speaking. To write is to tell about his mustached grin, the taste of his tongue, his grey belly—when I set these truths to paper, I make his monstrosity visible, familiar: one more regular old child molester. I lift up the rock he turned himself into when he lay upon me and reveal the white grasses, tiny bugs, balled-up roly-polies, ants, beetles with shiny stained wings—all the life still making a way down here.

Down here. To write is to go down, go in, to emerge with handfuls of something I smear on the page. I don't stop to read, reflect, reinterpret. I just stain what was empty, secrete the silenced, and move on with more handfuls. To write is to mix up the wheat paste and poster the *neighborhoods of my frightened inside corridors with noise & mess, to blur all the boundaries, remove and muddy the sharp crease between my good girl surface and the difficult things inside. To write is to lose track of identities, to loose tense muscles around neck, shoulder wings, belly, coccyx, thighs, to set vowels and variables into those muscles, transcribe a new calculus and slope new languagings for ease to ride itself upon into this swollen, unbreakable being.*

This is what writing does. It marks up what we work so hard to make smooth, it pulls tight all the lines cast forth from within us, knots together past present future, opens space and time to release the brilliant catastrophe we were meant to be. Our skin, this singular organ, contains every possibility we ever laced with might have been and the writing sets all that possibility free, helps it step ginger or fierce into the world, to discover ourselves again. (2002)

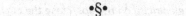

Why do so many of us who have suffered something unspeakable turn to blank pages, pen in hand or fingers on keyboard, reaching for the words to describe, clarify, or explain what we've been through, even if only for ourselves, even when we never expect to share those words with anyone else?

If you have written about or out of a place of shame or loss or trauma, you have your own answers to this question. Since I began offering writing groups for trauma survivors in 2002, I've found that when survivors write the true and complicated stories of our lives, our perception of our lives expands, shifts, opens and transforms—and when we share these stories with our communities, we are no longer alone with the many secrets we've carried for so long. Other survivors listen to our writing and treat us like creative beings whose words have power and make a difference, rather than responding to us like the terrible people our perpetrators convinced us we were. That reception changes everything.

The writing fingers open the tight fist of power and control and drops us out the writing opens up a chasm the writing throws over a bridge the writing topples buildings, walls and boulders fall steam risesthe room opens. The body opens. The future opens.

As a writer, workshop facilitator, and survivor of sexual abuse, I've witnessed first-hand what happens when survivors create the space (on the page, in our lives) for the whole of our stories, especially the stories that stick in our throats, the stories that hide under our lungs, behind our eyes, between our legs; the stories we aren't supposed to tell because our families don't want to hear them and/or our communities can't hold them with us—or at least we don't believe they can. All of us who are trauma survivors know: there are the stories we tell and the stories we don't tell. There's the trauma story that we have rattled off so many times that it rolls from our lips in one continuous breath, so polished and packaged we can barely feel it anymore, the story that is neat and clean and careful not to make anyone too uncomfortable—and then, underneath that, are the messier stories of our violation and survival, the many stories we never tell anyone, the parts that are still raw and throbbing and sore, wounded and tender and fragmentary. These are the stories that don't fit into a "good survivor" identity. These are the parts of ourselves that we're sure will get us turned out of our communities: stories of the things we did to keep ourselves alive, stories we fear make us as bad as our perpetrators. There are stories of what we long for, the desires and hungers we hold under our tongues, afraid of what it says about us that we *want* anything at all. The carefully-rehearsed trauma stories are only the tip of the iceberg that is our complicated, tangled, gorgeous human self. When I talk about writing ourselves whole, I mean writing out of the undulant enormity under our smooth surfaces, in order to bring forth shards of our as-yet-unarticulated real stories and selves.

First Nations writer Thomas King, in his beautiful book *The Truth About Stories*, says, "The truth about stories is that's all we are." In my twenty-some years recovering from sexual violence, using writing practice as my primary medicine and splint, I've found that writing—first freewriting alone, and then writing with other survivors—is a way to give myself the language for the stories I believed couldn't be told: the trauma stories I hid (or hid from), the desires I was afraid to articulate, the parts of myself and my experiences I trained myself never to speak.

•§•

I started journaling in 1993, when I was twenty-one years old and breaking away from my stepfather after nearly ten years of ongoing sexual, psychological, and physical abuse. As often as I could, I took refuge in local café, where I bought a large, dark roast coffee, and popped a tape into my portable cassette player—Ani DiFranco, Erasure, Zap Mama, The Crystal Method—slid my headset over my ears, folded the notebook open to a new page, uncapped my pen, wrote things I thought I'd never be able to say out loud. I spent years doing this, my butt planted in a wooden chair in some coffee house or other in Northern New England or around San Francisco. This is the way I found my tongue again. I wrote through the numbness that kept me protected—through writing I could feel the sadness, despair, depression, rage. The emotions had a weight and a shape once they found their way into words, whereas, inside me, they had all tangled together into a single inarticulate mass. There were few days I didn't break through into tears while I bent over my notebook at that corner table in the back of the cafe.

In the earliest months of my writing practice, I was often rigidly and "logically" truthful. I froze often during my writing sessions, straining hard to get every detail *right* so my stepfather could not accuse me of lying (should he ever come to read what I wrote—and, of course, I assumed he would; up to that point, he'd had access to every single aspect of my being). I wanted to compile a record of his atrocities, and was beginning the work of disentangling my feelings from the so-called psychoanalytical brainwashing that was a core component of his control over me, my sister, and my mother. If he ever made good on his threat to have me killed for leaving his bed, I believed someone would find this notebook and finally know who I really was. In those early years, as much as for any other reason, I wrote to survive my death in the form of a final, true story. I had told so many lies—I wanted someone, in the end, to know What Really Happened.

I wanted friends and former lovers and family to read the story that explained me: this is why I was so sexually experienced so young; this is why I'd be locked in the bathroom of my dorm room on the phone with my stepfather for hours; this is why I had rabid mood swings; this is why I was such an erratic friend; this is why I disappeared. *Oh,* this *was why Jen was so crazy all the time.* This *is what she was dealing with.*

After a year or so of "just" writing, I managed to get into individual therapy. I participated in groups for women who were incest survivors. I spent hours wandering around my small college town, listening to music and crying. I drank too much, watched too much bad television, spent uncountable hours reading books about incest, feminism, sex. But it was when I sat alone at the Dirt Cowboy Cafe in that small town in New Hampshire, one hand affixed to a big mug of French Roast coffee and the other hand moving a pen across the page, that things—life, loss, longing—slowed down and unraveled enough for me to be able to breathe a little better.

In *Writing Down the Bones*, Natalie Goldberg said we should take two years focused only on writing practice before we tried to write for publication, so that we could learn the contours of our minds, our inner selves. I couldn't imagine wasting all that time just journaling. *Two whole years? Is she kidding?*

I look up today and it's been over twenty.

They weren't relaxing, those hours with my journal. This was not a hobby or dalliance. I was learning to save my life. Writing came to be a way for me to be safely but intensely present with myself and with the world around me. Through writing, first and foremost, I (re)learned what it meant to be human.

•§•

This is the writing practice that has worked for me: write daily (or as near as possible), create open space for the words, keep the pen moving, don't let the censor/abuser stop the flow of words (sometimes I write down the censor/abuser's objections, when I can stomach it, just to get them out of the way), and follow the writing wherever it seems to want to go.

"Following the writing" means listening to the tug that wants me to write about my childhood dog or that moment of feeling triggered when I thought I was going to finally get to write about the sex I had last weekend. It means writing exactly the words that pop into my head—those first, often nonsensical thoughts—and trusting them, even if I can't see where they're leading. It means writing, word by word, into the terrifying places, always going slowly, listening to the deep wisdom of psyche that tells me when we are ready to go in and nudges me when we are ready to ease back out. I drop my pen to the page and go, trusting that I won't be the same on the other side. French feminist Hélène Cixous, in her brilliant essay "The Laugh of the Medusa," wrote, "When I write, it's everything that we don't know we can be that is written out of me, without exclusions, without stipulation, and everything we will be calls us to the unflagging, intoxicating, unappeasable search for love." *That's* what I mean.

When I started journaling in cafes back in the early '90s, I wrote fast and messy. Fast, because I wanted to catch those first thoughts as they came to me. There was no time to slow down—I needed to grab the thought and get it on the page right away because the stepfather in my head was sure to contradict, challenge, or change it. I learned to catch those thoughts and write them, too. I wanted all of it on the page, so I could look back at it later, so I could record all the madness in my head, so I didn't have to be all alone with this overwhelm anymore. The page could help me hold it. I wrote messily so that I could write anywhere—in public, at the coffee shop—without worrying that the people around me could easily read over my shoulder. I was afraid of being found out, yet I couldn't write at my apartment. *Home* wasn't a safe place, no matter that the physical danger lived 1,400 miles away. At the cafe, I couldn't hear the phone ringing, reminding me that he was (I feared) never going to stop monitoring me, never going to stop harassing me, never going to let me live my life away from him in peace.

I had a whirlwind in my head. I wanted to get it all down before I forgot, or lost the thread, or lost my nerve, before he came to take me back. I was sure he was going to track me down and make me go back.

In order to concentrate on writing, I needed noise outside to counteract all the noise inside, to soothe my hyperarousal and an overdeveloped startle response, to get to what Stephen King calls "the basement place" out of which to imagine and create. I needed a crowded cafe, loud music in my headphones, and my back to a wall, face toward the door. No one was going to sneak up on me while I wrote this history, while I wrote into the contours of my trauma. It took a great deal of effort and energy to be able to focus my attention at all. I wrote stream-of-consciousness (I have whole notebooks that are run-on sentences), fragments, flash images, and filled the page with shout-and-scribble when I was too angry to form words at all.

Over time, by following the thread of my writing right into the now, the now became a place that's safer for me to inhabit while I'm writing, even without all the distraction. Slowly, over these years of writing practice, I have come to be able to write even with no headphones on, no longer terrified of my startle response, no longer afraid of something bad happening to me when I get lost in the words.

•§•

Creativity is in us. Creativity *is* us. We who are survivors of intimate violence are always creating, given our ability to adapt to horrifying, unendurable situations. Without a profound creative capacity—our instincts and intuitions, the generative resource of our resilient psyches—we wouldn't have survived our homes or relationships or any of the other war zones we've endured. We couldn't have navigated the impossible landscapes laid before us. We wouldn't have been able to read the emotional street signs in our families, develop strategies for disappearing and reappearing inside our own bodies, or negotiate the simple, daily horrors of living with an abuser. Trauma and creativity are inextricably linked, and, I believe, creativity can pull us through the after-effects of what was done to us, and what we did to survive.

Changing our language, shifting our story even slightly, alters how we know ourselves. We are elastic beings ever becoming new. When we name what we have experienced—especially when we were told that no one would listen to or believe us, or when we were not taught the words we'd need in order to tell—we take power back from those who meant to silence us, and we reclaim control over the narrative of our lives. When we question, reword, or invert the stories we learned to tell about our ourselves, we are changed—we begin to be *restoryed*.

We are made up of the stories and memories we lift out of our pockets to share with friends over dinner, the remembrances we recite for ourselves in the thick of depression or in the bright morning of recovered joy, the stories we draw from film and TV commercials and pop songs and novels and Saturday morning cartoons, the anecdotes and gossip we heard our mother and aunts telling across the table at holiday suppers, that our fathers and uncles slipped through the sides of their mouths while watching the game, the stories that we saw whispered and pantomimed. We are shaped, too, by the stories we keep hidden. We were shaped by the stories our perpetrators told themselves and us, in order to justify their violence, and by the stories we told ourselves, in order to make sense of the violence we were suffering through. We were shaped by the response when we told what had been done to us: whether we were heard and cared for, or denied and shamed. The stories we grew up within determined what we experienced as possible—and impossible—for our lives.

There are stories that serve us for a lifetime. And there are stories that serve us for a period of time and then begin to harm us. Often, though, we don't notice that shift until we are in some kind of pain. Questioning our stories is risky and frightening. *Who am I if I'm not this person I've been telling for years? What do I mean if my foundational stories are malleable?*

When I began to lead writing groups with sexual trauma survivors, I finally thought to ask: What happens if we question the mainstream stories that get told about us? What happens when we tell the untellable stories? What if we challenge the stories our families or perpetrators or communities told about us, the normative, normalizing stories that tell us who and how we're supposed to be? I wanted to find out what happened when we wrote directly into the stories we were most afraid or ashamed of, when we turned our most-told stories upside down and inside out. What happens when we write the backside of the stories we have internalized about ourselves, about our communities, the stories of our healing or our desire?

In writing with groups of survivors (and other folks, as well), I found the strength and curiosity to write into and question some of my most deeply-held stories (that is, beliefs) about myself: that I was broken; that I would never feel safe in my body; that sex would always be difficult for me; that I was a failure; that I didn't deserve to call myself a woman; that I was culpable for my stepfather's sexual abuse because I hadn't been able to stop him for so long; that I didn't deserve family; that family didn't want me; that I wasn't worth caring about or saving. It takes heart and guts to tell the truth on the page, whether we ever share that writing with another soul. We grow, we transform, when we are willing to take that risk.

If we as a culture are immersed in story, then it follows that we come to know, to understand, ourselves through story. Therefore it's possible to be transformed by others' stories, by others' ways of knowing and experiencing the world and their own possibility, though this requires a profound vulnerability and willingness to be open to change. When we are present with other people's stories, we can learn different ways of looking at the world, looking at ourselves, understanding pain and struggle and desire and longing, than we ourselves have yet considered. I notice this happening quite often in the writing workshops, a note of, "I never heard it described quite that way before—that's just how I feel, too!" And there's a shift, a splitting open, a new openness of our perceptions, and thus ourselves.

There is a quality of magic that manifests when we gather with others in community and share our creative selves. The word *magic* comes from old Greek and Persian words that have to do with art and agency or power. I want that magic—that powerful art—for all sexual trauma survivors, because I believe this work can heal us, break open our isolation, reincorporate us into the human family, while transforming humanity into something more kind, expansive, and real.

One magic quality of story that I most value is the way stories show up for me when I am most alone and nearly lost. Dr. Rachel Naomi Remen, the author of *Kitchen Table Wisdom*, was one of the facilitators I worked with when I attended the Writing as a Healing Art conference in 2010. While she was with us she discussed the power of story, describing the ways in which stories are able to accompany people into their darkest places. The story that any of us tells about how we survive our own struggles will accompany those who've heard us when they, later, have to walk into their own difficult places. The listener receives these stories as a kind of opening, a faint and terraced map: *Look how they resisted, made it through, forgave themselves, told the truth—maybe I could do that, too.* I carry workshop writers' stories with me: they live along the skin of my forearms, they live in the cilia just inside my ears.

When I hear others' stories of resilience and resistance, I get the chance to revisit my own narrative, reconsider the parts I've labeled cowardice, betrayal, isolation, lack of integrity, lack of strength, and cover those old labels with sticky notes on which I've scribbled: strategy, resilience, patience, courage, generosity. I try on new naming. I remember, in the early 90s, sitting at an isolated desk in the dusty stacks of my college library. The timer that controlled the light above the study area ticked away while I flipped through an old collection of women's stories of abuse—maybe it was *I Never Told Anyone*—horrified that this was happening to so many of us, and, underneath that, so thankful to have discovered I wasn't alone. I don't think I ever checked that book out; I was too afraid of the librarian cocking an eyebrow my way, which would lead inevitably, I was sure, to my stepfather raging at me on the phone because I "told." But there in those stacks, when the timer ran out and the light clicked off, I held the book in my hands for a moment, breathing in the knowledge that there were women who made it out— that there were women who got free, that there were women who *told*.

We need one another's' stories as we learn to navigate the world post-trauma. For anyone struggling with the isolation of trauma aftermath, writing authentically— alone *and* with peers—can be transformative. Author and essayist Barry Lopez says, "The stories people tell have a way of taking care of them. If the stories come to you, care for them. And learn to give them away where they are needed. Sometimes a person needs a story more than food to stay alive." While we can never change what was done to us, we can transform how that history lives in us, take control over how it shapes and constrains us. We can come to understand that *creativity*, or *creative genius*, or *possibility* can be our name: *broken* and *raped* don't have to be our names. *Victim* doesn't have to be our name (nor does *stupid* or *shithead* or *selfish* or *crybaby* or *coward* or whatever other words they used against us to keep us tethered, afraid, and ashamed).

We can allow these experiences to take up a right-sized space in our souls without them having to be the whole of our being. We can story ourselves anew.

We who are survivors of horror—of sexual violation, of physical abuse, of mental torture, of emotional manipulation or disregard, of captivity; those of us who've had ties with our own blood severed, or who have wished to scrape out of our veins the blood that flowed there—who are we, without the roots of a shared (hi) story? We're not the first generation of survivors, we're not the first generation whose parents/caregivers/spouses thought we were worthy of abuse: part of our lineage is that truth, borne forward in the mouths of the ones who came before us, in the whispers and models of resilience, in the slow ways we learn to keep little pieces of ourselves safe. No one told us outright how to survive: that knowing is bone-deep ancestral memory, something in these cells that knows about staying alive when everything else says *die*.

We are of our own blood, true, and we are also of that other, larger family, the family that will never gather for a reunion, that averts its eyes from strangers or looks boldly into your curious face, the family of truth-veined human beings who made it through something horrible, only to have to live the rest of their lives carrying those memories in body and breath.

In this book, I mean to constellate some of what I've learned in twenty-some years of ongoing personal writing practice and over thirteen years facilitating sexuality and other writing groups with folks who, like me, survived sexual violence in one form or another. Throughout, I describe why I believe writing alone, and in a community of peers, is so revolutionary for sexual violence survivors.

The process I describe herein, that I've been working with for the past many years, has three parts, each of which can crack us open to transformation: *story*, *voice*, and *witness*:

- When we find words for our untold *stories*, we build new relationships with the fragments of experience, memory, and reaction that have bounced around inside our psyches with no tethering, no root; we allow the stories out of our bodies and into the world.

- When we read aloud our new writing, we give *voice* to both our story and our creative abilities, and we deepen our embodiment as writers and speakers.

- When we choose to share our work with others, we are *witnessed*: we hear how our writing, our craft, our story has affected others; our story isn't ours to carry alone anymore. We get to experience being truly heard and we get to return that kindness by listening to/witnessing others' stories as well. We come to understand that our attention is important, that our listening and observation matter.

In those first months and years of this writing practice, it felt like I was running for my life with words, and if I stopped to think too hard about what I was saying, I clotted up in doubt and fear and couldn't write at all. I needed the right kind of pen (Pilot Precise v7) and the right kind of notebook (8 ½ x 5 Artists Sketchbook, please); I needed the right noisy cafe, a corner table near the window, headphones and a cassette tape of music I knew well. I needed many cups of strong coffee adulterated with a lot of sugar. I was like that little girl, afraid of the dark, who needs a glass of water, *and* her blankie, *and* the same two stuffed animals, *and* the door left open just the right amount before she felt safe enough to fall asleep. Everything had to be just right for me, too; I was absolutely afraid of the darkness I was trying to write.

My stepfather had tried to occupy every fragment, every nook and cranny, every inch of my psyche—he believed, and trained me to believe, that he had a right to every thought in my head, every emotion, every instinct. He taught me to believe he (or someone in his employ) was always watching me, and through this training, taught me to surveil myself. A legacy of that surveillance took the form of brutal and byzantine inner critics who contradicted or challenged most of what I thought or wrote. So I learned to write very fast, in order to outrun these challengers—by the time the voice rose up to take apart an accusation I made on the page, I was already onto the next line.

The chatter of the other cafe patrons, the music pulsing loud and fast through the headphones: these occupied my hyper-vigilant consciousness, so that I could write from the place underneath—from the self that was terrified of exposure, from the well of knowing that had been forced into silence during the years my mother had been married to my stepfather.

At first, I used the pages to try and make sense of myself—quite literally. After finally escaping my stepfather, I first tried to write down—using the direct, clear, logical language my stepfather had demanded—all that I had been through and was feeling. But the words kept getting muddled. I stopped writing in the middle of a sentence, stuck between what I knew was true and the quarrelsome voice of an inner censor, which sounded an awful lot like my stepfather and challenged almost every assertion I tried to make about what he'd done. I stared out the window at my hale and happy-appearing classmates; why didn't they have this trouble? I'd lived so long inside the silence, and tangled in the Doublethink and

Doublespeak, required of those surviving long-term abuse that I no longer knew how to speak straight-forwardly. My stepfather had forced me to dismantle my own language and desire from the inside out, and reconstruct these in the image he preferred. I didn't know what anything *meant* anymore. That's not exactly true; I didn't know how to convey the layers of meanings inside my words to anyone else.

After I told my stepfather that I could no longer "continue our sexual relationship" (that was the language he required us to use) and broke contact with him and the rest of my family, he promised to harm or kill me and those I cared about if I told what he'd been doing. So I did not go to the police and I did not go to therapy. The trajectory of my life upended. He and my mother terminated their financial support for my education, so I had to withdraw from school after the fall of my senior year. I took a job with the on-campus library, went more than a little crazy, drank almost anything I could get my hands on, watched too much *Rikki Lake*, and wrote and wrote and wrote and wrote and wrote. It took almost a year after that terrifying conversation with my stepfather before I could let myself believe that I would not be physically harmed if I told my story to a therapist, and by the time I was able to so, I'd already developed the writing practice that I would use to suture myself back together.

In working to heal the damage my stepfather did, I haven't only written, of course. I also, as I mentioned above, went to talk therapy, as well as group therapy, feminist support groups, model mugging and self-defense classes, every modality offering tools I could use to further my healing, my sense of sanity. But my mother and stepfather were both psychotherapists: I understood how the language of talk therapy could be used to undo or contort or ensnare someone's psyche and sense of self—and though I have worked with kind, smart, wise and generous therapists, I don't know if I have ever fully trusted that process or relationship, though I do believe in its transformative potential. Writing, however, has been a steady and unwavering companion, able to listen and welcome without transference or countertransference.

The page has been the place where my whole self could emerge—my complicated, confused, petty, sorrowful, funny, jubilant, desiring, hopeful, despairing, pleased, depressed, hurt, enraged, spiritual, philosophical, playful, curious, certain, and uncertain self. The page introduced me to my human self—utterly imperfect and nonetheless acceptable. The page has been a place for beauty, for grief, for attempt, for starting over. And over. And over. *And over.* Freewriting is my yoga, my daily jog, my meditation, my spiritual practice—when I go without this writing for too many days in a row, I begin to lose touch with myself, become jagged and short-tempered; I can feel, inside, the shards of me banging against each other. I am too many pieces again, all of them demanding attention, demanding to be true. My sense of wholeness begins to disassemble when I fall out of this practice. I'm cranky, less pleasant to be around, less functional in my so-called adulthood.

People dismiss writing practice as "just journaling." I just did so when telling a neighborhood woman about what I was doing here, sitting in the sun across the block from my city's beautiful lake. She's been watching me here. She's small, slender, brownskinned, her hair cropped close to her scalp, wearing Bermuda shorts, a blue T-shirt, and green glitter flats. Her male companion is across the street, sorting recyclable cans and bottles, preparing the many bags to take to the recycling center. She comes over to me and says, "You must be doing schoolwork or something." I say, "I'm just journaling." She says, "You must have a lot on your mind then." I want to invite her to sit with me and write. I know she also must have a lot on her mind. The man across the street makes a noise in his throat when I comment appreciatively on the woman's shoes, and I am worried that any more kindness I show her will result in some kind of challenge from him when they're alone. (I never wanted anyone to say anything nice about me in front of my stepfather for the same reason.)

Just journaling. I don't say, *I'm continuing to teach myself how to breathe into this lifetime.* But, for me, that's what this practice really is.

•§•

Over time, my requirements for my writing time loosened—maybe I *could* go ahead and write if I only had a cheap ballpoint pen. I shifted from expensive unlined artist's sketchbooks to the cheap single-subject notebooks that I buy in bulk every August when school supplies go on sale. I began to be able to write at home, and, eventually, my startle response softened enough so that I could write in silence—no longer afraid of being heart-poundingly surprised by any sort of noise when I was deep in a write.

Writing groups helped me learn to write under conditions that weren't entirely under my control. More importantly, though, is that, throughout, I've worked to give my writing what the writing needed. For so many years, I was trained to believe that others' needs were more important than my own, that my creative or intellectual needs (to say nothing of the need for safety and comfort) weren't worth respecting. In my stepfather's house, if he was in the middle of working, he was not ever to be disturbed; woe to any of us who broke his concentration. Yet, of course, no matter what my sister or mother or I were doing, when my stepfather decided he wanted our attention or bodies, we were expected to be available to him.

After leaving his house, I came to be selfish in my work, to take my time back for myself and this practice.

Now, I'm in my apartment, writing this in a twenty-minute window just before a workshop is slated to begin. I put on a little Irish fiddle music, and I drop in to the writing. That's a miracle, when I stop and think about where I began, and is in part the result of these years of practice and patience, the result of giving myself years of care and structure—all the pieces in place just right as I taught myself it was safe for me to go into the dark, to find those stories still hidden, still isolated, still lost.

Think about how powerful it is to share a story, a necessary story. There are stories that live in me as a broken kind of breath because they haven't yet received the reception I need for them, a sense that they have been truly heard, understood, *grokked.* Former Poet Laureate Kay Ryan, at a *Granta* reading at Book Passage in San Francisco in the fall of 2012, talked about the work that the reader agrees to when she chooses to engage with a poem. Ryan said that the reader is part creator, part inventor, of the poem—without reception the poem has only done half its work. We need a listener/reader/witness to complete the process of storytelling or poem-making.

Story. Voice. Witness.

This process is so simple, and yet its impact is radical: Using a freewriting practice, we can take our creative transformation—and therefore our healing, our lives—into our own hands. We as communities have the ability to hold, welcome, and help reframe the difficult stories that keep individual community members feeling isolated and outside the fold. We don't have to relegate one another to the isolation of the therapist's office, and neither do we have to fix each other: we engage a healing practice when we *language* our true stories, when we share honestly with others who can hear us, and when we demonstrate that we are willing to listen and be present with one another.

This is a book that has sexual trauma survivors at its heart, but this practice of story, voice, and witness has made a difference in many people's lives, whether they identify as trauma survivors or not. I can't think of a group of folks or a community who wouldn't benefit from engaging together in this kind of generative, generous, shared creative community. Veterans, frontline crisis workers, PhD candidates, couples, sexual violence survivors, folks just coming out as gay or queer or trans*, survivors of genocide, teachers, coworkers, adoptees, refugees, foster kids, gender nonconformists, those folks of color who daily navigate white supremacy, religious communities, nurses, doctors, therapists, single parents ... we all have stories we want to tell, stories we feel silent and isolated around. There are none of us who haven't spent time living at the intersection of trauma and desire, and the stories at that intersection are stories that define us.

Many books have been written about the power and use of writing for individuals who want to heal. This book joins that lineage—another invitation to you to write your story because your words are necessary magic. We need our mainstream narratives about rape, incest, as well as those we tell about the survivors of these violences, to be complicated, messy, and thereby made more real. We need *all* the stories if we as a society are to learn the truth about intimate violences, and if we are to undermine and transform the conditions necessary to allow those violences to continue to run rampant in homes around the world.

This is not a how-to manual or a guide or a workbook. This is a love letter, a series of stories, an exhortation. Like author and memoirist Lidia Yuknavitch said when she spoke at the Association of Writers & Writing Programs Conference (AWP) in 2015, *I am here to recruit you.* This book is a revelation and a hope. This is how I did it and how I think about things, one more piece of the conversation about what writing can do for us whose bodies and other parts of ourselves have been fragmented in various ways by intimate and/or sexual violences, offered in fragments, small essays, long rants, curiosities, listsicles, and prayers. This is some of what I've learned and thought about after writing myself (more) whole these twenty-four years after escaping my stepfather's violence, and after writing with hundreds of sexual violence survivors (and others) since the first queer women survivors erotic writing group I convened at the San Francisco LGBT Center in the summer of 2002.

•§•

I have structured this book as a collection of short essays: you can read the whole thing straight through if that's your way, or you can drop in to different sections randomly, open the book and see what has chosen you today. Read to be inspired, read for prompts, read for ideas or possibilities, read for challenge or to argue. This book is meant to be consumed however you prefer. Go front to back, back to front, skip around, or begin in the middle, read to the end, and then go back and finish up with the beginning. There's no wrong way to do it. Though a collection of writing prompts appears in the Appendix, I consider this whole book a spark for your writer's imagination, and the beginning of a conversation.

If you find yourself responding strongly to what you're reading, I invite you to put the book down, pick up your notebook and pen, and write whatever is coming up for you, what you're agreeing with or pissed off about, how you wish I'd said it differently or how you're surprised by a particular phrasing or consideration. You'll notice that I sometimes drop into poetry (as at the very beginning of this chapter)—much of this book was generated in freewrites, either in my journal, for the Writing Ourselves Whole blog, or in writing groups, and I include these more poetic pieces as examples of what can emerge when we let the pen go where it wants to go. First and foremost, I want to convey the power of writing for deep inner change, and, more than anything, want to encourage that small, quiet (or clamorous!), persistent part of you who just wants to drop everything else and write.

My invitation is to let yourself write slow. Write your story in chunks, in stages, in fragments. Respond to writing prompts. Do this for a month or six months or three years, every day or most days. You certainly won't (nor do you need to) write about trauma every time you pick up the pen (and any time I write, "Pick up the pen," please add, "or place your fingers on the keyboard"). Your story is more than trauma—*you* are more than trauma. It's good to give yourself permission to write anything. Turn your writer's eyes away from the images at the back of your head and toward the flowers just blooming in your neighbor's window box or the taste of a ripe peach or the daydream you had about the bike messenger you saw flying down Market Street on her fixie while you sat on MUNI waiting for the streetlight to change.

•§•

The essays in the book are gathered into five sections between this introduction and the conclusions: Initial Preparation, Story, Voice, Witness, and Self-Care. These sections aren't strict confines; more like loose collectives, or affinity groups—you'll see a lot of overlap in themes and ideas throughout.

In *Initial Preparation*, we begin to lay the groundwork for our writing practice, what it means to write ourselves whole, and why we would ever want to try it.

The *Story* essays tangle with the work involved in finding, finally, the language for the unlanguageable: the unspeakable, the unspoken, and the unheard. It has to do with deciding to find the words for the stuff we were told would never be believed. This is the part where hands are on the page or keyboard, the alone work part, the communion with self, finding words for embodied and disembodied experience, and dis-ordering what has been sanitized, made too neat and nice so that others listening will be comfortable.

In *Voice*, we get into what it means to take our narrative back for ourselves, to say (in writing and out loud) what we were never supposed to say, and to allow our bodies, finally, to "speak" those stories that they have held for so long.

The *Witness* section contains writing about creating and sustaining a peer-led sexual trauma survivor writing group: what happens when we write together, how to navigate some of the challenges that arise, how to sustain yourself and your group.

In the *Self-Care* section, we think about both how to use writing as a self-care practice, and how and why to take care of ourselves as we write these beautiful and difficult stories of ourselves.

The *Conclusion* essays aren't terribly conclusive—more like launching pads, explicit invitations to begin now, and then begin again and again, to find words for your own stories: as poetry or prose, as fiction or testimony, in any form you wish, and write yourself complicatedly, messily, fragmentedly, gorgeously whole.

Please take care of yourself while you read, and while you write. There's explicit language about sexual violence, and about living in the aftermath of trauma, in these pages. Please be easy with yourself as you read, stop when you're uncomfortable, and write when you feel drawn to write. You have enough time; please don't feel you need to rush yourself to get it All Done Now. Think about ways you can take care of yourself during or after your writing, and consider how to be kind and gentle with yourself during this time, how best to receive the support you'll want, and make some mental plans for that.

Some ideas for self-care: call a friend who can listen to you without trying to "fix" anything; talk to a therapist; go for a run; punch a pillow; journal at a café (maybe treat yourself to an almond croissant, too); call someone from your writing group; play with your dog or cat or ferret or another animal in your life; visit the ocean at high tide and yell along with the thunderous waves; make chocolate-chip cookies or a big batch of buttered popcorn; prepare a whole meal that tastes good and feeds you well; rest; put on your favorite music while driving and sing along at the top of your voice; look for four-leaf clovers; go dancing; take a hot bath; write in your journal; snuggle with stuffed animals; spend an hour in the sun with a good book; take a "nature bath"—that is, a walk somewhere that you can be immersed in nature; garden or find another excuse to dig your fingers into some dirt; watch the birds; smell the roses (really!); bake bread; make yourself a cup of strong tea or just exactly the sort of coffee you prefer; go for a bike ride; binge-watch a ridiculous TV show; find an old movie that is sure to make you cry, and then one that makes you laugh...

This is just a beginning, of course. What else is on your self-care list?

What I hope for every single person reading this is that you *write:* if not inspired by the words, then by the energy behind them. Writing has saved and changed my life. May it do the same for you. Begin now to write yourself whole. Gather your own circle of writers in which to share your stories. And throughout, please, be easy with you.

initial preparation

suturing the rupture: what writing about trauma can do

This is my aftermath, this writing. This is where grief or something more unlanguage-able has brought me. Medicine is supposed to ease hurts, soothe spasms, turn the knots inside out, is supposed to quiet the voices, allow focus or a little joy or peace return, is supposed to settle the stomach or senses or skin, is supposed to make something better. This is homeopathic practice: writing brings me into the pain, the misunderstanding, the trauma, the loss, and turns them around for me to examine. There is an inoculation, a lancing and letting off of infection, a suturing together again. There is deep medicine in this, in bringing the terror up, shining a light on its vulnerable edges, then letting it back down. And there is an offering left in the aftermath, a transcription of procedure, a tracing the outline of a fragile, fractured, healing psyche and body. This artifact shows all the stages we go through: what we were, what fire we went through, how we shadowboxed and strove through to the other side to find what remained of our soul and pulled it back through to live again. (2013)

•§•

Trauma has impacted nearly every single person I know, directly and/or indirectly. Is this true for you, too? We may take trauma into our bodies and lives through our parents' physical violence, or sexual misuse or molestation, through their name calling or threats or mind games or psychological torture. It may be an assault by a stranger, someone who took us by surprise on the street or in our home. It may be a natural disaster, like living through an earthquake or hurricane. It may be a physical illness, like cancer. It may be living under white supremacy, and/or other forms of oppression. It may be living or fighting in a warzone. It may be the legacy of our parents' or grandparents' traumas, our ancestors' experiences of political, cultural, or intimate violences.

Merriam-Webster defines *trauma* as, variously: an injury to the body (as a wound, a cut); a "disordered psychic or behavioral state resulting from severe mental or emotional stress or physical injury;" and an emotional upset. The word *trauma* derives from the Greek word *trauma*, meaning "a wound, a hurt, a defeat."

A disorder state. A defeat.

In my workshops, I define trauma, quite broadly, as any experience which confounds understanding, and which leaves a person feeling silenced: either without access to language to describe it, and/or unwitnessed/unheard/shut down when they attempted to speak about the experience. I think of a traumatic experience as one that causes damage to bodily or psychological or spiritual integrity, one we're not able to immediately integrate or process, that overwhelms, and then transforms, our understanding of ourselves and our reality.

A traumatic experience is generally thought of as something out of the norm— except, of course, for those living with incest or domestic violence, living in war zones, or experiencing political persecution or race-hatred: this *is* our normal.

In its most recent criteria for Post-Traumatic Stress Disorder, the Diagnostic and Statistical Manual of Mental Disorders (DSM), the diagnostic "bible" for psychotherapists, psychiatrists, and insurance companies, defines *trauma* as "exposure to actual or threatened death, serious injury or sexual violence," whether directly or indirectly. When I talk about it, I tend to expand this definition somewhat. Trauma is a site of shock in the body and/or psyche. It's a rupture, a bifurcation, a disassembly. Trauma marks the moment when what *was* ended, and something new emerged.

•§•

But what was the moment of trauma? Sometimes you can't ever put your finger on it. There is no warp of scar that separates the Before from the After. Not in this body. There is only the fuzzy and ephemeral, unmappable distance of memory. The way I cannot mark when it started. The way I cannot tell you, It was here, when he rubbed my back over my summer tank top. Or, no, it was here, when his hands lifted the tank top a week or a month or who could say how long later? And why am I still looking for this line of demarcation, the moment when that brown-haired girl on the couch went from a regular tomboy with a handsy stepdad to someone not exactly there anymore at all. But that's how it is with ghosting. Could you say when exactly the Cheshire Cat began to disappear? You simply saw his whole curved self, a ball of striped, grinning fur, tucked up into that tree, and only after he was well into his evaporation did you begin to notice what was missing—by the time that understanding took hold, he was all and only teeth. No obvious moment when you could point and say, Look, his edges have blurred. The blurring comes across gradually. You don't know, when it begins, that some part of you will be blurred, ungraspable, forever. You think it's just going to be for a minute—just until he takes his hands back to himself. Just until your mom says something to him. But then he doesn't take his hands back, and your mom presses her lips together tight, and those edges that thought they were just pretending, just practicing the art of disappearance, shimmer more finely, get harder and harder to feel again; you can't make yourself reappear whenever you want to anymore, like the Cheshire Cat could. You don't know that one day you, too, will be only teeth—and that then those sharp knowings will disappear from your grasp, too. (2015)

Many of the folks I've written with over the last decade are survivors of sexual violence, domestic violence, child abuse, sexual assault or rape, extreme or ritual abuse. Others have survived or are living with cancer or other life-altering illness. Some have had to live with sexual harassment, neglect, emotional abuse, forced prostitution. Some will never have a name or a clear visual memory of their traumatic experience: instead what they have is a body telling them that something terrible happened. Often, these writers without specific memories reach hard for language that can put a name to physical sensations like nausea, nightmares, discomfort in certain situations, discomfort around certain people, depression, hyper-vigilance—that is, want to make sense of these symptoms of PTSD. Despite the DSM's languaging of trauma as an experience that is "exceptional" or "out of the ordinary," trauma is a *common* experience—it's a rare person who has experienced nothing traumatic in their lives.

Trauma lives in us in individual ways; through trauma, our relationship with language is ruptured. What has happened to us makes no sense because we cannot find words, because *there are no right words* to make anyone else truly understand. Our storyline fissures, and we fragment. We experience ourselves as voiceless, sometimes for many years. Trauma shocks us out of alignment; we are removed from our own story, and we have to, each of us, find and even create the language to articulate what we've been through and what we've become. We are left having to rebuild our whole narrative. The story of ourselves is what gets broken. The story of ourselves is what we have to suture together again.

In 1994, when I was twenty-one, twenty-two years old, you could find me most days holding up a table at a cafe on the edge of my college campus, filling unlined notebook pages with long stretches of writing. I was scared and I was angry and I felt broken open inside and most days I didn't feel like I made any sense at all unless I was writing. On the page, I didn't have to pretend to be "together"; all my brokenness and fragments, questions and desires jumbled together in one place. I was trying to figure out my relationship to words, as much as I was trying to get out of my body and onto the page everything my stepfather had done. In the process of writing, I both discovered and created the story of my life. I met my (new) story and (new) self on the pages of those blank notebooks.

My stepfather attempted to sever me from words. He worked to render words—up to and including the words *yes* and *no*—meaningless. Maybe that's not exactly right. What he wanted was for words to mean only what he wanted them to mean, and as soon as I thought I understood what meaning he wanted me to make, using the words he'd defined, he changed the rules. It was like living inside an Orwellian Newspeak generator. From my stepfather I'd learned that words don't have to do or mean what the dictionary says. I was required to say *Yes* to my stepfather every time he wanted access to my body, even when what lived inside my mouth and skin, and could not be spoken, was *No*. He dismissed the word *No*. I learned that *No* could have no meaning at all.

Having to say one thing while meaning another, over and over again, drives us more than a little crazy, forces us to question how we can possibly communicate. *What do words actually do? What good is language if it can be so easily stripped from its moorings, its connection to the real and lived experiential world?*

Twenty-four years and thousands of pages later, I still don't fully trust that words will do what I ask them to.

An experience of trauma—either long-term or instantaneous—rocks us out of our familiar relationship with words, as it rocks us out of our familiar relationship with everything else in our lives. Part of what makes an experience traumatic is that we are without sufficient language to convey to others what has happened to us. We are at a loss for words. Words fail us. We clutch for clichés, or we clam up and let someone else do the talking. We are a verbal species, we humans, and it is terrifying to be without the words for something important in our lives. Even when we are able to matter-of-factly communicate the violence we've experienced, if the people around us don't respond to our words as we would expect or anticipate, as when a parent gets angry with *us* when we disclose abuse, or pretends the abuse was no big deal, or acts as though we haven't said anything at all, we can feel crazy. At a fundamental level, we wonder if our words have any impact. Are we not saying what we think we are saying? Do people really not care? We may wonder if what *we* are doing when we are speaking is the same thing that other people seem to do when they speak.

We who, as young people or adults, survive sexual or other violence are also taught, paradoxically, that our words are *too* powerful. My stepfather was hurt and disappointed when I resisted his advances—his suffering was my fault. He told me all the ways I would harm my mother if she found out what he was doing to me; her anguish would be my fault for telling, not his fault for sexually abusing me. I learned how dangerous a misspoken word or slip of the tongue could be.

I spent years with a sense of impotence and fear around my speech: *maybe what I say* is *unhearable, is* actually *incomprehensible; maybe I'm still not working this language thing right.*

When I was finally able to write about my stepfather's violence, just a few months before I would start the process of untangling myself from his web of control, I detailed every damn bullshit threat that he'd made, took it apart, raged at it, questioned it, turned it over to see the impotence on the other side. I wrote down everything he did and forced me to keep silent about or to rename. The actions he called "teaching" or "lovemaking" or "sex" or "help," for instance, I called by their true name: rape. I began to undo his occupation of my very mouth. He had infiltrated even my *words* with his violence, and after he was gone from my physical body and everyday life, I had the distance I needed to roll out my words on the page and risk examining the wounds, and begin to discover how to put myself back together again.

•§•

We want to get back into "right relationship" with our own words—meaning, we want to feel a sense of agency with and through language. Our words *do* have power, though not in the destructive sense that our perpetrators, families, or communities often claim. The story we tell *about* our words also has power. For years, I repeated to myself what my stepfather had trained me to believe (and what society and media reinforced)—*that I didn't* deserve *to speak, that no one would listen to me or care even if they could hear me, that my words didn't matter.* Writing practice is what finally broke into and through those lies. Writing brought me, and so many of the writers I know and have written with, into a different relationship with words, language, stories, and with the words, the language and stories used against us.

So this is what writing practice can help us accomplish: finding right—and even playful—relationship with creativity and language. We are writing about our lives, and while we deserve for our lives to be received seriously, we also deserve laughter, silliness, and play. Through laughter, we find breath. Through play, we reconnect with our intuitive, creative being, what Black lesbian feminist author Audre Lorde describes as the "*yes* within ourselves." We get to have that *yes*, our *yes*, back, as well as our *no*, and have them mean exactly what we want them to this time.

•§•

My dictionary says the word *heal* means, first, "to make a person or injury healthy and whole." A later definition: "to repair or rectify something that causes discord and animosity."

Is healing more than the cessation of bleeding? More than simply having the bone set, wound scab over and begin to physically mend? When we talk about healing from sexual violence, I often hear the language of *psychic* wounds: the wounding of our trust, our relationship with instinct and memory, the scarring of our sexuality, our sense of being able to be safe around other people or in the world, even within ourselves. How do *those* injuries find succor, when there's nothing to set in a cast or suture up? How do we heal the stories of brokenness, heal the belief that we're no longer whole, that we are unfixable?

Many authors have written about the transformative power of creativity. Pat Schneider, in *Writing Alone and With Others*, reminds her readers that when we write, we are *writers*, and that through writing, we can "begin at any time to be free." Julia Cameron's *The Artist's Way* encourages a "recovery" of and through creative expression. *Live Through This*, edited by Sabrina Chapadjiev, is a collection of essays by artists and writers who've battled deeply self-destructive urges using creativity and artistic expression. Social psychologist James Pennebaker, in his book *Opening Up*, reports on the results of his studies with college students at the University of Texas at Austin, which revealed that "excessive holding back of thoughts, feelings, and behaviors can place people at risk for both major and minor diseases," whereas "confronting our deepest thoughts and feelings can have remarkable short- and long-term health benefits." Dr. Pennebaker found that those students who wrote deeply and expressively about one of their most difficult life experiences for just twenty minutes a day, for four consecutive days (and *only* for those four days), subsequently received better grades in their classes, showed an improved immune system (as evidenced by fewer visits to the campus infirmary), and reported that they felt happier and less depressed. What we hold inside us impacts every aspect of our lives. Writing about that which has been inhibited (unshared or unexamined) can not only free up the mind to higher levels of thinking, but can also improve our physical health.

The creation of art enacts release and transformation; exposure to art invites different ways of thinking, feeling, and being into the rooms of ourselves. Creative practice reengages us with our deep instinctual self, with the life-flow of our erotic self, which is our whole, embodied and empowered self. Creative practice can be a suture, a cleansing of the wound, a soothing of the inflammation, and a manifestation of the scar.

•§•

Art makes (a) way. Art reveals what's possible—enacts possibility. A brave and engaged poet once commented, in one of my writing workshops, "You can say things in poems you don't really say in casual conversation." We heal when we transform a wounding—either physically, through the body's regenerative capacity, or psychologically, though an alteration in our understanding of the experience that caused the wound, our ability to express it (concretely or metaphorically), or our sense of, finally, being heard and understood, of no longer being all alone with the violation and pain. Because it offers a way to express difficult or charged experiences or thoughts (such as sexual trauma or sexual longing) through metaphor and other abstract means ("Tell all the truth but tell it slant," Emily Dickinson advised us), creative expression provides outlet and inlet, deep risk and safety, camouflage and exposure: creativity is large, contradicts, contains multitudes, just like us, as Walt Whitman proclaimed.

I have come to believe that we can change the world this way, through writing deeply and openly—I mean, with this and other practices of discovering and living ourselves into the vast *elemental* of our creativity. "Art, in its living and working out, is not about accomplishment. It is about energy and time and discipline and self-criticism and pursuit and letting go. Art is not about being. It is about becoming," wrote philosopher Ladelle McWhorter. Don't ever think that our work, the very practice of writing—the *very fact* of taking the time to sit down with one's own thoughts and commit them to paper—is not revolutionary. We undermine the old teachings. We take the old language and turn it inside out. We name our hidden truths. We true our hidden names. We crack the surface of the advertised world and take hold of the reins of our lives. As long as we keep on writing and knowing each other as constantly changing peers in this process, as long as we are free to tell ourselves and our stories however we choose, as long as we play in the memory and myth of the thickness of poetic language, we will walk ourselves, together, into freedom.

Use your pen to thread the needle

Give yourself ten minutes. Find somewhere you'll be
comfortable writing, whether that's at a quiet kitchen table
or noisy cafe. Open your notebook, turn to a new page, and,
at the top of the page, write, "This is what I want my words to
do..." Complete the sentence with whatever comes up for you,
whatever wants to be written. Then write the phrase again, and
complete it again. Begin again as many times as it takes, until
you find yourself in a flow, and follow your writing wherever
it seems to want you to go. If you get stuck, you can always
begin again.

writing that changes its writer

Freewriting is the one practice (well, besides really good dancing) that most consistently drops me into a transformative experience—that is, a sense of being different somehow, on the other side of writing, than I was at the beginning. When I am able to let the writing flow, get the editor out of the way and write without stopping for at least fifteen or twenty minutes, I often find that something in me has shifted, loosened (as though I've done some psychic stretching); many times I write something I hadn't known I wanted or needed to say.

Transformative writing is writing that changes the writer in the process of its creation. A transformation is a thorough or significant change—one dictionary I consult gives a definition of *transform* as "to change completely *for the better*" (emphasis mine). I think of writing that's transformative as writing that surprises the writer as it's emerging, either with respect to form, content, structure, or some other factor. It's writing through which the writer may learn something about themselves (even—sometimes especially—if the writing is fiction).

So, when I talk about a transformative writing practice, I mean a regular and consistent freewriting routine that, intentionally or not, enacts a transformation or series of slow, deep changes in the writer. I mean a practice of deep communion with the page, which is also both a deep communion with self and not-self.

I describe this as a writing practice, rooted in the body, that engages the fullness of our creative power. When I am at the page and the words are flowing, when

I let the words come exactly as they arise in me, when I'm not worried about control or how I look or whether I'm writing *right* but rather have the sense that something is writing through me, that I am a vehicle for the words that needed to get written, then I say I am doing transformative writing practice.

This writing, right now, is not about craft—absolutely *not* about grammar or punctuation or the other parts of the editing process. This is learning to release and reclaim all the words, every one: all the language of and for these selves that we are. We who learned to talk in code and split tongues, who learned to communicate through gesture and glance and dyed hair and torn clothing, through the size of our bellies, through thin scarring on our wrists or thighs, we who were not allowed to *say* our lives or experiences directly—we now have the opportunity for a new articulation. Through a transformative writing practice, we can realign with our instincts, our intuitions, our values, our wishes; we can learn how our true inside self/selves look and feel and sounds.

Here is an example of one of my workshop writes, sparked after listening to Sweet Honey in the Rock's "Ella's Song":

This is what I want to say: It won't end. You won't get fixed. You won't reach a place where your name is only Healed and incest doesn't ever feed you breakfast anymore. The people who tell you You'll get over it don't know what they're talking about, because they live in their own closed cage of denial. You have been transformed. You are not the same as you were Before. And you will never not also be who you were Before—but it may be some years before these layerings of yourselves can sit in the same room with you and have coffee in the morning. There is no such thing as getting over it. There is the business of living through and with. There is learning to breathe again, there is learning you are worthy of the air you breathe, there is having to breathe when you know you are not worthy. There is you, just breathing. You will have years called Night and years called Drunk and years called Weep and years called Frozen and years called Broken and Fuck. You look at this and think you can't bear so many years of pain—but what's true is that all those years are also called Freedom.

You will not always be in pain. Your heart will harden and soften at the same time. You will forget all the names you ever had, you will climb into a skin so different from the one you were fucked into that not even your mother—especially not your mother—will be able to recognize you. This may or may not be a cocoon. It might just be the true face of your new eyes. Every stage is a phase, like this breath you are taking is a phase, like this heartbeat is a phase, like a single kiss is a phase is an instant an instantiation of your personhood. Phase means nothing except you are still alive. Ignore them when they tell you that whatever you're experiencing now is just a phase. Ignore their relief, if it comes, when you enter a different phase. They do not sing with all the tendons of your body and they can't speak the truth of your soul. Sit with the people who can hold your surfaces and your undersides, both.

One day you will say yes to your skin, yes to sex, yes to the feel of your body alive and inhabitable. The next day you will wrench up with No again. There will be years like this. There will be two yes hours in a row. There will be days when you don't say his name. There will be come a night when, in your dreamtime, you will take the knife brandished against you and turn it on the ones you've been running from. That will be a good day.

Know that this place you're in right now will transform. Be with people who can hold the shimmer of insurrection that is the space between who you were raped to be and who you are becoming. Be with those who can open their hands out to rage, who are imperfect in their holding, who want to fix it, and who understand that there is nothing to fix. Understand that you will emerge from broken, that broken is a necessity, that no human passes through life whole and that none of us are anything other than whole. Believe that broken is necessary if one wants to see all sides of a thing. Know that you are because of and in spite of, you are *of and not of, you are welcome in this human family, you have never been outside its true skin. We live among people who have forgotten how to open their hands to those who need receiving, people who deserve explicit welcome, and, yes, deserve apology. Know that the platitudes people offer you exist so that you can climb inside something together, that they are a doorway that you can see each other through when the words don't work anymore. Know that words will sometimes fail you but you will keep trying to unwrap them to find what lives inside because for all the pain there you will never stop wanting to know and to share what lives truly inside yourself. (2013)*

I began this freewrite with a desire to offer something hopeful to the survivors I know and love, and to those who are just beginning their process of recovery, and found myself at first writing things that didn't feel very damn hopeful at all. And then, of course, I found I was writing this as much for myself as for others in need of words of encouragement: *Know that this place you're in right now will transform.* No matter how many years I've been actively recovering, I still need reminding. One more time, I get to be tender to the still-aching parts of myself.

I initially met the word *transformative* in conjunction with writing when, in 2000, I read in *Poets and Writers Magazine* about Goddard College's Transformative Language Arts (TLA) program. Transformative Language Arts is described as "the intentional use of the written, spoken and sung word for individual and community growth, development, celebration, and transformation," and called to me when I was searching for a way to integrate anti-violence activist work and writing. I imagined developing a creative writing methodology to use with LGBTQ women who wanted to write about sex as a way to reclaim and recalibrate their relationship with desire.

(Please note that I don't mention initially envisioning work with trauma survivors—when I first began my studies, I wasn't intending to work with survivors; that was a transformation in itself, the moment I allowed myself to understand that I was going to (have to) navigate my own survivor experience, that I would write with survivors. That particular understanding brought on big mourning and loss, as I'd somehow convinced myself that I could write about sex without writing about trauma. Denial works in powerful ways, doesn't it?)

While studying for my master's degree in Transformative Language Arts, Ladelle McWhorter's book *Bodies and Pleasures: Foucault and the Politics of Sexual Normalization* introduced me to the concept of "*askesis*, an exercise of oneself in the activity of thought." McWhorter describes *askesis* (which she learned about through studying the philosophy of Michel Foucault) as "a self-transformative, self-overcoming practice, whose purpose is 'to learn to what extent the effort to think one's own history can free thought from what it silently thinks, and so enable it to think differently.'"

When I speak of writing as transformative, I mean a practice in which the writer opens themselves to just this sort of in-depth exploration and metamorphosis.

Of course, not everyone wants their writing to catapult them from caterpillar into the thing with wings. Sometimes you just want to jot down the notes of the day. I understand that. The thing is—sometimes the wings begin to emerge anyway, and it is useful to have a practice in place to help them unfurl fully, when you are ready to risk leaping into the air. Transformative writing practice has helped me— and many of those I've written with—not only excavate my wings out from under years of scar tissue, but also learn how to fly.

Transformative writing is often risky, genre-defying, full of metaphors, stream of consciousness, deeply connected and unconsciously-driven. Over time, through the use of this practice, we are not only able to improve our writing, but we are also able to witness ourselves in the process of changing. This is writing that takes chances, is not censored by our inner editor. Sometimes the results of this kind of writing are linear, straightforward. Sometimes the results are an almost surreal conglomeration of verbs, nouns, and adjectives with no distinct structure, conjugation or form—often the resulting writing is somewhere between these extremes. Every time, *every time*, though, this practice of dropping onto the page and following the words wherever they seem to want us to go results in emotionally-resonant work. I have found the process of freewriting to be an erotic, embodied experience, after Audre Lorde's definition of *erotic*: "I speak of the erotic as the deepest life force, a force which moves us toward living in a fundamental way. And when I say living I mean it as that force which moves us toward what will accomplish real positive change."

When we write freely this way, over a period of time, we give ourselves the space to examine our inner curvature, the contours of our minds and experiences. We write ourselves into new ways of perceiving, new ways of knowing—profoundly intimate experiences, both, if we allow them to be, because they open the door to new ways of being in the world. Transformative practice in action: the slow and gorgeous effort of learning to communicate (with) all parts of our inside selves again.

The music of transformation

Locate and download a copy of Sweet Honey in the Rock
singing "Ella's Song" (buy it if you can—support your
revolutionary artists!—or find a video of the song online).
Play it once you are in your writing place, with your notebook
ready, pen uncapped, coffee steaming next to you, whatever
you need to help your words flow. Let the lyrics wash over
you. Notice what images or feelings rise up in you as you
listen. If a line or a phrase catches your attention, copy that
down into your notebook. You might begin writing from any
of these associations or words, or you can begin with the
phrase, "We who believe in freedom..." Follow your writing
wherever it seems to want you to go, even if you end up
writing about something completely different from what you'd
originally intended.

the page has room for my incomprehensibility

Today I don't want words, I want the juice of this river, I want to play in the garden. I want to plant new seeds and then listen to the neighborhood birds until the seeds throw up shoots. Some days it's all white butterflies and green tea. Somedays it's all the dog and her orange ball and the kids screaming at the school a block away. Some days you've done enough healing, it's been years enough, and you can set something down, remove the practice barrier, the training wheels, you can roll down the window and let the air in because you've done enough. You've done enough. There are more tears to come, yes, there will be more big ache in this lifetime, but you recognize now that that's the human condition—not only about incest, not only about recovery, just the whole life fact of this existence. We don't stop crying and there is laughter in our eyes, the puppy sprawls at my feet in the shade. I let the sun take my shoulders to a dark brown, bake this old, oldest, tension out of muscle and bone. (2014)

The page has room for all of this, has room for my incomprehensibility, for what's belabored, for the poetry that lives inside all my pretense. The page has room for the scars and scabs, the boll weevils, the torn leaves, the torn skin, the nonsense phrases, the bird calls, the butterfly with the wet and torn wing. The page has room for text messages and daydreams, the old fantasy and the hummingbird right now putting its green beak into the scarlet runner bean blossoms. The page has room for my wilted leaves, for the gangrenous selves, for the parts half clipped and dying, has room for what's still to be resurrected and room for what he just could not figure out how to kill.

The page has room for as much as you can give it, and only accepts it one way: a word at a time. You can give it whatever words you want, in whatever order they arrive, but you have to stroke them out letter by letter. You give the chaotic story a bottleneck to push through and it will frame itself into a kind of sense. Write it again and the frame, the sense, will be new again. You never write yourself the same way twice. The hummingbird flies overhead—you grab it out of the air, you press its luminescent feathers and rusted-hinge song to the page. You open your eyes wide, wider, to find more of yourself existing. You are how you see. That apple tree, how the breeze reshapes its flow around you, how you eavesdrop on the conversation between those two city birds. You are the dreams you lived and the dreams you left behind. You are everything that got you here and you are *here*.

How does transformation happen? Minute by minute, and word by word.

As is true for so many of us, writing saved my life. I'd been trained out of the ability to be a friend, had been instructed to trust no one, did not open myself to even my most significant others. The person who knew me best in the world, during my adolescence and very young adulthood, was the man who sexually abused me, and even *him* I didn't tell everything (despite his very thorough attempt to convince me that, since he could read my mind and already knew what I was thinking, it was simply a measure of my trustworthiness for me to reveal to him my every thought). The only safe place I could find was the page. I came to realize that he couldn't get in there (nor, actually, could he get into my mind, but allowing myself to trust that fact took much longer). Finally, I had a place for all of myself to belong. I let the worry, remembering, panic, desire, sorrow, rage and fear out there. Writing helped me to figure out what I knew, what I thought, who I'd been and who I was becoming. I read *Writing Down the Bones*, and followed Natalie Goldberg's instructions: freewrite every day, follow any surprising or ridiculous thought, get it all down onto the paper, don't stop to analyze or decipher, just write, just write, just write. The practice became exercise and meditation, and a process of recreation and resurrection.

•§•

They say—those voices of writerly authority—that we should write what we know. But sometimes what we know is denial and silence. What we know is discord. What we know is our words squelched or torn from our throats.

So we write what we know, *and* we write our "unknown"—that which is uncertain, hazy, confusing, diffusely remembered, unrooted in us. Write what you don't know, or what you don't know *yet*. Write what you think or imagine or wonder. Write your certainties and your fears. Write what unknowing feels like. We need a language for what it's like not to know what one's own body has done or been put through. Write the fuzziness and numbness. Write the cycling of emotions. Write exactly what happened—what you know happened and what you don't know happened. Write the uncertain as if you were absolutely clear, and then write it full of questions and confusion. Write it grammatically incorrect, as it exists within your body and memory: confusions, fragmented, broken, metaphorical.

•§•

As young children, if we are lucky, we are taught by those who love us to listen to our instinct, intuition, curiosities—to listen to our "gut." We need guidance and encouragement to heed that deep inside wisdom, though, and most often, even for those of us not abused, the process of growing up means learning to ignore our intuition. We are taught to do what others expect from us, what makes others comfortable or happy. If we are female, we're taught to act small, get quiet, and stuff our voices down while baring our bodies for the viewing and approval of others; if we are male, we're taught to get loud and big, force our voice into a room, take what we want and stuff our emotions down. If we are genderqueer, well, we're mostly just taught to disappear. We are—all of us—taught that what other people think of us is more important than what we think of ourselves. And we are taught that being ourselves, if that self is at odds with the expectations of our community or those in power, can get us hurt. Our survival instinct kicks in and teaches us how to follow, even if following chafes.

In the workshops I talk about what it means to come back into a relationship of trust with our intuition, that small quiet voice inside that has always wanted to lead us in the right direction but that we were trained or forced to ignore, especially if we were children of violent homes. It didn't matter that there was something inside us screaming, *No, stop, let's get out of this situation, let's get away from this person!* If we live with our abusers, we can't leave, at least not physically, most of the time. We are forced to turn our attentions *outward*—to focus on the smallest nuances of a parent's or abuser's mood, voice, actions, so that we can get a sense of their emotional state and thereby hope to keep ourselves a little more safe. We learn how to read their tone of voice when they call us to dinner, learn how the evening is going to unfold by the way they shut the door when they come into the house. We give so much attention to the violent or unstable people around us, and we turn our attention away from the voice inside that knows what goodness and brilliance we're capable of. We have to ignore that voice if we want to be safe.

I've used writing as one way back into a relationship with my intuition. And part of that practice, for me, has been writing messily, taking risks, following whatever thread is pulling at me. I write the words that call themselves forward, even if they make no logical sense, even if I'm confused by where they're going, even if I'm scared or feel stupid about what I'm writing. Maybe I just hear syllables or nonsense words—write them. Maybe there's a phrase that wants out that I don't understand—I have to write it; otherwise those words or sounds just keep repeating themselves until I do.

This is a languaging of trauma, the real world's song, with its own grammars and choruses. Repeat what bears repeating, and then rewrite the rest. Follow your instinct, and let your pen guide you.

Using metaphor to get under everyday "sense"

On a sheet of paper, number the lines 1-10. (I always liked the numbering part of any assignment when I was in elementary school.) Draw two vertical lines down the page, separating the page into three columns. In the first column, next to each number, write the names of people or places that are important to you. Try not to think about this; write the first thing that comes to mind. Now cover that first list (with your hand or a piece of paper). In the third column, write 10 common nouns (everyday things like, *cow, mountains, governor*). Fill the in-between column with "is" or "is like," then add articles (a, an, the) and do whatever else you need to make the sentences read smoothly. You'll end up with lines something like this:

1. *Mother is a foot* (a metaphor)

2. *San Francisco is like orchids* (a simile)

These will usually be metaphors and similes that don't really make "sense." Read through your list, and let one of these prompts choose you. Copy it onto a new page in your notebook and begin to write: what could this line mean? Give yourself ten minutes. Don't be surprised if your writing veers off into strange places. Let yourself go there!

we are not trauma but we know the words for it

We get all the words. We get to write everything. We get to not be ok and be absolutely ok at the same time. We get to take this work slowly—write a memory for ten minutes, then breathe and cry and beat pillows for twenty. This isn't work we need to rush through. We're building a relationship with our deep inner self, our surviving self, our material, our memory, our creative genius. We are meeting our own idioms, a linguistics of loss and determination, a semantics of our own particular triumph. We write phrases that don't make sense anywhere outside the context of our own subconscious—even we may not consciously understand our writing sometimes. We keep writing until we understand what the sense that lives in us could be. We write something that completely contradicts what we wrote yesterday, and then we keep writing until we understand that we have not contradicted, we simply exist in multitudes—we are Whitman's heirs.

Some days you might write all around the edges of the violence you suffered. Some days you might avoid euphemisms: instead of entering the written picture with the relative soft-focus of "that was the day he molested me," you might choose to describe precisely what of him went where on you. You might describe the full gloss of your body's reaction. You might describe it as though it's happening to someone else, or it's happening to someone you're talking to. You might choose a third person point of view (that is, using *she*, *he*, *it*, or *they*) that puts some distance between the reader and the experience, or use the passive voice (e.g., "The body was abandoned") to center the action and draw attention away from the actors. One scene of your story could use all of these framings. Use all the tools at your disposal.

Then write it differently. Write yourself fighting back, then write yourself fighting back differently or not fighting back at all. Write someone walking in. Write from the point of view of the bed, the couch, the closet, the garage floor, the basement walls, the kitchen table, the office chair—the inanimate witnesses to your experience. If someone had walked by, walked in, what would they have heard or seen? Write it inside out. Every different telling brings forth new details, new remembering, and new art.

Then write about the birdsong in the summer birch tree, the smell of sea salt roses, the deep blue of the thin autumn sky. Or take yourself for ice cream or go for a run or have a long cry or a swim.

When you write trauma, your body will fill up with memory and emotion. Consider how you want to take care of yourself after, how to thank your body for this effort of recollection and creation, for tangling itself back up in the old (sometimes not so old) memories, how to communicate to your psyche: *I will take care of us through this process of reclaiming and restorying.* I take long walks, cry into the notebook, get into the garden or watch silly sitcoms. I go for long drives, roll the windows down, turn the radio up, and sing loud. I browse bookstores, play ball with the puppy, make myself a cup of strong green tea.

Notice when, during the writing, you find yourself suddenly so sleepy you think you could lay your head down and fall asleep right there. Listen to what your body tells you: are your muscles tense? Does your skin go tingly, or numb? This is your intuition speaking to you. Sometimes these body messages will mean, *Write more now.* Sometimes they will mean, *Get me the fuck out of here.* You'll learn the difference—maybe the hard way, by trying to ignore the body totally, like I did (which—spoiler alert—didn't work all that well).

We claim every word that could fit into any mouth. We do this every day, or most days—we claim regular and consistent space for our creative emergence and delight. We write until we don't understand what we're saying anymore. We write until we're bored with the trauma. We repeat ourselves, think we are tapped out, and then we stumble over a scent and we describe it and that leads in to a story that taps into a vein of new memory, so we write more.

We are not trauma but we know the words for it. We know how to speak to it. We know how to reach inside of it. We know how to recognize its underseams. We have stories that can save children, save sisters and daughters, brothers and sons, the mothers lost to themselves, the men who think rape will save them—we want to strip them all down. Those who pretend not to know this song cannot help but hear our chorus. We hold no room for pretense. We call out the names anyway. We tell the true stories anyway. We describe tactics, smooth smiles, rage. We teach each other lost languages. The liars don't have to read our stories, but their women are, and their sons. Girl children are sharpening their blades on the stones of our stories. This time we name endings. We feed the young ones what we know and they will save their own lives. (2014)

We use poetic language or the conventions of science fiction, we write mythologies and fictions, we use legalese or academese or our mother tongue— we write trauma as a business letter. We write trauma as a movie script. We write trauma as a novel, a piece of flash fiction, as a shopping list, a letter to the editor, a to-do list, a song, a piece of art criticism, a recipe, a series of haiku, notes for an essay, a blog post, a guide book, an encyclopedia, a dictionary, a thesaurus; we write it as a travelogue, as erotic fiction, as pornography, as a poli-sci textbook, as chant, as spoken word, as a map, as a series of blueprints, a guide to a demolition. We write it as translation, as a phone book, a contact list, as religious ceremony, as a bible, as a how-to manual. We write it as pulp fiction, as noir, as a series of public service announcements, as ancient spells, as feminist polemic, as a letter in a bottle; we carve it into rock, cave, treebark, write it in sand and beach glass, sing it to deer and ducks and hawks. We tell it with eagle eyes and up close like flea bites.

Write the rage. Write letters that will never get sent. Say everything you wanted to say, everything you *did* say, everything they should have been able to hear you say.

We take every angle, every form. We use what works, and as we write, we discover, uncover, recover and (re)create ourselves. We are naked and named, we declare ourselves. We find the language for the normal, everyday evil in the world. We don't just say *Me, too*—some days we also say, *Fuck you*. We take our tongues back from between their teeth. We name exactly what they did. Their language is only part of our story. Their daily and commonplace violence is only part of the story. How they meet us with big smiles and generosity later is only part of the story. We must write, too, our aching bodies, the breadth of our laughter, how our mouths still know how to smile: we give the whole story of our lives to the page.

Practice trusting your own words

Set your timer for ten minutes. On a new page in your notebook, start with the phrase, "This is what they told me to say..." (If the prompt isn't clicking, try changing the pronouns: "This is what they told her to say," or "him to say," or, "This is what he told us to say." Let yourself notice what works). Write for about five minutes, then stop. Take a breath. Begin again, on a new line, with the phrase, "This is what they told me *not* to say..." Write for five more minutes. If you want to continue, pick up your pen, take another breath, and then dive into anything that came up for you during the first two writes.

finding your own routine

For twenty years, I put myself and my healing psyche in front of a notebook, nearly every day, opened the notebook to a fresh page and begun to write. My mornings often look like this: wake up to the electronic harp of my smartphone's alarm, make some green tea, settle into my writing room with my notebook and light a candle—I like it to be early enough that it's still dark, early enough that there's nothing else I *should* be doing. So often I've felt like I've got to steal my writing time: from partners, from my job, from chores that need attending to. There were years when I rose at 4:30 or 5 a.m., well before my partner woke, so that I didn't feel guilty for taking time alone to write. For me, this regular practice of morning writing is saying to writing, "My first and best breaths are still yours."

Long before I read Julia Cameron's *The Artist's Way*, I was waking up early in the morning to write for an hour or so, as close to every day as possible. I called these morning writes my "core dump" times. In computing terms, a core dump is a file that's created to collect everything that was in the computer's memory when there's a crash. When I apply the term to my writing life, I mean a write in which I dump onto the page anything and everything that's in my head and heart at a given moment—no matter how random or seemingly disconnected. Poet and artist Brian Andreas describes the spaciousness with which I try to hold such inner disorder: "he tried for days to put / it all back in the proper / order, but finally he / gave up & left it there / in a pile & loved / everything equally." These were the hours that I could get everything out in front of me, my worries and frustrations, trauma memory and work struggles, trouble or longing in my relationship. It was like a long talk with a good friend who listened intently and accepted me unconditionally.

Writing has been the place I trusted the most—the place where I learned to trust *myself*. And I have been fortunate to live with significant others who treated my writing with respect, who did not read journals, who treated my journals as if they were as private and inviolate as the inside of my own beating heart. I've rarely shared with anyone what I wrote in my notebooks—the notebook was a place for me to work things out, a steady and long-suffering companion who didn't judge or criticize or interrupt or tell me what I ought to do. I needed this kind of sacred, protected, nonjudgmental space—that is, I needed to learn to treat my whole self as sacred, to release myself from judgment.

Even after all these years of daily practice, though, I can still struggle to give myself what best serves my words: those earliest morning hours devoted to the tender skin between dreamtime and waking life. Things get too busy, there are too many jobs or a love affair just beginning (or suddenly going down in flames) that needs all of my otherwise-creative energies, and suddenly there's no time to write three pages in the morning. It's so easy—even after twenty years of practice that proves otherwise—to convince myself *I just don't have the time*. And then, slowly but surely, my well-being begins to unravel.

Fortunately, every day I get to begin again. I get to decide to show up for my creative and healing self all over again. Writing practice brings me back into my human realness: I don't have all the answers, I am complicated and ridiculous and loving, I am not as shiny as I pretend to be, thank goodness.

At the 2010 Healing Art of Writing conference, an attendee asked how one develops a writing practice, how one gets in the habit of writing. The questioner was new to writing, and she wanted to do it right. She'd heard, maybe, that the way you become a writer is you write every day, no matter what. Underneath her question, I heard: *What do you do to become a real writer?*

Responding to the question, poet Jane Hirshfield spoke of her own writing practice: she doesn't especially have one—well, not one that looks regular and regimented, anyway. She told us that she writes when she's drawn to write, and when she is not drawn to write, she doesn't force herself: when she tries to force writing that's not ready to come, the writing's not good, doesn't work for her at all. Amid all the voices telling new writers that they must make space for writing every day, I'm grateful for Hirshfield's example, her reminder that, as creative folks living creative lives, we get to learn and honor our own rhythms, trust how the words want to flow in/through us, and make our lives work in that direction.

I encourage you to give your writing what it needs, whenever you can. One friend writes in the morning, sitting on the sidewalk outside her apartment building, where with the sun on her face, she writes the day awake. Another friend can only write at night, after her child has gone to bed and all of her tasks (both for her job and her family) are completed. Some folks I know only really write in workshops or writing groups—their writing craves the company of others. These folks pay attention to what the writer inside them is asking for, and try to make those conditions available for their writing as often as possible.

We who survive trauma are endlessly creative and find our healing all over the skin of possibility: we paint and draw, we sing, we have open-hearted conversation with good friends or with anonymous folks online, we fight, we write, we run, we dance, we read the same book over and over again, we watch terrible TV, we drink, we use, we cut, we have sex that doesn't serve us, we have sex that brings us into our bodies bit by bit, we use anything and everything to get us to where we are willing to see the awfulness through just one more day until we reach into a day that isn't all about awful anymore. Sometimes therapy is an answer. Often and for many it is a very good answer. In the years I couldn't afford the therapy I needed, I wrote, and I believe I had to write myself into a place where therapy (meaning the deep work of figuring out how to do true human connection through sharing, risk, transference and countertransference and all that) could even be a possibility.

•§•

Maybe you've heard the recommendations. Write every day. *Nulla dies sine linea*: no day without lines. Julia Cameron says three unbroken pages every morning. Novelist Madeline L'Engle is to have said, "Just write a little bit every day. Even if it's only for half an hour—write, write, write." Anne Lamott says to try and sit down at about the same time every day, in order to train your creative unconscious to kick in for you.

For me, being at the notebook in the morning, each time, is a returning to that place of presence and safety, a returning to that place of non-judgement and discipline, that place of structure and freedom. There are plenty of productive writers who do not write every day; Toni Morrison once told the *Paris Review*, "I am not able to write regularly. I have never been able to do that—mostly because I have always had a nine-to-five job. I had to write either in-between those hours, hurriedly, or spend a lot of weekend and predawn time." We do it when we can; if it works to write daily, then do that. If you can only really get writing when you're around other people, then get thee to a writing group! If you write when your muse grabs you by the hair, then make sure you know where your notebook is when she starts hollering at you. Above all, try not to beat yourself up for not doing it the way "the experts" say you're supposed to—because even the experts can't agree.

There's a book I love that I discovered while I was at a Hedgebrook residency in 2012—*World Enough and Time: On Creativity and Slowing Down*, by Christian McEwen. In this thoughtful, thorough book, McEwen describes how necessary it is for writers and other artists to slow down, feel our rhythms, be all the way in our lives. Through personal anecdotes and examples from writers and other creative folks, McEwen makes the case for a slower—rather than fast and multitasky—creative life: she describes the artist's need to wander (literally and figuratively), to have space for silence and dreams, to do one thing at a time, to have space for deep connection with others and room in our lives for alone time. Not everyone will resonate with her arguments. I myself bought a copy of her book as soon as I returned from Hedgebrook and dip into its pages whenever I need to counter the voices in my head (not to mention all those business-coach types out there on the interwebs) clamoring at me to do more and go faster and do it all *now now now now now.*

Whatever your rhythm, keep listening to and honoring it. Write every day if that's right for your work. Find what works for you for awhile, and do that. And then what works for your writing will change. And you will change, too. That's just as it should be.

It's not necessary to write every day in order to call yourself a writer. "A writer is someone who writes," my teacher (and the founder of the Amherst Writers & Artists workshop method) Pat Schneider always says, quoting William Stafford. While many extoll the virtues of morning writing, you might work better in the slow energy of the afternoon, or the quickening of first dark. You might prefer just to write on weekend mornings, if you don't do other work on the weekends, in order to have hours free and stretched out and open for your words. You might prefer not to have any set schedule at all, instead just following the pull of your creative urges, waiting for some writing to shove hard against the insides of your fingers, needing you to set it free into the world.

Write into your rhythm

Take ten minutes and write about dancing—any sort of dancing, whether you yourself *like* to dance or not.

Then take ten more minutes, and write into these questions: What would an ideal or dream writing life look like for you? Where would you write? What time of day? What would you write, if you suddenly found yourself living that ideal writing life? Try and get into the details, the specifics. Let yourself really *see* it, feel it, move into and through the possibilities.

what they take

All over the country, all over the world, illuminated by that insouciant yellow moon, bright, clever, curious children are being suffocated under the weight of the violence done to them. They are turning themselves inward. They are turning away from what they love, because what they love is used against them. They are learning to distrust their curiosity, their intuition. They are learning that there's no room for wonder—how can you take time to explore the world when so much of your creative genius must go to keeping yourself alive and as safe as possible?

•§•

I imagine what I might have been able to do with the last twenty years of my life if I hadn't been, first and foremost, focused on surviving.

Yes, I know we are to be grateful for the places we get to, eventually. We are to be grateful that, *eventually*, we heal enough to find a way back into intimacy, find a way back into joy. We can find a way back into these bodies that have carried us around, even through hell. Eventually we find a way home, into ourselves and our real lives, if we are lucky and persistent and don't die in the meantime.

Please hear me: this isn't about self-pity. I just feel sad.

When we say they steal our souls, steal our lives, this is what we mean—they impact what we can do with our capacity, our incipience. They leaked their barrels of crude oil into the complex and nascent pool of us, they poison all of the very many different selves we had before us to possibly become.

And so, instead of having the chance to focus our energies on *becoming* one of those many selves, we must spend our years cleaning the slough, trying to remove the crude. We bring in big booms to collect and clear out *en masse* what remains of the spill. We clean off the bigger animals—the ducks and muskrats and deer and raccoons. One by one, we wipe out eyes, wash until most of the residue is gone. We clear away what died, spend years fertilizing, tending the soil, hoping life will return to the places that were decimated. We spread fire-retardant material, we post sentries and guards at the edges of the pond, trying to keep watch on all sides, wanting to keep out anyone who'd try to pollute us so badly again. Sometimes we are successful. Sometimes we are not—but the energy is expended just the same.

Regardless of what else we wanted to study and learn, we have to teach ourselves biologics, become environmentalists, scientists—we learn to develop little organisms that will feed on what's left of the poison, that will consume what molecules are left in the water and will seek out the bits that fell to the floor of the pond, permeated the water, soaked into the sand, coated the tadpoles and minnows and frogs and turtles, got inside their mouths, ate into the grasses and pond marsh and tilted the ecosystem toward death.

We spend the bulb and blossom of our lives cleaning up a toxic waste site.

Meanwhile, we watch our friends come into full flower: making connections, reaching out, writing books, making marriages and families, developing their crafts, their skills, themselves. We watch them build careers, and wonder what is wrong with us that we can't do what they're doing. But we are still salvaging the superfund site inside of us. We painstakingly wipe off every blade of grass and feather of every bird that is a necessary part of our inside selves. The oil is never completely eradicated. Some of the areas impacted never recover, never bounce back, never become what they ought to have been able to become. And then we simply have to mourn their loss, grieve what they might have been. "Meanwhile the world goes on," Mary Oliver wrote. *"Meanwhile the sun and the clear pebbles of the rain..."* Meanwhile, there are other oil spills, everywhere. Meanwhile, those who polluted us are allowed to continue their devastation. Meanwhile, the balance of power is not upset, meanwhile you and I spend years teaching ourselves and then teaching others how to clean up the mess that our perpetrators made of our souls, made of our lives.

What if there was something else we had in mind to do?

There is a Dorothy Allison poem that lives in me. Entitled "boston, massachusettes," it was written in the aftermath of the homophobic murder of a lesbian in Boston, who was splashed with gasoline and set on fire. The poem imagines the voice of that woman who'd been lit: "This is not all I am / I had something more in mind to do."

Something in me, in us, screams this as well. *This is not all I am. I had something more in mind to do.* We are forced, through someone else's actions, to turn our precious attentions, the energy of our "one wild and precious life," to the effort of cleaning up someone else's mess—and for many years we feel like that mess is us.

What if I'd had something else in mind to do?

Some choices are made for us. But sometimes—eventually—we get to make different choices for ourselves. We clean the last feather of the last duck, we rope off the wild grassland long enough that new life emerges; the songbirds return, we can see bees and butterflies in the wildflowers that have just blossomed, little fish come back out of hiding. The landscape, the habitat, is never returned to the exact state it was in before the disaster—but it *can* recover.

Rehabilitating a wild ecosystem is an enormous undertaking, one that takes time and money and resources that we might have otherwise devoted to other efforts, other work, other interests, other curiosities. And it's labor that often goes wholly unseen.

We are reclaiming what another human being—or, sometimes, a whole society—decided to ruin, to take for themselves, to spill all over and into and leave covered with his (or their) garbage. We are not garbage. We deserve all the effort of cleanup. We deserve the time it takes to have every bit of our ecosystem attended to during the cleanup process—every microbe, every biological organism, every single-celled paramecium, every shellfish dug into the mud, every clump of wild rose, every spray of marsh grass, every layer of water that expands and contracts through winter freezes and spring thaws and the hot labor of summer.

And the truth is that we might have done something else with that time and attention. And it isn't fair. And yes, we do it anyway. Yes, we ought to have been able to do what our classmates or neighborhood friends did and just turn our attentions outward, toward our curiosities, our growth and potential. We ought to have been able to sit back and celebrate the wild complexity of our inner self and, while tending to all of the layers, inner and outer, deep water and treetop, live into the complex diversity that would emerge in us and of us.

I'm trying to find a language for what is stolen from us when we're violated as young people. It's not our souls—our souls are always with us. What's stolen is our time. We have precious little time in this life, and that is what they take from us. That is what is irreplaceable. Our bodies and hearts recuperate, because we are extraordinarily resilient, because we are capable and adoring, because we don't take no for an answer from the bits of inside self that want to give up and die. Many of us don't die. But our trajectories are forever altered.

(And those who wreak the havoc in the first place? They're off in their lives—maybe unaffected, maybe continuing to create destruction elsewhere around the world, maybe confined to a cell, having only themselves to desecrate. So very rarely do they clean up after themselves.)

Of course it's not too late—it's never too late to be the selves we might have become. e.e. cummings said, "It takes courage to grow up and become who you really are." We become hybrid—old and new growth in the same patch of self—and we learn from the labor, the effort, the attention paid, from blisters and aching backs, from sorrow at what has been lost, and joy at what emerges from the ashes. Life persists, renews, in the aftermath of destruction. That's what they can never kill. We rise to the surface, again and again and again.

Take it back

Did this chapter bring up feelings/responses/longings? Let yourself begin by writing those. What happens for you when an alumni magazine arrives, or when you read an update on social media about childhood friends doing well when you are struggling? Give yourself ten minutes.

Give yourself ten more minutes to write what was taken from you. What would it look like to take any part of that back?

Then give yourself something sweet (a new book from the library, maybe an ice cream cone...).

put on your own oxygen mask first: writing as radical self-care

In my community, a lot of folks are talking about radical self-care—not just self-care, but *radical* self-care. But what makes self-care radical?

I think you have an idea. I think your deep heart knows. It's the *other* voices that demand this explanation—the inner critic, the internalized perpetrator, your inner radical activist wanting to know how you can possibly justify an hour for a walk around the lake at the heart of your town or even, god forbid, several days' vacation when the revolution is nowhere near at hand and people are starving and beaten and suffering while you decide you're just gonna take *a little down time*. Really? "Who do you think you are?" ask all the voices in unison.

We are not supposed to take care of ourselves. We *know* we're not worth taking care of. Those meant to care for and protect us when we were younger didn't care for us. Who are we to do otherwise?

My work has been about discovering how to get—how to even *know*—what you want when you've spent a lifetime learning to maneuver around other people's wants, when you've learned every tactic, every trick in the book, to live through having somebody else's desires forced upon you, when you only know what you want in reaction to someone else's demands.

We live in a culture that trains us in dissatisfaction with our bodies and lives, that values workaholism, materialism, the acquisition of More. If we are activists, we inhabit a culture of overwork, in which direct and secondary trauma impacts everyone around us. We see our comrades doing too much for too little (if any) pay. We see frontline activists and direct action workers burn out; we see old-timers harden into a professionalized cynical mindset that protects them from the pain and stress they see every day. We learn by example that our self-care is never supposed to take priority over the work. *The work.*

I don't believe this anymore. I used to, but after hitting a massive burnout in 2008 and then *continuing* to overwork myself for several more years, I've finally opened my eyes to the idea that there might be other, maybe even more effective, ways of engaging in a long-term and sustainable relationship with trauma and social change work.

Our self-care is radical because so many of us were trained from birth to tend to others' needs first. Our self-care is radical because it sustains us for the journey, it keeps us in the game, it makes our work more effective, it opens our hearts, it brings self-love back to the table as a necessary goal and practice.

I know, you say. Yes, self-care, right. I just have to finish this grant proposal, do my shift at the co-op, organize tonight's transformative justice roundtable, answer these twenty-seven emails and cover the hotline...

Then *I'll take care of myself.*

There's no good time. There's always something else *really important* to do. To-do lists are only marginally useful when they include items like "upend patriarchy," "write healing book," "undo white supremacy," "end rape culture." I don't know about you but I've *had* to-do lists like that. The work seems endless, because it is: we're a part of an enormous social, cultural transformation. For us to be able to show up for this work we love, for the people and communities and world we believe in, we have to attend to our hearts and bodies and souls.

The choice to sustain ourselves is radical—especially for those of us whom our family, community, or society deems not at all worth saving. Audre Lorde said, speaking as a Black lesbian feminist, "Caring for myself is not self-indulgence, it is self-preservation, and that is an act of political warfare." Self-care is radical when it directly contradicts the messages all around us, telling us we deserve to die.

•§•

What we pay attention to reveals what matters most to us. Spanish philosopher Jose Ortega y Gasset said, "Tell me to what you pay attention and I will tell you who you are." I became aware some years ago that I consistently put everything else in my life ahead of this work that I so adore and need: the work of pen to paper, of imagination, wool-gathering, wondering and dreaming and remembering and resurrecting and restorying, this work of words. I did my day job, the dishes, tended to the people in my life; I did the second (and sometimes third) jobs, I prepared for writing workshops, communicated with other writers—then I obsessed about relationship struggles, got overwhelmed and exhausted, drank wine and watched TV to decompress, felt guilt and shame, then went to bed. No time to write, once again.

For me, developing and sustaining a daily writing practice has been about learning to put on my own oxygen mask before I try to help anybody else. I know quite well what happens when I decide I don't really *need* to write every day, or convince myself that I just don't have the time: resentment builds up in me like a toxin. As soon as I sit down with my notebook and journal for twenty minutes, though—not necessarily writing about whatever's bothering me in the moment, but describing the smell of the morning breeze, the sound of the birds, the colors of the morning light, what happened yesterday, last night's dreams—my whole outlook shifts. I don't know what makes this happen. It's like an inner realignment, a rebooting and system recalibration.

Some years ago, one of my teachers and mentors, Caryn Mirriam-Goldberg, the founder of Goddard's Transformative Language Arts concentration, recommended that we who are writers or artists make time for our creative work first thing in the day, before our attention became scattered. Caryn's inquiry was this: what if you gave the first and best energy of the day to the thing you loved the most? What if we trained our muses to believe—through our actions—that we were devoted enough to put our creative work first?

This challenge made me stop and think. How many of my friends complained that they had no time to write, between our many jobs and our responsibilities to home and family? How often had *I* complained about this? Many parents I know, for instance, wait until their kids are asleep, until all the work of the day is finished, before they sit down to write—already exhausted and depleted—only to find themselves watching cat videos on YouTube instead of developing that next scene in their novels. I used to believe I should get done with my *real work* before it was ok for me to write. I felt guilty about taking time out to write at all. Selfish. Ashamed. Like I was stealing something from somebody else in order to get this soul-feeding work done.

We who are survivors of intimate violence often don't believe we deserve what we love. I used to describe in detail, to friends, other workshop facilitators, other writers, how much I *wanted* to be writing, but *then I didn't write*. I created spaces in which others could write, and then watched, with jealousy and frustration, as they wrote. Eventually I got so hungry, so desperate for writing time, that I felt justified in shutting out everything and everyone else in my life, forgoing work, canceling workshops, in order to binge-write. This is not a sustainable rhythm (to put it mildly), this swinging from creative anorexia to creative binge and back again. I don't recommend it.

We have, as a culture, this myth of the solitary (lonely) writer, the one who needs a little cottage all her own, and empty, open days in which to work; in the midst of my creative self-denial, I convinced myself that this was what I needed, and that when I had a room of my own, *then* I'd be able to write. The truth is so much less romantic and dire. I need at least thirty minutes every day to sustain my creative self. That's bare-bones. It doesn't have to be the pale, unwashed writer secreted away in the garret above the house, locked away for years: It's twenty to thirty minutes in the morning, first thing, every day. I will not simply wait for the muse to strike—if she shows up, beautiful, and if not, I'll still open the notebook first thing in the morning (preferably with candle and cup of tea nearby) and let the pen loose on the page. This is what saves me. This is what I know works for me.

I apply stricter discipline when I want to bring an essay, story, poem or other structured project to fruition. But this is the standard: tell that inside-self every day that you will show up for her, and every day the stories will start to flow. Show up for her about the same time every day, and she'll start being ready for you at about that same time every day. Maya Angelou said, "What I try to do is write. I may write for two weeks 'the cat sat on the mat, that is that, not a rat.' And it might be just the most boring and awful stuff. But I try. When I'm writing, I write. And then it's as if the muse is convinced that I'm serious and says, 'Okay. Okay. I'll come.'"

Poet Richard Hugo, in his brilliant book about writing, *The Triggering Town*, shares this anecdote when he talks about developing a regular writing practice: "Once a spectator said, after Jack Niklaus had chipped a shot in from a sand trap, 'That's pretty lucky.' Niklaus is suppose to have replied, 'Right. But I notice the more I practice, the luckier I get.'"

Through this practice, you develop a relationship with your storyteller, that part of you that got ignored and walled away for safekeeping during the years of your trauma. This part didn't die, and she didn't disappear—she was always with you. This daily writing practice is simply reengaging with a very old conversation You open the notebook and say hello when you uncap your pen and start writing. She says hello back by offering up words you can slip onto the page, by inviting you to write into your deepest, scariest, most beautiful songs. When we are willing to find language for the stories our bodies still hold, we can gain greater control over those traumatic memories. We create a place and a container into which to release these stories of loss and shame and horror and grief—as well as a place to honor our survival.

Self-care is uncomfortable for many of us: we fear judgment from our friends and communities, our comrades, our families, those around us who are not taking care of themselves. Of course it's uncomfortable at first—and maybe for awhile: it's discomfiting to act in direct opposition to the voices of those who told us we didn't deserve to *live*, much less have joy, pleasure, creativity, and celebration in our lives.

Radical self-care looks like acting with intention, looks like small daily or regular centering practices, looks like creative intervention in a way of life designed to sap all of our energy into the daily grind and away from love, intimacy, and cultural change.

Radical self-care looks like leaving work on time instead of staying an extra two or three (unpaid) hours to finish "just one more thing."

Radical self-care means releasing ourselves from the pressure to be like everyone else—either in mainstream culture or in our various so-called marginal communities. It means listening to our energy patterns, hungers, curiosities.

Radical self-care means knowing that what works for us today might not work tomorrow—and what today we think is *ridiculous*, indulgent, woo-woo or way *too Berkeley* (Body work? Ecstatic dance? Yoga retreats? Somatic energy healing?) may very well be just the thing that works best for us tomorrow.

Radical self-care means unscheduled space in our lives, time for wandering, time for wonder.

Radical self-care looks like learning to listen to our bodies. Down time. Breathing room. Resting is as important a part of exercise as contracting, after all.

What else can be acts of radical self-care? Consent. Sobriety. Quitting the day job. Therapy. Going back to school. Quitting school. Social media breaks. A movie marathon. Masturbation. A month of celibacy. A sex party. Tending a garden. Adopting a cat. Planning a vacation. Finding a different job. Leaving activist work.

Returning to activist work. A cup of tea. Meditation. Making yourself a delicious lunch. Grieving. Watching movies that make you laugh or cry—or both. What would you add to your list?

I think one of the reasons we call our self-care *radical* is that we want to assert its importance. Things that are edgy, dangerous, and transformative are deemed radical. Radical is about roots, is about shifting the core of a thing: in this case, ourselves.

So, sleep is radical for those of us raised on exhaustion. A long talk with our best friend is radical for those of us isolated from community. Deep, prolonged belly laughter is radical for those of us fed despair. These are transformative practices. Radical acts.

For me, radical self-care meant writing every day (and then reaching beyond writing practice into other healing modalities, once I found the limits of what writing could do for me). Writing practice has helped me discover when I needed a break, and has also helped me understand what I might need to do to take care of myself or make a change in my life. When I take the time to be in reflection (itself a practice of radical self-care), then I can respond to what my body and life are asking for. In the end, this is about crafting a life that is sustainable and consistently nourishing me so that I can engage in work that nourishes others, so that I can be of use in the ways I am *meant* to be of use.

Rooting in the body

Give yourself ten minutes for one of the following:

What would a day look like if you got to take exquisite care of yourself? What would you do if money/time weren't of any concern? What's one aspect of that ideal day that you could incorporate into your life right now?

The word "radical" comes from a Latin word meaning "root," and, in my experience, many of our roots reside in our bodies. Our self-care is rooted in our bodies. Write about a place where your body (or a character's body) is comfortable: Is this place inside or outside? Is this place "real" or fictional? What do you do there? What don't you do there? (Feel welcome to write in the third person (*her/his/their* body) or in the second person (*your* body) instead of in the first person (*my* body), if you choose.)

getting our whole mouth back

This is about my stepping back into language by swimming away from the abuser's so-called "logical" sense. This is about a writer whose words fell out of her mouth one at a time, just one at a time, until she thought she had none left. She turned to find them and was met with the blank bright face of silence. Powerful, uncommon creativity requires attentiveness, a willingness to play, a willingness to risk: all things that those in power seem to wish to squelch in us, we who are the victims of their abuses. Stories can collude with silence, in their occlusion of some aspect of an experience, but they can also be the opposite of silence: speaking truth to power in a fresh and embodied way, which power cannot help but attend to, if even for the instant of metaphorical resolution. And an instant's all it takes to change the world—and ourselves. (2002)

This is what a regular, consistent freewriting practice can do: it can make room for all the mess that we are. Give me those thirty minutes of writing, first thing in the morning, and my fragments and filaments begin to realign. I feel less piecemeal, less a la carte. I am more congruent—more whole.

Freewriting can erupt us with story.

When we make story, we create a kind of order—we put sequence, logic, organization (linear or not) to what had been just a random constellation of events. And when we are too tied to a particular story of ourselves, freewriting can offer us space for complication, questioning, disordering. Sometimes we need our old stories to come apart.

Writing ourselves whole doesn't mean writing ourselves into something neat and clean and grammatical; it means writing ourselves *wholly*—the ugly stories, the fragments of memory, the selves as yet unvoiced, the unwavering and terrifying desires. It means claiming and/or reclaiming the fullness of our language.

Many of us who were sexually abused were told what was being done to us wasn't happening. We were forced to say we liked what our perpetrators did. We were forced not to speak of it. We had our words used against us. We felt culpable if some of the violence was pleasurable. Words were snatched from our tongues. *Nos* were turned into *Yeses*. As much as we may have felt betrayed by our bodies, we may also have felt betrayed by our words. We had to speak with forked tongues, we had to use the words they fed us, we had to swallow, unuttered, the words that rose up in us to speak the truth.

Writing led me to look at my adolescence from different perspectives: yes, there's a girl inside the story with a penis shoved into her mouth who tells no one. *Keep writing*—remember that she was terrorized into silence. Can I find forgiveness for her inability to speak?

We can take our voices back for ourselves. It's no one's job to *give us back* our voices: our voices were not stolen or lost—they exist in us always and still. We were simply ignored. When we speak, we are defying that cultural edict to silence. When we write, we defy the norm that says, *You have no tongue to tell with.* The longer we tell the story that our voices were lost or stolen, the longer we believe that story, the longer some part of us remains silent. Writing down our story undermines that narrative, fissures it, creates the space for our real stories to emerge.

Writing ourselves whole is getting our whole mouth back, our whole throat back, our whole consciousness back, our whole creative genius back, our whole intuition back, our whole language back. Writing ourselves whole is claiming all the words and all the stories for ourselves to do with as we wish.

•§•

Writing trauma is always writing the gap, claiming not only what can be explained, shown, but also holding room for the rupture, the thing too sore or swollen to find its way into words, into the throat, too inflamed to move with grace down the forearm through the pen onto the page. *Here is a hollow place. Here is the place I still feel his hands. Here is my body spent with joy. Here is my body too fatigued to move. Here is where depression lives beneath my skin.*

This morning, to choose to write the gaps is to explain about the pornography on the bottom shelf of my stepfather's bedside table, those laminated pages filled with splayed and penetrated bodies, how I knew where the magazines were when I was fifteen, sixteen, younger. See me in my bedroom see him in my bedroomfind the magazine there by my face where I could focus my attention, how pornography gave me somewhere else to look while he was raping me. Leap to the unarticulable conversation between my younger self and those women on the pages who taught me how to bend myself open, taught me the value of what's pink within us, taught my face how to take a woman's shape of pleasure. As a girlchild unlearning how to be human, I needed to be taught how to wear other masks, and my mother could only show me the faces for silence and acquiescence and betrayal.

Write those gaps. Find what terrible beauty lives inside them.

•§•

Consider the stories we are ashamed of, the stories we are taught to be ashamed of: stories about hunger, desire, sex, illness, the intimacies of the body—its noises, excretions, breakdowns. The stories our society teaches us that it doesn't want to hear, doesn't know how to respond to, can't hold.

Poet Richard Hugo, in *The Triggering Town*, invites us to write into our obsessions: "Your triggering subjects are those that ignite your need for words. When you are honest to your feelings, that triggering town chooses you. Your words used your way will generate your meanings. Your obsessions lead you to your vocabulary. Your way of writing locates, even creates, your inner life. The relation of you to your language gains power."

We don't choose what we will write about; our subjects choose us. I am obsessed with putting words to our body-stories: stories of the difficult or unruly body, the stories of the engorged and ecstatic body, the excavated body, the disembodied body—stories that are stuck inside us, clogging our throats, tacked and clustered around the edges of our vision, tightening and thickening our belly, untold stories taking up space in our consciousness, in our skin, and keeping us from fully inhabiting our lives. These are the stories we rehearse, consciously or unconsciously, so that we won't forget. We rehearse the way the room was quiet, what the sun looked like against the walls or grass, what his eyes looked like, what we said or didn't say, what his hands smelled like, how our mouth tasted, how cool the breeze was. We remind ourselves to remember the noises he made, the sound of a ringing phone somewhere that no one answered, the voices of kids walking home from the parochial school a few blocks away. We rehearse the bird that flew to the feeder, during. There's plenty we've lost, but we remember that bird.

We are strong enough, big enough, to write these stories that take up so much room inside of us. If you write it, if you choose to share that writing, you will bring others into the room, or car, or gully with you—you won't be alone there anymore.

Start now

Pick up your pen, drop your fingers to the keyboard, and start now to write yourself whole. Just let the words come. Don't lift the pen from the page, don't censor, don't make sense. Don't stop to worry about whether your grammar works or if you ought to use a comma or a semi-colon or if it's time for a new paragraph. Give yourself these ten minutes, maybe fifteen. Give yourself the half-hour of a lunch break. Give yourself a morning hour, an evening hour. Shut off the phone and turn away from the computer. Set down in ink or pencil whatever words come up, non sequiturs and nonsense and to-do-list reminders alike, stories and complaints, wishes and dreams and frustrations and remembrances. Let it all come and commingle on your page. Let it flow through the boundaries we build within and around ourselves, the containments and separations, the work stuff and play stuff, the now stuff and then stuff. This writing is just for you. No one else ever has to see it.

Start it now. Do it again tomorrow. Keep up this pattern as many consecutive days as possible, over several years. If you miss a day, a week, a month, just begin again. Continue for a lifetime.

Writing ourselves whole means entering the mess, means inviting imperfection and wonder, means visiting with our humanness, means getting to welcome the full humanity that so many of us have felt denied access to in the aftermath of trauma.

story

our stories are our world

There is a riot of native birds narrating the live oak out back. They sound like a swarm of country crickets. The heat is dry and steady. The day falls open; no— it contains.

Our stories create the world around us. Stories—and the words we have to tell them—shape what we can see, what we can know, what we can envision and imagine for and about ourselves and those we love. We write and we can learn to look beyond the grammars we were given, learn to be more than outline and patchwork, learn to allow ourselves to touch and taste the skin of *all* the words— even, or especially, those they told us we weren't allowed to hold in our mouths.

This is a way we make ourselves free. This is a way we allow freedom to grow in us.

Thomas King, in *The Truth about Stories*, writes, "You have to be careful with the stories you tell. And you have to watch out for the stories that you are told." And Laguna Pueblo writer Leslie Marmon Silko, in her novel *Ceremony*, says, "I will tell you something about stories. They aren't just entertainment. Don't be fooled. They are all we have, you see. All we have to fight off illness and death. You don't have anything if you don't have the stories."

You understand how our culture is a story—I don't have to go back to the pilgrims, to the myth of America as a land of peoples persecuted who only wanted the freedom to live and worship as they desired, or the story of our land of the free and home of the brave, the story our country's forefathers told about our manifest destiny, about God and entitlement, about people with white skins, people with skin that was darker, features that were broader or slenderer, people with other beliefs, ideas, or voices.

These stories do a particular kind of labor. They impact our understandings of our history and our place in society. If we accede to their tenets, if we allow ourselves to live inside those old myths, our vision is constricted—there are possible realities, interpretations of history, we are not able to imagine if we accept these stories as truth.

Consider the stories we told (and tell) to justify war: in Korea, Vietnam, in the Middle East; consider the way those stories are repeated by politicians and media, even when we *know* those stories are lies, utter falsehoods crafted by those in power with the hopes of swinging popular opinion in their direction long enough that they could get their way, do what it is they wanted to do in the first place.

Consider what violences are referred to as war, and which aren't.

We tell a story that in this country we put family first. Politicians stand at podiums, pound their fists on the hardwood, wipe sweat from their foreheads and tears from their eyes, reiterating their fervid belief in family values, the well-being of children. And many of those men (and a few of those women), if not later revealed to have beaten partners or abused children themselves, vote to undermine or do away with resources and support systems for women and children across the nation.

My stepfather taught me about these sorts of stories. He was a politician of a different stripe. He taught psychology and human sexuality at two universities, where, among other things, he studied the impact of child sexual abuse. He developed (along with my mother) a recovery program for sexually abused kids, and ran that program at Boys' Town, a Catholic child advocacy home, based in

Omaha, NE. He wanted to learn how sexual abuse affected the brain, proposed study after study to be completed using brain imaging.

All the while he was abusing his wife, raping her daughters.

Now, when a man stands at a podium and bangs his fist and proclaims the evils of child sexual abuse, I wonder: What's under the story he's trumpeting? Who he is hunting at night? Every upstanding community hero, I wonder who he's fondled or tortured or shamed, who's afraid of coming forward because they are sure no one will believe them. After all, *everyone loves the man who tells a good story.*

•§•

Most adolescents get to experiment with different selves as they learn who they are and who they want to be. We sample the stories of different identities; through trial and error, we find, if we are lucky, selves that fit us most of the time: writer, queer, working-class, musician, friend, coffee-drinker, vegetarian—these are some of the labels we use as shorthand for the (more complicated) stories of ourselves. And as we grow, we learn (and often this is not an easy lesson) that even those seemingly-intractable stories of identity can shift and grow.

In my adolescence, a grown man fed identity to me, shoved it down my throat. The stories he gave me went by these names: woman, smart, beautiful, narcissistic, overly-trusting, slut, raped, owned. Once I got away from him, I needed to tell different stories, to escape the identities he'd insisted I wear, in an attempt to undo what his violence and my resistance had embedded in my psyche.

It's a difficult thing to root a self out of a soul—I mean, to take apart a self and look inside it to see what's worth saving, what can be torn out and discarded. The tendrils of the stories my stepfather had built into me, built me into, threaded around every bit of my sense of myself: who could I be if I wasn't what he made me? When hatcheting back the kudzu of lies that make us hate ourselves, we are sometimes left with emptinesses where the old stories lived. Though we want those narratives gone, the ones that camouflaged and protected us, the truth is that they have become familiar, become home. It's frightening to be without them—we feel naked without their blanketing of ivy and shame, while we are discovering new stories to try on in their place. Opening up room for a new self is not light-hearted work.

What happens when we begin to question the stories that have shaped us?

In *Women Who Run with the Wolves*, Jungian psychoanalyst and poet Clarissa Pinkola Estes says, "Stories are medicine." When we story something we have experienced and had to keep silent about, we gain a new control over it; it becomes our *material*. We find the words for our story, and when the right words/ stories don't exist, we invent them.

I have been a writer since I was a child; maybe you have been, too. I wrote stories on paper, I made up stories with my dolls or other toys. I told stories into the neighborhood while riding my bike around and around and around the same blocks. I loved Shel Silverstein and wrote little poems in a small book that had clamps at the center of the binding to welcome in more small pages. My sister began giving me beautiful cloth-covered blank books as birthday and Christmas gifts, and I had a place to keep the things I wrote.

But little by little, as I moved into adolescence, my writing dried up, folded in on itself, away from me. Writing was not a safe outlet in my stepfather's house—just as there was no safe outlet at all, of any kind. My job, in that house, was to keep my surface clean. Any cracks in the costume, and he'd dig his fingers in to pull me apart, seeking out the tender and vulnerable parts, the not-yet-conquered parts. Hide what's compassionate and curious. Put away the confusion and sorrow. I tended my emotions so that I showed only what he believed he'd trained me to be.

Beneath the armoring and pretense I'd built up in order to survive, the stories I told the world about who I was, there was a twelve-year-old girl who was outraged to be living in a house where a man could call her names, choke her, violate her body, separate her from her mother and father and sister, and she had to pretend to be grateful for all of it. That astonished, indignant little girl never died, though she got buried deeper and deeper. She held fast to her story, her truth, anyway. And when at twenty-one I found myself in a cafe with a notebook, finally willing to risk writing down the stories of what my body had been through, I had to reach down and pull that little girl up through the strata of all the other selves and stories I'd been forced to live over the previous, highly-formative, decade.

That girl didn't come up clean or unsticky—she came up coated with the residue of all the lies I'd had to inhabit. I wrote and wrote, trying to make sense of all those lies, questioning the stories I'd had to train myself to believe so that *he would believe that I believed them*: that I was a bad person, I made decisions based only on fear, I was selfish and narcissistic, I didn't want to evolve, I was resistant to change, I didn't care about other people's feelings, I was a liar, I was a slut, I was frigid, I was a dilettante, I was stupid, I was driven by what other people thought of me—

The thing was, some of those stories had truth in them: I *had* been a liar; I *was* afraid; I'd *absolutely* had to care more about what someone else thought about me than what I thought about myself. So many of our stories are complicated and messy, given that we have to pretend to believe messages like this:

This doesn't hurt. This isn't incest. This isn't rape. You don't have anything to cry about. You're selfish. You don't really mean to tell me no. You have to ask me for sex if you want me to believe you've really changed. What do you mean you didn't want it—you asked me for it. It's ok to be curious—all kids your age want to see other people's bodies. It's ok that this feels good.

What happens when you grow up with no stable story of self, no stable stories at all? What happens when words can change meaning at one person's will?

What happens when—fifteen years later—you find yourself at a cafe with a blank notebook trying to write the "real" story?

What, at that point, can "real story" even mean?

•§•

This is where most humans live: at the intersection of loss and longing, pain and want, history and future, trauma and desire. We are not supposed to acknowledge this. Don't talk about those things that drive you. Don't mention the hungers or terrors. Don't cry at the office. Don't tell anyone about the *miracle* of the amazing sex you had last night. Keep it to yourself. We're supposed to put on our business-casual khaki pants and our button-down short sleeve shirts and slip our feet into loafers and go into the world, contained, and of a single, unscarred, unfragmented piece.

(There are reasons for this, beyond the white American cultural ideal of quiet and calm and bootstraps and containment. Capitalism needs smooth and well-molded cogs to fit into its machinery. When we are jagged with loss or slippery with desire (or vice versa, or both), we fit less well into these warrens of cubicles with their grey plastic computing boxes and aerodynamic chairs, into the hairnets and plastic gloves, into the time-clock punch-in-punch-out of the streamlined American dream.)

We are supposed to be "Together." We are supposed to be "Functional." We are supposed to be a single story, a single unbroken trajectory from birth through adulthood to death, a sheer pane of glass through which our neighbors can peer and see only a comfortable backyard, a house and garage and 2.3 children and a spouse of only one of two genders.

We are not supposed to be multifarious. We are not supposed to wear our desire for *more* on our sleeves—unless that *more* is for money or goods. More love? More healing? More compassion? More peace? More justice? More nature? More creativity? More laughter? More layers, more trajectories, to the stories of our lives? Put those away, please.

When I say "at the intersection of trauma and desire," *desire* doesn't only refer to sex—it also refers to our many creative desires: for engaging work, for relationships that feed us, or for healing; our desire to paint or sing or write or draw or dance or build. When we allow ourselves to tap into awareness of any one of the desires we've attempted to tamp down, *all* of our ignored desires begin to trickle forth (and then flood), which is why we are trained to keep our desires under lock and key, hidden even and especially from ourselves.

It's our humanity that exists at the intersection of trauma and desire. Writing our real, complicated, embodied stories—and allowing those stories to be heard and held by others—can be a way back into our full, messy, complicated, hungry, embodied humanity. For those of us living in the aftermath of childhood trauma, the idea that we might be able to inhabit a humanity at all, not to mention an honest, imperfect and complicated humanity, can feel like nothing less than a miracle.

The stories we tell ourselves about ourselves

Take a few minutes, and generate a list of stereotypes/myths you've heard about sexual abuse survivors. Select one and respond to it: "This is what they say about me, but I..." Give yourself ten minutes to talk back to those stories.

what's outside the broken story?

Thomas King writes, in *The Truth About Stories,* "Stories are wondrous things. And they are dangerous."

A story is a rehashing of events, a narrative, an anecdote, a lie, a truth. It's a telling or a making up. A story offers an account of an experience, so someone else can come to know or understand what happened. It's a fabrication, a weaving into existence something that *wasn't,* that didn't exist, until we put it into words.

Story is contextual. And who determines a story's context? "She's telling stories" is a way to call someone a liar. But we know what truths come from storyteller's mouths. Dorothy Allison, the author of *Bastard Out of Carolina* (among many other life-altering books) says, "People want biography. People want memoir. They want you to tell them that the story you're telling them is true. The thing I'm telling you is true, but it did not always happen to me."

Survivor is a story, one we buy into or not, one we step into or out of, just like *woman* is a story, or any other identity label is a story—that is, a place-holder for a much larger and more complex narrative. Our culture tells us what "survivor" means, and if we don't look like the porcelain victim doll that gets held up as an example, then maybe (we think to ourselves) we don't get to be a survivor.

Survivors are broken and brave, ruined and stained, feel culpable for what happened to them, will never be the same again.

Thomas King also writes, "The truth about stories is that that's all we are." We create ourselves, we know and understand ourselves, through the stories we learn and listen to and repeat about ourselves, about those like us, about our communities, society, families, world.

Identity is a story. We don't just take on a label when we identify as something, we take on the narratives that accompany that identity—we have to interact with that identity's story.

Trauma is a story. Survivor and victim are stories. Religion is a story. Sex is a story. The body is a story.

Yes, the body is also bone and tissue, chemical reactions, pulses, electrical leaps. The body is fluid and organ, emergence and excretion, breath and heartbeat. The body exists as an object in this precise moment, entirely independent of its context, its historical situation, its experiences. But what would this body be, independent of the stories I have told about it, the stories others have shaped for it? What is this body *without* its accumulated stories, its histories and herstories?

Is DNA a story? Musculature? What can you learn from the record of someone's skin, his scars and stretch marks, her stains and curves? What can you read in the intricate interweaving of neuronal infrastructure (which grows more complex when the stories we tell about ourselves grow more complex)?

We use story every day, throughout the day. When someone asks how we slept, we offer a story of dreams and waking. When a friend calls to tell us about her morning, she gives us a story, an anecdote. We tell childhood stories, baby stories, coming out stories, the story of how we met a friend or lover, the story of an illness, the story of our experience of abuse, the story of our recovery.

Every story is an illumination and an occlusion. Every story highlights one side of a situation while leaving out other information. This is out of necessity. We can't remember or apprehend every detail of an experience. We tell what we remember and, over time, what we remember is what we've told. We believe our own stories. We can forget that there are other ways to tell, understand, envision those stories; that is, different ways to tell ourselves. Each new recounting provides a different lens through which to decipher our lives.

How we tell our stories matters. The words we use for our stories matter. The metaphors and symbolic language, the imagery, all matter, all influence how we perceive our bodies, our physical being, our agency, our history, and our possibility.

Consider the story of the word *broken* as it gets applied, metaphorically and not, to survivors of violence. Consider how often you've heard *broken* in survivor narratives: *he left me broken. He ruined me. She left me in pieces. He tore apart my soul.*

I climbed into *broken*, that narrative of fragmentation, when I began to understand that I was an incest survivor. The incest/trauma survivor story contained words like: "broken, ruined, dead." This is the language big enough to describe how the body feels, how the victim feels, how the raped child feels when she is violated by someone meant to be a protector, when she is physically and psychically assaulted, silenced, shamed and threatened, then psychologically tortured so that she will comply with the abuser's demands of silence. We need a brutal narrative to match the brutality of our reality. We need a story that will wake people up, a story that will make bystanders understand why we need help. We are counteracting and attempting to supplant the other, deeply entrenched stories: *the child is the parent's possession to do with as the parent wishes; children often lie and are not to be believed when they say their parents or priests or other adults are hurting them; child abuse is a family problem and outsiders shouldn't intervene; she wanted it—children are often so seductive.* Those stories have been around a long time. It makes sense that with the rise of an Incest Survivor advocacy community, we would reach for language as incendiary as the experiences and silencings we suffered through: *he broke me apart; he left me for dead; I felt like a ghost; I didn't exist anymore.* These metaphors and similes convey our extreme disenfranchisement from our own agency.

I grabbed the story of *broken* and swallowed it completely: I was no longer whole. He had stolen something from me. He took me apart. He turned me into a shell, a carapace, a carcass. A ruined and broken thing.

And the more I told this story, the more the story is what I inhabited.

Just a few years ago, I began to question the story of broken that I'd so fully believed: What if broken, a story I'd made a core part of my identity and self, was just a *lens* through which I was looking at the world? What if there were another stories, other lenses, other interpretations? What if *broken* didn't have to be my name?

What stories do you have about yourself and your experience that no longer serve you?

"The truth about stories is that they're all we are."

I was invested in the story of myself as broken, in part because I believed that if I was not broken, if I could be whole and well and healed, then that meant my stepfather had gotten away with his years of torture and violence and manipulation and rape. And I needed to be the evidence of his crimes. No matter that he'd already been tried and judged and found guilty. I would be the walking, wounded reminder.

As a senior in college, when I was finally able to hear my stepfather use the word *incest* not as a taboo to be interrogated and evolved beyond, but instead as an act that *he understood that he was and had been perpetrating*, I began the long process of breaking away from him, and stepped into the story of Incest Survivor, which meant stepping into the story of *broken*.

Broken was irrevocable, irreversible. A shattered vase might get glued back together but you can always see the cracks, the scars—and that vase was now weaker, easier to break the next time. I joined with others who were broken and proud of it. Fuck you, we said. We might get better, but we were never going to be the same. We were ruined, worthless, broken.

I spent nearly twenty years telling this story, wearing it, breathing it, trying to have sex and relationships through and around it. I'd told it so often it seemed indelible: I hadn't *been* broken—I *was* broken.

Broken makes for good and poignant writing. It also hurts. I focus my attention on how broken I am—how unloveable, unhealable, how wrong—rather than recognize how I am changing, growing, healing. It's all about the lens I'm willing to look through, the story I'm willing to consider.

•§•

My stepfather taught me (directly and indirectly) to maneuver around the truth with language; he required a precise articulation of silence(s). When I used his linguistic strategies, denying my truth in the process, I lost more of myself. My words hid under my tongue and tried to move it, ran into my arms and tried to force them into fighting, tensed up my thighs to get ready to run. Is this why language resists me now? Is it still frozen in that fight or flight stance, the words flying out of my head like startled birds?

Today, silence still hesitates in my peripheral vision, having a smoke with its back to the wall, scruffy in work clothes, unshaved face, ready to be called back to the set of my mind when my eyes drift off to the left. Those fast, deep silences were like diving deep into quiet water: no sound, no words, just the hazing of all that was around me. A trance state. A fugue.

They work hard to ensure that we won't be able to talk about what they do. They don't want us to have a language—they wanted our mouths, our throats, empty when they opened us up to shove their cocks in. They take words from our mouths and eat them: they feed on us.

The fucked girl is a cracked vessel: How do we get outside stories so pervasive that they've shaped cultures' thinking for thousands of years? "Damaged goods" is not a true statement, not a *factual* statement—and yet, because this is the prevailing metaphor that our society uses for those who've been sexually violated, we who are survivors come to *know* ourselves as damaged; there's no other commonly available language to describe this state of being in the aftermath of violence like this. Thus, when I start to question these stories, before the experience is liberating, it's terrifying—I feel the earth shifting under my feet and dropping away. For a time, there's nothing to stand on once we move away from the stories that have shaped us and we have not yet found the words for the selves we are still unearthing.

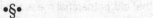

•§•

After almost two decades of recovery, I noticed a shift. I began to think, what if I'm *not* broken? This, you understand, was a revelation, a kind of coming out—a bright line of possibility around the edge of a story I thought shaped everything I saw, everything I would ever see. It was terrifying to question this fundamental story of me. What if I am whole, my sex is whole, my complexity is whole? What if I struggle, still have questions, but am whole, intact? What if nearly everyone struggles with their relationship to their body, whether or not they spent their adolescence being psychologically tortured? What if that's not just a sexual abuse survivor's experience, but a common, shared, *human* experience?

What if I could tell a different story?

Broken proved to be a hard story to shed. *Broken* gave me license not to try, to be depressed and miserable; broken's the reason I'm a failure—he never gave me a chance. Broken means it makes sense that I'm not close to people, that I don't return phone calls, I don't keep my commitments. *She's broken, you know. Oh, right. Forget it, then.* Broken gave me a pass.

Broken things aren't alive. What if I wanted to live?

How could I tell another story?

I've come to believe that we were never ruined or stained or inherently broken. I don't believe that our souls got warped or that we are somehow made *wrong* by someone else's acts of violence and violation. (Sometimes parts of our bodies literally are broken, of course, through the act of rape. I do not mean at all to discount that reality, or the need to speak that truth.)

One reason we are called "broken" is that once we were property—and a raped female (child or grown) was less valuable to those marrying us off: our fathers or other male relatives. Our literal commercial value dropped once we were no longer virginal—and so we were ruined. When we accept the story of broken, we're saying that old, patriarchal mess still has merit.

Taking a stand against a cultural meta-narrative is resistance work. If I'm not broken I must be resilient. In learning to live outside the lens or silo of Broken, I am flung (if I'm not careful) headlong into the relentlessly cheerful Gratitude story: whatever doesn't kill you makes you stronger, praise be to god.

I was ready for a less-than-simple story, something more complex, more complicated, more real. A story that took awhile to tell.

In our survivors writing groups, this is what we hold out hope for: the messy story, the fragmented telling, the rape story with jokes and laughter in it, the story of the loved and loving parent who put his hands inside his child, the story of turning still for support to the mother who abandoned you. The stories that friends, surveys, some therapists, family, nonprofits, social workers, activists and advocates have a hard time hearing (sometimes literally have difficulty comprehending) because these stories don't match the language we have acquiesced to as a culture: us and them, ruin, devastation, dismal, hopeless, broken.

Our human, lived stories are more complicated than one lens can reveal. Outside of one story are a hundred other stories. Not *broken or unbroken:* rather, intact and imperfect. Wounded, sore, struggling, scared, funny, hopeful.

"Translating a phenomenon into language alters the way it is represented and understood in our minds," writes psychologist James Pennebaker in *Opening Up.* I'm saying that there's a sense to be made of self through writing. It is a transgressive self, a shifting, silvery slippery self. We are not broken. Our souls were not murdered. We ached and felt lost and scared and were not protected the way we needed to be. We are *always* changing. We are—I am—never the same from one moment to the next. All my meanings are always already changing and so are yours and so are yours. The girl who was raped is and is not you. The woman who had sex with her lover last night is and is not you. *We are free to allow for the remaking of ourselves.* We are free to know ourselves un-parenthesized and un-encapsulated. We write to bear forth, and to bear witness to, this growth. We write to help ourselves become more comfortable with this change in ourselves, so that we can also be more comfortable with this changing in/of others around us.

We may have felt like part of us died when we were violated—but we did not die. We lived, whole and resilient and terrified and lost and in need (as all humans are in need) and weak (as all humans are sometimes weak) and stuck and then not stuck and then stuck again, and so we go about the business of writing ourselves out of the briar patch once more.

Put the story together again

There's a quote I have often used as a prompt in workshops: "I want things whole but I love things broken" (from poet Ellen Doré Watson). Do you, or have you, felt "broken"? In what ways have you believed yourself broken? What if you *weren't* broken in these ways—meaning, what if these aspects of you were not broken at all, but completely normal, understandable, human responses to horrific experience? What would it mean if you weren't broken? Give yourself ten minutes; follow your writing wherever it seems to want you to go.

permitting permeability: rewriting (our) desire

"Oh, I'd love to do that, but I never could—I'm such an awful writer."

I can't count the number of times people have told me, after asking what I do for work, that they're terrible writers: they love to read but could *never* write; they aren't creative. And then they laugh, a little wry and knowing, with sadness in their eyes. This is how we talk about ourselves. It's hard for these folks to hear me when I say I imagine they're fantastic, inventive writers, and that I'd love to have them come to a group. No matter how strong their desire to write, they're blinded by the societal myth we Americans have of The Writer: someone with a magical (if off-kilter and drug-addled) life, endless access to perfect prose and, often, lots of schooling, privilege, and prestige.

My allegiance is to the Pat Schneider-Natalie Goldberg-Peter Elbow school of thought, which testifies to *anyone's* ability to write powerfully. All you need is: a) the inclination (the desire) to write; b) a safe, supportive, and confidential place; c) a writing implement; d) something on which to write. And I've found that even when all of these elements are in place, many of us *still* don't write, because we have learned—after years of defeat, badly-behaving teachers, criticism, and an elitist (mostly white and male) literary tradition that doesn't reflect the lived experience of so many of us—that it's easier on our hearts if we simply deny that desire.

The word *desire* itself comes from the Latin phrase *de sidere*, meaning "from the stars," and its original sense may have been "await what the stars will bring." Those of us who are survivors know how to deny ourselves awareness of what the stars are delivering to us. We understand that we don't deserve anything but leftovers and castoffs, that we are supposed to want what our families or lovers want. We know intimately how much it hurts to want something (like freedom or love, safety or bodily integrity) that those with the power over us won't ever give us; we know how it hurts to want something we can't have. So we teach ourselves not to want at all.

A few years ago, I heard poet Jane Hirschfield in an interview on the radio. When the interviewer asked why we should welcome poetry into our lives, the poet talked about how poetry made her life more *permeable*:

> We human beings. We're very strange creatures. We think we want order. We think we want safety. We think we want security. But we really want—or what I really want—is to be absolutely overwhelmed, disordered, thrown into chaos and disarray by something absolutely fantastic which is larger than I am. [...] [P]art of the work of poetry is to make you permeable to the experience not only inside your own skin but the experience all around you.

When Emily Dickinson says, "If I feel physically as if the top of my head were taken off, I know *that* is poetry," she is articulating that experience of permeability. Poetry—as well as other forms of creative writing—insists that we allow life to move through us. That's the deep intimacy of poetic language, the vulnerability required of us as we read, the way the poem draws us into itself through our engagement with associative leaps and metaphorical imagery, the way we lace ourselves into the poem's universe: suddenly, we are intimately interwoven into the mind and experience of the poet. Poet and reader are bound: there is no separation.

How deeply erotic. And how challenging—even terrifying—for those of us who've worked to close down our bodies, secure the borders, as a means through which to keep ourselves safe.

•§•

Writing can be erotic in a couple of different ways. The first and most familiar
to many of us is on the level of content: stories you find in the romance or
sexuality section of the bookstore. But writing can also be erotic in *form*: work
that slips genre boundaries, uses poetic language, refuses linearity, leaps into
surprising metaphors, or otherwise risks experimenting with structure and
readers' expectations. Even if this writing is not explicitly sexual in content, we
nonetheless can have an erotic experience of this sort of writing, writing that—
because it demands our participation as readers, *permeates us*, shakes us out
of complacency, wakes us up. In her essay "A Meditation on Metaphor," Alicia
Ostriker writes that "the pleasure we take in metaphor is a pleasure of consent."
We *allow* ourselves to be penetrated by the writing, to be opened and changed.
The erotic is a border crossing, a shifting through the sands and watery edges
between us and within our selves. What bravery required from all of us who have
been initiated into the sharp painful oblivion that is the anti-erotics of sexual
abuse to re-engage with language and self in this way, to risk the blurring of
edges when we have worked so hard to fortify our ramparts to keep everything
not us out. I think of Audre Lorde's essay "Uses of the Erotic: The Erotic as Power,"
which, when I first read it, blew open what erotic had meant in my life, and gave
me access to this life-affirming power again:

> The erotic is a measure between the beginnings of our sense of self and the
> chaos of our strongest feelings. It is an internal sense of satisfaction to which,
> once we have experienced it, we know we can aspire. For having experienced
> the fullness of this depth of feeling and recognizing its power, in honor and
> self-respect we can require no less of ourselves.

The process of writing itself can be a permeating, liberatory experience, can allow
our containers and compartmentalizations to get slippery; our solid sureties
become luminous and translucent; our hearts expand, we breathe deeply, we feel
all the way out to the edges of our aching, beautiful, precise bodies.

•§•

For many years, the only person with whom I could speak "freely" about sexual matters was my stepfather. He trained me to confess to him any and all sexual thoughts. Inevitably, he wanted to try them out, using my own desires or fantasies to further ensnare me. I remember, when I was twenty or so, on a road trip with my then-boyfriend, I bought a copy of Pauline Réage's *Story of O*. My boyfriend drove through tiny New Hampshire towns, all white clapboard and slush, while I read, getting turned on in spite of myself. This wasn't my introduction to the idea of BDSM "play"—a dear friend had already introduced me to Pat Califia's stories of queer women doing amazingly rough and dirty (and consensual) things to one another. I'd wanted this curiosity to be just mine, something I could keep to myself, away from my stepfather. But, like every other sexual discovery I made as a young person before getting away from him, I ended up "confessing," as I'd been trained, that I'd bought the book and was thinking about exploring this sort of play with my boyfriend. My stepfather was enthusiastically supportive of my delving into this sort of sex—and the next time I went home, he "asked" to play master and servant. As though I had a choice. As thought it was an option to say no. Hadn't I said I was curious? Hadn't I said I wanted to try more?

And so one more piece of my burgeoning erotic landscape got trampled on, teaching me, again, again, never to tell anyone what I fantasized about.

It was through writing that I was finally able to explore my fantasies without feeling like I had to put them into practice immediately. I have greater access to language as well: the tongue-tiedness and frozen throat that can afflict me when I am speaking extemporaneously does not occur when I am writing. The words flow quickly and I have learned to play gently and hard with the sense that can be made of nonsense. This writing, then, becomes something other than straight or traditional "truth telling," something other than the confession that I was trained to bring to sexual conversation.

That which is ignored or shoved into the unconscious (or sublimated, as Freud might correct me) has a way of reminding us of its presence. We have to use a lot of energy to keep denying awareness of the hungers we've taught ourselves to disavow. Eventually, for many of us, it becomes more tiring to continue to deny than it does to allow ourselves the terrifying experience of desire. I'm reminded of the quote attributed to Anais Nin: "The day came when the risk to remain tight in a bud was more painful than the risk it took to blossom."

Often, it's not safe for us to acknowledge our desire (for writing or anything else) when we are still living under the control of those abusing us. It wasn't until I'd been out of my stepfather's home for three years that I felt safe enough, secure enough, to risk writing honestly in a journal, to begin to reclaim my desire to write. Sometimes being true to our creative selves means finding a way to survive—to stay alive—while keeping our deep selves under wraps until we are old enough to leave the house of our parents, escape our abusers, and find our own space in the world, where we can open our notebooks and write with safety, with no fear that our private words will be rousted out of their quiet beds and used against us by parents, caregivers, lovers, mates. Sometimes we are able to find writing groups, where we can create with others who have similar desire and are going to support us in our need.

After awhile, through this writing, something dangerous and beautiful arises. Once I have conscious access to desire, to any desire, it becomes harder to deny the other things I've longed for but pushed aside. Once those long-buried longings come careening out, you're going to want to have someplace to explore them, to turn them over and examine them from all sides, to take the time to discover if it's really even something that you want anymore—or if it's been shoved down so long that it just needed to pop up and hold your attention for awhile and then go ahead and fade, like a burst bubble or a sunset or a crow flying off into the stars.

The early stories that permeated us

This is one of the first exercises I offer in sexuality writing groups. Write for five minutes in response to each of the following fragments:

This is what I learned about sex...

This is what I didn't learn about sex...

This is what I *wish* I'd learned about sex...

Then pause, and take a deep breath. Then, for ten more minutes, freewrite about anything that came up for you as you wrote. Follow your writing wherever it seems to want you to go.

the lexicon of our longing

Trying to use words, and every attempt
Is a wholly new start, and a different kind of failure
Because one has only learnt to get the better of words
For the thing one no longer has to say, or the way in which
One is no longer disposed to say it. And so each venture
Is a new beginning, a raid on the inarticulate
- T.S. Eliot, "The Four Quartets"

This is what we do: find new words for what lives inside us, and struggle with the inarticulate, with the feeling that there aren't enough words for what we experience when we have been traumatized, to say nothing of trying to put into words the complicated longings inside our bodies, under our tongues. Because women (and queer folks and genderqueer folks and...) are raised without a full language for our sexual lives, sexual language becomes a foreign language: *a different tongue.* Those of us sexually abused as young people grow up with a sexual language that is profoundly confused, one we often want nothing to do with. So how do we learn to inhabit our whole, complicated, messy, beautiful sexual selves?

The groundbreaking literary scholar Carolyn Heilbrun writes, "Women must turn to one another for stories; they must share the stories of their lives and their hopes and their unacceptable fantasies. [...] We know we are without a text, and must discover one." Those of us who have not been able to tell, or even fully *know*, our own stories have to seek out the positive representations of ourselves—and when we do not find them, we must become the positive representations we wish for. We seek out the others like us, listen to the stories they have to share—and share our stories as well. How do we do this if we have been denied access to the very language required to communicate authentically? We must take the language we were given and stretch it out. We can write *anyway*. We can play. We must trust ourselves enough to create our own images. In *Sister/Outsider*, Audre Lorde writes, "And where that language does not yet exist, it is our poetry which helps to fashion it. Poetry is not only dream and vision, it is the skeleton architecture of our lives. It lays the foundations for a future of change, a bridge across our fears of what has never been before."

In my experience, women tend to find it psychologically and socially easier (that is, less taboo) to discuss sexual matters if they occurred in a violent context than they do describing to friends the amazing thing a lover recently learned to do with their tongue and how *good* it felt. Have you noticed this? We make room to describe ways in which we've been hurt sexually, but we feel weird, we feel shame or guilt or other illicit naughtiness, when relating stories about intense sexual joy or pleasure. Our current American society has more comfort with violence than pleasure, and has allowed us greater access to the language of violence than to the language of sexuality. (Could this have something to do with the way we conflate sex with violence, or tend to use the language of violence in sexual conversation?) Lesbian poet Kitty Tsui writes, "Chinese is my first language. But I was fluent only in the words my parents deemed it necessary for me to know. I was certainly not taught the words for breast, cunt, ass, orifice, or orgasm. *There were no words for sex; therefore, sex did not exist.* We never talked about the acts between married men and women, never mind lesbian sex!"

If putting words to erotic feeling or desire is uncomfortable or even upsetting for you, please know that you're not alone in that response. As we step into this part of our process, it's important to remember that no one controls language, even though words that are not comfortable or feel "foreign" may seem to belong to someone else (i.e., the oppressors): *every bit of every word in every tongue is available for our perusal, our play.* We claim our power when we tell our stories, whether we write them in our notebooks alone or we share them with friends, a counselor, a stranger at the bar, or a writing group. We change the course history might have taken when we write, "I want you to put your hands on me." And again when—if—we read that writing aloud to someone. And *again* when we risk sharing *any* authentic desire with a lover. We change the world when we defy our training as survivors. In this defiance, somewhere, a child realizes new possibility for herself. Perhaps she moves differently in the world as a result. Perhaps her daughters and sons will as well.

Here's why this matters: When a child tries to describe to her mother what Daddy is doing to her at night and she has *no language*, no words to describe the part(s) of her body affected or the behavior itself, the violence continues. When a mother turns red with embarrassment and instructs her child not to talk about such things, the violence continues and has been compounded. Sexual silence and ignorance nurture sexual violence. They prepare a bed for that violence, make fertile the ground where it can lie down and do its dirty work. When there's something that children are trained not to talk about, that they grow up knowing they ought not to talk or think about, you can bet that someone's going to take advantage of the situation. Piece by piece by piece, moment by moment, history reinforces sexual silences: physical silencings, linguistic erasures. Child abuse requires specific and particular silences: the perpetrator's silence, the victim's silence, the witnesses' and bystanders' silences. Everyone has to play their part just right for abuse to continue unabated. We ourselves reinforce the power these silences have over us each moment we don't speak, each time we don't risk articulating our desiring selves, each time we set aside our desire in favor of another's. Anything done to decrease survivors' shame around their sexual desire, the better off we will be—the better off this *world* will be.

How can we trust our knowledge of, understanding of, *trust in* our own erotic power? One way I've found is to write it: we can write, and we can help others to write. Through writing, we take action. We may also take action other than writing, and utilize our erotic power in other ways. "Power is the ability to take one's place in whatever discourse is essential to action and the right to have one's part matter," author and critic Carolyn Heilbrun writes in *Writing A Woman's Life*.

To *take* one's place: we cannot wait for someone to offer us a seat at the table. Frederick Douglass told us, "Power cedes nothing without demand." Kick aside the chairs and start dancing on the meat and potatoes. Take your sister's hand, pull her up on top of the table with you. In addition to knowing the truth of our own erotic desire, we need to listen to the truth of other survivors' erotic desire, rather than continuing to allow the patriarchy to divide us with the misinformation, lies, and hatred that they disseminate for their own gain.

The erotic in so many of us is ripe and ready for authentic and messy release, for a complex and honest truth-telling. An embodied, erotic writing practice reminds me how to be in my body, how to be in love with small and intimate details, how to notice and respect vulnerability, how to play, risk, and experiment. When we who were violated at the site of our sex find words for what we want (carnal desire or long-held dream), when we access our embodied, erotic selves, we are engaging in an act of insurrection.

We are afraid of what people will think of us if we say *this is what I want*. We are afraid of ridicule and shame, of isolation and shunning. We are afraid of what it will mean about us if we want or get this thing. We are afraid of saying it and then never getting it. We are afraid of someone using our desires against us. We have been taught not to ask for things, not to want. Our parents taught us that we don't get everything we want (and that we get a lot that we don't want): that's the way life is.

The erotic urges us to slip the constraints of conformity that have been demanded of us if we wish to be accepted, acceptable—if we want to be safe. And, of course, naming what we need, even just articulating a desire, any desire, can leave us feeling like everything is breaking—because, maybe, everything is. In allowing our longing to come to voice, the closed and clotted places within us shift and tear, release what they were holding in. We feel messy, exposed, raw, because, finally, we are.

They used to say *an army of lovers cannot fail.* When we are fully embracing our erotic, our embodied selves, we are powerhouses. We are in love with possibility, fiercely present, and moving forward out of a sense of adoration rather than hatred. This force is unstoppable.

A glossary of desire

Take a few minutes, and create a "dirty word" list: write down words you think could come up when writing about sex (body parts, sex acts, euphemisms and slang, and so on)—sometimes, one of the hardest parts of this writing is just allowing ourselves access to these words! (In a group, we create this list together, on a whiteboard or flipchart, then we read the list aloud together! That way, we move past the nervousness about saying these "dirty" words in front of strangers.) Then, for ten minutes, write in response to the phrase, "This is how I want you to touch me..." (As always, feel free to change the pronouns: *This is how I want her, This is how he wants me...* whatever works for you.) Follow your writing wherever it seems to want you to go.

---

writing the difficult stories

This morning, my beloved's best friend died. I want to describe for you this good man, with tubes obscuring his face, his lips as full, his chin as furry, as it'd been when I'd spoken with him outside the Lake Merritt BART station just five days before. I want to show you the weight of his family gathered in sorrow and hope around him, his brother bent clear over his face, whispering *Shhh* as our friend's body struggled to inhale, rattled with exhale. I want to give you the smell of that room—the sticky sweet of sickness, the too-clean hospital floors, the antiseptic, the scent of gardenia and one relative's heavy cologne, the sweat and tears of all those gathered around his breaking-open body. I want to give you the moment when we, certain he was dead, began to cry, his sister now bent over his chest, my beloved with her arms wrapped tight around her body, trying, maybe, to keep inside what was about to disappear forever—and how shocked we all were when he gasped suddenly, a fat sharp intake of breath, his mouth gaped wide, his body not yet done with life.

There's more I want to share, details that are too intimate, that aren't only mine, perhaps aren't mine at all. Yet his death is embedded in my body now. It is a story that has remade me. It is a moment that already I am finding form for, so that I can have some handle on my terror and sorrow at being so close to a body in the deep work of dying.

At one point, needing a break, I let the elevator carry me to the main floor and I walked as fast as I could without running out through the lobby, past the gift shop display with the angel tchotchkes in all different races standing still on glass shelves, and made it down the hospital's front stairs and across the driveway, over into the sun, before I began to sob. I walked into some bushes, squatted down, leaned back against a cement wall, and let my face fall into my arms, stretched out in front of me. I wanted to collapse with exhaustion.

I'd only been in that room an hour. How did people spend days, months, years tending to loved ones on the precipice of death?

I haven't told anyone this story, though—it just doesn't feel like something I can talk about this way. As a whole, mainstream American culture doesn't deal well with the real stories of death—nor of sickness or violence or abuse or mental illness or war. We don't do well with sorrow or loss, with anything but the most surface and sensationalized stories of divorce, breakups, layoffs, foreclosures, abortions, miscarriages, disappointments. We don't want the details; we don't want the day-to-day reality. We want the happy ending. We don't deal well when we hear what really happens during a rape, when we're told about the neglect and abuse of children, about the mistreatment of animals or the environment. We don't know how to have tender, complicated conversations about race, class, gender, body size, disability—we don't like to hear that you're hungry or homeless. We have a hard time holding your sorrow or rage. We want to make it better, and if we can't, we mostly get defensive and we want to get away.

Possibly paradoxically—but probably not—we also have trouble with talk about rapture, passion, desire, and sexual delight.

My experience is that Americans are most comfortable with the stories that don't discomfort or destabilize us, with stories that don't make us feel the things we're busy trying to avoid or deny or ignore. We are surrounded by the tools we use to mollify us and keep us safe in our bubbles of conformity: how many hundreds of TV channels do we need, how many movies, video games, how many Top-40 radio stations and apps and social media platforms will it take to keep avoiding all that we don't want to think about—that there is pain all around us, immeasurable loss that cannot be fixed, that everyone we love will die, that there is not language enough in the world to express all that brings us joy, and that many humans choose to act in unconscionable ways toward other humans and other beings and the planet in order to satisfy their own desires and serve their own comforts first and foremost?

Back in the '80s, one of the survivors interviewed for *The Courage to Heal* said, "Incest is not a taboo. Talking about incest is the taboo." If incest were *actually* taboo, it would happen *much less frequently*. But we know the numbers, don't we? Non-perpetrating parents and other adults deny the reality of the child who is being abused, or get angry with that child (or later with us as grown adults who have finally remembered or reached a willingness to disclose our experience) when we speak up. And, as grown ups, when we want to share the stories about what shaped us or about what still hurts us, we are often asked, in one way or another, when we're going to get over it, or when we're going to forgive, or how we have moved on.

These questions aren't meant to soothe us or witness our pain or our real human experience. They're meant to shut us down. They're meant to bring the conversation to a close.

There 's so much of our real lives that we are expected not to talk about so that other people will be more comfortable: abortion, miscarriage, cancer, AIDS/HIV, sex, desire, erotic or passionate joy, death, religious ecstasy, adoption, rape, incest, molestation, acts (or the very fact!) of racism, sexual harassment, hunger, child abuse, soldiers' experiences during war, civilian experiences of war, military sexual assault, rape by priests and other spiritual leaders, sexual violence in sex-positive communities, violence against women by women, extreme or ritual abuse—the list seems endless. We could fill many pages just *naming* all the topics we're not supposed to broach in polite company.

In my own writing and in groups I've facilitated, these are exactly the stories I'm most interested in holding space for. We need space for the stories no one told us how to tell, for the stories someone told us *not* to tell, for the stories that make our partners or siblings or parents or friends uncomfortable.

When I am in a room with other people in it, *any* other people, I understand that I am in a room with trauma survivors. Almost all of us have been through something traumatic in our lives. Still, folks tend to become uncomfortable if I start talking about my stepfather's violence during a casual evening out with friends, or at the bowling lanes, or at the Seder table. If the rest of the room is discussing their experiences in high school (say, what it was like to lose their virginity), I have two choices: I can participate honestly, and shut the conversation right down, or I can keep silent, and remain isolated. In "polite" company, we're not supposed to talk about most of what our bodies experience, whether pleasurable or painful. Many people are uncomfortable with the language of the body and the words that describe the bodies we inhabit, what we experience, where we feel whole, and where we feel injured.

Silencing people in service to this cultural discomfort is an act of re-traumatization.

The silence around these "taboo" parts of our lives increases our isolation, deepens our belief that we are the only one who ever has or ever will go through something like we did. We start feeling like *we're* taboo. We are afraid to say anything for fear that this will be confirmed. What if we make people uncomfortable? What if they can't look at us, can't hear what we're saying, judge us in some way?

This, of course, is one of the reasons these proscriptions around certain topics of conversation exist—not talking about it furthers a survivor's sense of isolation and disconnection. A disconnected and fragmented people are a more easily divided and controlled people. When we speak out, when we share our true and messy, real life stories, we do our part to undermine our own and others' isolation, and to undermine the conditions for further violence to occur.

When we write and share our silenced and secreted experiences, often someone looks at us with surprise and says, *Me, too.* Two isolations are disrupted in that moment.

•§•

My stepfather was in my dreams last night (the memory of him, the specter of an old terror that haunts my frontal lobes and hind brain all these years later), but I can't quite remember what was going on. He was in my bedroom, or I in his. I had been in the house alone; he'd been kept late at work, at a training. He said, *They kept us late*, with a kind of wistfulness, like if he'd been there sooner, he could have joined me in my nap, or in the bath. He talked to me like a lover—again he was trying that tactic. The room was soft, full of shadows, afternoon moving into evening, and I was going to have to talk my way out of having sex with him—or was it too late for that? Under the surface of his speech was that layer of disappointment that I was supposed to collude with: too bad we didn't have enough time. I wake up not quite remembering, and feeling lost.

All I'm left with now is the oily, gentle, sure way that he'd smiled, like everything inside him was greased butter-soft and kind, like he thought I was stupid and had no memory—like I would believe his unctuous gentility the way that people in other parts of his life did. Like I didn't remember his viciousness, the names he called us, like I didn't hold his violence in every fiber of my being.

I need to be able to show you that kind-surfaced ominous smile, so that you can feel the foreboding—that's my job as a writer. I need you to see the worried fold in his pale forehead, dashed with a few stray greying hairs, that made him appear concerned but actually reveal the work he was doing to figure out how to convince me to go back into the bed and take my clothes off without having to physically force me to do so. I need you to hear the strain in his chuckle, the way his mustache would furrow, the places his pretense frayed. See him there in his canvas pants and shirt, a big man pretending to be young, cradling books in his arms, swaying just slightly, in response to my desire to escape, so that he blocks the door.

•§•

I used to believe that I should come away from every writing session wrung out and exhausted. For years I only wanted to write what I struggled with, what hurt. I pushed hard into every wound, wrote into and under scabs. If I didn't cry while I was writing, I didn't think I was doing it right.

(I felt this way about therapy, too, incidentally. If I wasn't making a breakthrough every single time, what was the point?)

I wanted to get it all *down* so I could get it *done*.

I believed there was a *done*, by the way. I believed that once I wrote everything, I would be better. This is the psychopathology my mother and stepfather had indoctrinated me into—a therapeutic mindset that dug and dug and dug into me, always searching for something new to use to explain my so-called rebellious behavior at home.

I wanted the writing to save me. If I had to do it over, I'd probably do it all the same way—though I'd like to think I'd give myself permission to go slower, to take care of my body, write about something besides sex and trauma (and relationship drama) now and again, join a writing group or class earlier. As it was, I spent the bulk of my writing years doing this work alone—and writing every day still didn't ease the parts in me that needed to stay awake until 2 a.m., weeping and drinking red wine while watching bad television, convinced that the rest of the world was Doing Something Really Important while I wasted my life with these stupid notebooks.

I had to do it the way that I did it. Writing taught me patience, taught me structure and consistency of practice. Until very recently, I wasn't able to show up for any relationship the way I could show up for writing practice. Writing the truths of my life taught me that these words could emerge into the world without killing anyone (and I don't mean that euphemistically). When I say "difficult writing," I mean I am always writing toward and for the twenty-one-year-old young woman who was sure she had something important to say and was also convinced that she was going to die before she got to say it.

You might not push yourself as hard as I did. I would recommend that you don't. I got addicted to writing only what hurt because I would get an endorphin or adrenaline rush from the fear: writing what I was terrified to write, writing until I was enraged or sobbing. Afterward, I crashed, felt emptied and depleted, and my abuser had trained me to believe that that's what "successful" ought to feel like.

You might do it differently. You might let yourself write your grief and terror in shorter bursts, giving your psyche more space to assimilate the stories emerging—I mean, taking small bites that are easier (though not always *easy*) for your healing self to digest. You might not try to push yourself to write it all out in a sitting—though sometimes the words catch hold and you find yourself just needing to follow them. Suddenly you find you are *ready* to write That Part, the thing you never tell, or you get an idea for a story that will illuminate some particularly complicated aspect of your experience—and you drive right through the twenty-minute timer and utterly lose track of time. These are good days, even when the writing is hard, the material is hard—and if it *is* hard, write until you feel ready to stop, then treat yourself very, very well. Make a healthy meal for yourself, something with vegetables, something with good flavor. Call a friend who can be with you right where you are. Have a good cry. Go for a long drive. I used to prefer to take a long walk to and from the writing cafe, sometimes, afterward, letting myself talk to the air, and weep.

Writing into what hurts, what's difficult, what others have asked us not to talk about or don't want to listen to, allows us to give the experience breath and bone. Something that feels unrooted, too terrifying to touch without mental oven mitts, is suddenly and literally in our hands. A situation that feels like it's unravelling in several directions at once has to slow down enough for us to write down each piece, one word at a time. A situation we've had to be "rational" about is allowed to get messy, loud, violent, angry, sad, or scared.

I want you to write it down because I believe you'll find yourself in the writing. I want you to write because when we write, we claim the language that our abusers and antagonists have wrested from our mouths, have told us we don't deserve or can't be trusted with. When we write it down, we see that we are not too much—

that our emotions are not too much. Some of us are afraid to write a particular story or memory because we're afraid it's too big for us to handle—or, really, that our *feelings* are too big for us to handle. So we keep it contained, we think, by not writing it.

That situation will let you know when it's ready to be written. I'll encourage you to take small bites of it. Write it a little. Twenty minutes at a time. Write loud, violent, small, quiet, strange, surreal, opaque—all in small steps. Use Anne Lamott's suggestions of shitty first drafts and short assignments. Understand you will write it poorly and there are parts you will write over and over until you've written it to your satisfaction. Let yourself not write it right, especially the thing you have avoided writing because the voices inside say you won't do it justice and the other voices rise up to contradict every statement you make. Thwart them with surrealism or fiction, or by writing really, really fast so that they don't have a chance to catch up (this last one was often my solution). Write it wrong. Write it over and over. Understand that you won't just write the difficult stories once. Understand that you will eventually get tired of writing it, that you will feel called to write something else. Write until the tears come and write even when you can't get to the tears or when you laugh instead. Rejoice at the times you laugh instead. Those, too, are good days.

Storying the hurt

In her book, *Writing Alone and With Others*, Pat Schneider
offers the "simple" prompt: Write something that scares you.
Write something that scares or has hurt you.

Notice what comes up for you when you read the prompt, and
let that association/idea/memory be the place where you begin.
Give yourself no more than ten minutes. Then stop, breathe,
get up and walk around. If you really want to keep going after
the first ten minutes, consider writing in these ten-minute
increments. When you are done, do something very nice
for yourself (see that list back at the end of the introduction
for ideas).

writing the delicious stories

When I started writing on my own, when I was coming out as both an incest survivor and a queer woman, I did a lot of writing about sex. (*A lot* of writing about sex.) Not quite ten years later, when I started leading writing groups with other trauma survivors, I was still curious about how we found words for our want: What stories do we tell about our desire, about what was ok to long for and what wasn't? What did it mean, what did *we* mean, as survivors of sexual trauma who wanted to have good sex?

My initial impetus for the erotic writing groups for sexual trauma survivors was to create a space where survivors of sexual violence could express their full, lived, complicated, and consensual sexuality—a sexuality that was, explicitly, at the intersection of trauma and desire. This would be a space where we could acknowledge the trauma embedded in our sex, even if we never wrote about the trauma/violence itself. These were groups where we wrote sexual fantasy about fictional characters and read them aloud to people who understood how dangerous and revolutionary it was for us to entertain the idea of a fun or silly or "light" sexual fantasy. What did we think we were doing, sitting in molded plastic chairs in a room with painted concrete walls and writing in public about having sex? Didn't we know it would be safer to keep these things quiet, to put them still unworded back in our bodies?

During those eight weeks of my first writing group, in the summer of 2002, something in each of us writers softened, as, week after week, we allowed ourselves to risk writing what we really wanted, out of our particular healing and desiring humanity. In these groups, our definition of "erotic" was expansive, after Audre Lorde's definition in her essay "Uses of the Erotic": the erotic as a site of our grounded and embodied power, our profound creative fullness. When we write from that place, we write from and with our breath, our bodies, our whole human experience. Each word passed through our musculature, our bones, our veins, from head through body to page. Through this writing, we practiced trust for and gratitude toward our bodies. We restoryed an eros that had been desecrated.

Then something surprising happened: the women I wrote with began to write about desires other than sex. Each of us in that room wanted more, better, more connected, more *healed* sex, of course; we also wanted to write books or paint pictures or make music or find more satisfactory work. Articulating *any* longing— having it witnessed and held—creates space for *all* of our longings to begin to shuffle around and ask for the attention they've been denied. Each of the writers in that survivors erotic writing group started to pursue not just sex that was more true to our actual desire, but more of what we wanted outside the bedroom, too. We wanted more joy, in all parts of our lives.

Turns out, hunger is hunger is hunger. Desire is desire. In America, we've tried to confine eros to the sexual realm, because we think we can contain and control it that way, but eros is bigger than deep and authentic sexual connection (which, itself, is pretty damn big, whether with someone you've just met or with a long-time lover). Eros is embodied power. Eros is our longing for realization, for fulfillment. Eros is our creative expression. In "Uses of the Erotic," Audre Lorde wrote, "We have been raised to fear the yes within ourselves, our deepest cravings. But, once recognized, those which do not enhance our future lose their power and can be altered. The fear of our deepest cravings keeps them suspect and indiscriminately powerful, for to suppress any truth is to give it strength beyond endurance."

•§•

We can get stuck, some of us, writing the difficult stories. We can repeat the shame and terror that still clenches our shoulder muscles, takes up residence around our lungs, shallows our breathing, invades our dreams. We can forget that our bodies were designed to experience joy. We succumb to the belief that we don't deserve pleasure, that our bodies are only crime scenes and therefore not worthy of ease or comfort or delight.

When we write the delicious body stories, the stories of desire, of deep longing, of sex that is wanted even when it's complicated, we begin to (re)write a different and older story into our skin. Consensual pleasure is our birthright, if and when we choose it, and our bodies are entitled to as much kindness and generosity as we would offer anyone else.

Our bodies are resilient: we hold loss and sorrow and rage, longing and pleasure and joy. The fact that we can experience pleasure does not undermine the awfulness of what was done to us. It does not indicate that the trauma we experienced "must not have been that bad," as you might fear others will say about you. I was afraid of that, felt it was my job to be the display of my stepfather's violation and violences. I believed that if I were ok, if I were healthy and successful and enjoying life, that that would mean he had gotten away with it. Can you see the bind that I tied myself into? *You cannot be successful or joyful, Jen, because that means he wins.* I had an analyst tell me just a few years ago, "You don't have to be the body of evidence anymore."

I initially started writing sex stories "for" my stepfather, but continued it for myself. Writing about sex was a way to explore my emerging sexuality. This process became a lifeline, a highway I built for myself upon which to drive away from him.

•§•

Early on in my sex-writing practice, I was able to get around my triggers and trauma aftermath because I wrote fiction. I wasn't writing *myself*—exactly. Instead, I sat behind my character's eyes and came in through the back door, as it were, to the safety and power of my sexual self. I found solidarity with my characters: the sex they wanted that they were afraid to admit, their struggles to break through the confines of particular identities. I was able write a home for their desire, and, in so doing, without having to admit it directly, wrote a home for one more piece of my own sexuality.

There have been times when writing about sex in and of itself was sexual, was *sex*, for me. Erotic writing can bring me into the heart of my own sex, into my power and fear and lust and longing. This writing is a means through which I continue to heal myself: when my body feels broken and unredeemable, when I am afraid that I will never again be wildly and joyfully sexual, I remind myself that at least I am wildly and joyfully sexual when I write (or, anyway, I can write characters who are).

Writing about sex is rarely triggering for me—I know that isn't true for everybody. In my experience, there's something powerful about the one-step-removed, the *I'm just writing this down, I don't have to do it*, the *this is someone else's fantasy and life I'm stepping into right now*. There's something powerful in writing another's desire, taking this character and asking, *Ok, what happens now if we try this?* And I get to see what it's like for her, and wonder (maybe, sometimes, I let myself wonder), *Would it be like this if I tried it myself?* Other times it's enough to follow this character into all her desire and her risk and bravery and fear and shame and orgasms (or not) and feel all that possibility move through my body as I write.

•§•

This is just some of what I have discovered that writing about sex can do, in my years both as an erotic writer and working with many, many others exploring the power of writing their own sexual desire:

- Writing about sex can bring the sex we write (back) through and into our skin.

- Writing about sex invites us to use *everything* as material—making even that terrible first date at the sex club worthwhile.

- Writing about sex allows us to play with a subject that we take so very seriously.

- Writing about sex can unlock the fantasies we are proud of and the ones that shame us, can give us a place to explore what we want, imagine, or fantasize about without having to act on any of it. Writing about sex can also teach us things we didn't know about ourselves: we often find ourselves surprised by what turns us on while we're writing.

- Writing about sex can provide a space where we can be in all of our feelings about sex without worrying about protecting or taking care of anyone else: while writing about the sex I had with my lover last night, I might find myself washed over with shame about my body and old loss or a flashback—on the page, I can flow with those feelings, fully. In this practice we find that nothing about our sexual experience has to be contradictory or wrong. Our sex is more than the violence inflicted on us and more complicated than pure ecstasy—just like everyone else's sexuality. We find an ever-shifting normal that is the full body of our lived erotic experience, and we transcribe what constitutes *our* normal.

- In writing, we create fictional characters to try out some of the things we ourselves would *never* do in the flesh.

- We can language all of our body's memories: the painful, yes, and the enjoyment, too. There's as great a taboo around writing about physical/ sexual/erotic ecstasy as there is around naming the specific traumas we had inflicted on us through "sex." Every body-naming is a revelation.

- Writing sex connects you to a lineage of brave and brazen sex writer- revolutionaries.

- Writing sex is a way to get more comfortable with our body's particular language of pleasure. Especially when in a writing group, erotic writing exercises can offer us the opportunity to say aloud those words we're not supposed to say, the "bad" words, the shameful true words of our bodies. When we can say those words, even if our voice shakes (to paraphrase the Maggie Kuhn quote), we become someone formidable—we will not be shamed this way, and so we become harder to control. We can teach the children we love a language for their body that is accurate and respectful, and we are able to hear them when they have questions about their body or when they want to tell us about something being done to them. In this way we undermine a primary currency of sexual violence: silence. We tell the perpetrators, *I have no secrets you can hold over me, and I won't keep your secrets for you.* We can untie our tongues from the anvil of shame.

- We can have a lot of fun writing about sex! It's hot, it makes us flush with how defiant we are, and we witness our prowess: What kind of woman says things like that? What kind of man is so vulnerable?

- Writing about sex invites us into empathy with others. Through writing or listening to others read sex we ourselves haven't been interested in, or have been prejudiced against, we undermine our unexamined stereotypes (and expand our own erotic repertoire!).

- Writing about sex reminds us that we are, by birthright, erotic, sensual, sensuous beings.

- Writing about sex reminds us how *eros* is interwoven through our whole lives, feeding the heartbeat of everything we do.

- Writing about sex unlocks other desires we trained ourselves to ignore. When we unleash our erotic creative voice, we never know what will arise. We may find ourselves remembering how much we used to love to dance, or that we really wanted to be a marine biologist when we grew up, or that once upon a time we wanted to learn to play guitar or plant a garden or have a child or write a fantasy novel: passion doesn't center solely around genital sex, as we know. No wonder those in control have worked so hard to cultivate shame and stifle our erotic awareness: when we are fully engaged with our erotic selves, we are slippery creatures, harder to control, harder to contain, harder to taunt with visions of unattainable and disposable consumer goods. When we are in full possession of our creative joy, we are more interested in cultivating connection and creation than in the mindless pursuit of a sterile life of consumption. (So: writing sex can undermine the soullessness of advanced capitalism—how about that?)

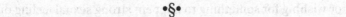

If you're just getting started writing sex, be gentle with yourself. Let yourself consider the details: what something tastes like, what a certain texture feels like against your or your character's skin, what a favorite piece of music sounds like or does to the body. That's all embodied writing. Erotic writing doesn't have to be carnal: erotic writing, by my estimation, is embodied writing, writing that's in and of the body—the character's body *and* the writer's body.

It doesn't matter if anyone else finds your erotic writing sexy or hot: others' perceptions of what is or is not erotic ought not to be the focus when you're struggling to access the language, the metaphor, of your *own* erotic. What matters is that you begin to become thickly aware of your own juices, your own unguent self.

In her essay "The Laugh of the Medusa," Hélène Cixous writes, "A feminine textual body is recognized by the fact that it is always endless, without ending: there's no closure, it doesn't stop [...] a feminine text can't be predicted, isn't predictable, isn't knowable and is therefore very disturbing." (And a "feminine" text/textual body doesn't have to reside in or arise out of a body that was sexed female at birth.) This option of an experience of internal delirium on the way to some uncertain outcome can seem frivolous, illogical, or stupid. But, when I allow myself to follow a line of thought, without trying to control its direction, but instead trusting what I might find there, I am engaging in *erotic* writing and it becomes a *reclamation* of self, a reclamation of the vast *power* of body and/in words.

Storying the stars

Go back to that definition of desire:

> *desire*: noun: a strong feeling of wanting to have something
> or wishing for something to happen; strong sexual feeling or
> appetite – verb: strongly wish for or want (something); want
> (someone) sexually; express a wish to (someone); request
> or entreat. – original sense might have been "await what the
> stars will bring," from the phrase *de sidere* "from the stars,"
> from *sidus* gen. *sideris* "heavenly body, star, constellation"

Read that definition aloud to yourself. Take a moment to notice
what reactions arise in you in response. Write for ten minutes:
What are you (or a character) waiting for the stars to bring?

story and intimacy

The word *intimate* comes from the Latin intus, *within*. It means, "pertaining to the inmost character of a thing; fundamental; essential." Intimacy is therefore, by definition, familiarity.

Familiar, of course, is rooted in the word for *family*. And so we understand why some childhood sexual trauma survivors have trouble with, want nothing to do with, intimacy. Our most intimate selves were violated. That which was meant to be held sacred—our bodies, our trust, our care and well-being—wasn't protected or respected by those charged with keeping us safe. As a part of our healing and our self-care, we might, for a time, choose not to live in the place of intimacy.

Trauma contorts and hollows the gifts of intimacy. Writing can be a practice that returns us to a place of intimacy within ourselves and then, too, with others.

For the years he abused me, the person I was the most intimate with in the world was my rapist, due to the nature of his violation and control. I spent six years in his house, and another three under his control from a distance. He taught me about sex and relationships—that is to say, he *controlled* my sex, and all my relationships were mediated by his psychosis and my trauma response. I had to hide the awful reality at the center of my life from friends at junior high (then at high school, and then again at college), from my mother and other family, from *everyone*—even from my sister. My stepfather was the only one who knew all my secrets. There was no one else in my life I was as intimate with as my stepfather. I was allowed to trust no one else.

A victim's intimacy and authentic connection with others are dangers for the abuser: a friend, teacher, neighbor might notice that something's wrong and try to help, to support a fractured self-esteem, to counteract the abuser's narratives that the victim is alone, can't get away, and has asked for or otherwise deserves what is being done to them. In our isolation, it comes to be the case that we are more intimate with our perpetrators than anyone else in our lives. They know all our secrets. They know the awful things we're capable of. They have seen us debased, dehumanized. They have watched us do things we said we would never do. They tell us they are the only ones who'll ever really know us, ever really love us, and we start to believe it.

This is what isolation does: it leaves us with no place to turn. We might eventually have friends, communities, partners and/or children with whom we want to be close—and still there's a distance between ourselves and those important people in our lives. Intimacy has been a place of danger and shame. It has been a place of violation. We may be drawn toward a deep connection with friends or partners, might feel a desire to be authentically known, but we are also profoundly terrified of being exposed in another's eyes. If we are vulnerable in front of them, will they also misuse us? What will happen when they learn what awful things we've done?

The man who abused me called me horrible names, mistreated me, shamed me, did everything he could to take me apart psychically and reassemble me according to his desires and whims—and there was no one in my life who could contradict all he was teaching me. No one who could undermine his lessons. No one who knew me better. The abuser was the most consistent person in my life.

Or that is what I believed for a long time. That's the story I told: the only person who really knew me was my rapist.

And it's true, there was much that he knew about me that others in my life didn't know, experiences that defined me for which only he and I were present.

But just because he made me into a tool for his use didn't mean he knew who I was, or wanted to be. My desires were of no interest to him. Control isn't intimacy; in fact, he couldn't truly be intimate with me at all.

Authentic intimacy requires vulnerability on the part of all involved parties. Intimacy requires a capacity for connection that sociopaths can't offer. That he only saw me as a pawn to be manipulated in his reach for more power and control denies the possibility for actual intimacy.

Maybe this means that for a long time in my life I was intimate with no one. This brings a different kind of sorrow. We as humans have a deep longing for intimacy, don't we? But those of us who have come through some experience that sets us apart in some way from those in our family or wider communities— sexual assault, child abuse or neglect, domestic abuse, war, mental or physical illness—we understand that we are no longer known, may even believe that we are no longer *knowable* by those we love and who love us. Our communities— those who aren't survivors of violence or trauma, and some who are, too—have difficulty with the stories of what we've been through, the stories that make us who we are now. Violence flings us out of the circle of shared story, which is part of the circle of intimacy. To tell our truths, then, is to risk having those we love shun us—and yet, in *not* telling, we internalize the idea that intimacy is conditional, that our stories are "too much" for those who love us, that we are "too much," that we are unknowable. We are alone with our stories. We remain isolated with what we've been through, what was done to us. We may try to "get over it" or "move on" without sharing the stories with anyone, even ourselves.

But we are made of story, as much as we are made of stardust (like Langston Hughes told us). If I can't share something that has significantly impacted my understanding of myself, if I try to ignore that story, shove it aside and forget about it, I don't know about you, but I start to come apart. I begin to act on my rapist's assertion that people won't love me if they know this about me, if they know my truths. I start to shape my life, consciously and unconsciously, around *that* story, instead. And I get both profoundly lonely and certain that lonely is my destiny.

It's a terrible cycle.

For years there were parts of my story that I never told—I could easily rattle off many terrible aspects of my years under my stepfather's control, but could not fully accept others' responses of shock and support because they didn't know the Really Bad Things, the worst parts. The things I'd done, things I'd been forced to *behave as though I wanted to do.* Those were the stories I kept hidden in a deep box inside my gullet.

We—my listeners and I—would be more intimate after I told, remember—and intimate was not a safe place.

My first step toward a transformation was to approach these tellings on the page. I didn't undertake any coordinated or intentional process to find language and expression for my most volatile and shame-dense memories. No, this work, like all the other parts of my work, came haphazardly and over time. Now and again, I would choose to write about my sister and our shared reality in that home, or about ex-boyfriends I'd had to hurt according to my stepfather's instructions; these were the tenderest parts in me. Writing about these things felt like oozing pus onto the page: foul, toxic. At first, all I could do was put words to the shame and guilt that took up so much space in my psyche, like some kind of parasitic fungus. I wanted to externalize these memories, so they'd exist somewhere outside the secret I'd kept for the man who'd abused me.

You know what happens when you clean out a wound that's become infected. It hurts like hell. It's gross and ugly. But after it's done, the wound can heal. These places in my psyche were deeply infected with the secrets I'd kept. In writing these stories down, piece by piece, I felt nauseous. Why did I have to remember these things? But, most often, by later that day, the nausea lifted. The writing brought me new questions, which acted as antibiotics: What if I wasn't the person I had been taught I was? What if I couldn't have done anything differently? What if I did exactly the best I could under terrifying and violent circumstances? What if I'd been an abused, brainwashed, and manipulated teenager?

Could I write myself into some compassion for that young woman?

These questions stretched the wound, both stung and comforted. Subsequent writings still hurt—these were deeply infected sites. But after awhile (sometimes years), those extra-awful parts of me came into the fold of my whole, complicated story. I even began to find a way to be intimate, tender, with those parts of my history, those most wounded parts of myself.

Reading others' writing helped with this process, too. Talking to supportive folks helped: friends, significant others, therapists, family. Another step (for me) was to write about these awfulnesses in writing groups—allowing trusted others in a confidential setting to share with me in holding these stories. It turned out that peer writers were willing and able to listen to the stories I shared, respond with support, and then not treat me like an untouchable thing who has said "too much." In fact, it's been my experience that when any one of us in a survivors writing group shares anything particularly vulnerable, writes about something taboo or especially unspeakable, there is a palpable honor in the room for the risk that writer has taken and the tacit permission they have offered, inviting the rest of us, too, to go deeper in our own writing.

What a profound risk, to tell those things that we were trained to believe made us pariah, that made us monstrous. When we do so and are met with kindness, respect, and generosity, though, that pariah story is eroded. One more layer of that old isolation is stripped away, and we move closer to an authentic relationship—a true intimacy—with those who love and support us, even with ourselves.

The intimacy of our tenderest stories

Take a couple of minutes to create a list of things you're ashamed of (just two minutes – don't try and create a comprehensive list!), then let one of these choose you, and write about that place of shame for five to seven minutes. When you're done, read it aloud to an empty room (whisper if you have to, or just mouth the words). Then write for another five to seven minutes, looking at the situation through tenderness and compassion for the self in that situation. Follow your writing wherever it seems to want you to go. After writing, be very kind to yourself—maybe now's a good time for a terrible '80s movie and a big bowl of popcorn (at least, that's what I would probably do).

the words to become—
and unbecome

Do you remember a time when you first came out to yourself? Maybe you came out as lesbian, bisexual, gay, or queer—or genderqueer, or trans. Maybe you came out as a survivor or a victim of domestic violence. Maybe you remembered abuse that you'd forgotten. Maybe you came out as straight or kinky, as butch or femme, as a man or a woman. You realized that, in some important respect, you were not what the world said you should be, that you were not who or what *you* thought you were or should be, and you were terrified that if anyone saw who you really were, you'd be cast out by those you loved.

I was rewatching an old lesbian movie recently, *Desert Hearts*, remembering when I first saw it, in my early twenties. In the film, there's a scene with the women lovers out at a bar/restaurant after they have first had sex. For one of the women, it's not only the first time she's laid hands on another woman, it's the first time she's even imagined this possibility for her life. She is raw, in love, terrified, overwhelmed, and hungry. For the other woman, the situation looks different: she is ten years younger, but has been out to herself for a long time and has had other women lovers. It's 1959 and she has found a way to be herself in her world: most people in her life know who she and how she loves without it being of much contention or overt violence. So she is more comfortable being out in public with a lover. She touches her lover's hand, but the other woman is terrified, pulls her hand away. She wants to return to the hotel room where they have been making love for days. She doesn't understand why the world has to come in.

As I watched, I remembered going out to breakfast with the first woman I fell in love with, the afternoon after the morning that I came out to myself when we kissed for the first time. It's a beautiful, complicated story that I'd love to share— maybe someday over a cup of tea. That's not the story I want to tell right now, though. I want to tell the story of my fear—how I sat with her in that diner booth in the middle of our little college town, and we ordered waffles piled with fruit and whipped cream, coffees with cocoa and whipped cream, and all I wanted to do was reach back across the table and put her whole body in my mouth— but what if somebody saw us? I was sure every single person in the restaurant *already knew*. Surely our waitress—a tall, rangy woman with short hair and broad shoulders who looked like she belonged in a '50s bar in Greenwich Village with a pack of Marlboros rolled in one sleeve and a femme on her hip—could see what we were.

This fear astonished me: was I really someone who cared if strangers knew I'd had sex with a woman?

It wasn't as simple as that. The truth was I was afraid my *stepfather* would find out—and that when he did, this would be taken away from me, too. His was the kingdom I dwelt within, he the arbiter of what sex could be, he the boundary-maker and namer. I sat in that Sunday-morning diner, packed as it was with hungry college students and fresh-pressed families on campus tours, and ate breakfast with a woman who had showed me something I hadn't known about myself. And I knew if—when—my stepfather discovered it, he would take this, too, as a tool of his terrorization. He would use it against me.

And he did.

•§•

Where did incest end and homophobia pick up for me? Is there any way to untangle these threads? No one at school knew about my stepfather's abuse; as far as my lover knew then, I was just another straight woman having sex with a lesbian, getting worked up in the nighttime and wanting to keep my daytime surface smooth and unrumpled. It wasn't that we weren't obvious to all of our friends, a community of queers of all flavors and shapes and sizes; it was that I couldn't have it or us publicly acknowledged. Anyone might be his spy. Someone might tell him.

The story I like to tell, now, is that coming out as queer was no problem for me, that it was an enormous positive in the middle of the horror that was the rest of my life. I didn't experience the wracking shame and self-loathing that I later read about in all the coming out books. I would tell anyone who asked that, compared to being an incest survivor, being queer was a bright spot, a blessing, a gift and a joy.

In 1992, when I first had sex with a woman, I hadn't ever thought about my sexual orientation. I was just a girl who got fucked by boys and men, most of the time sort of consensually—that is, the boys my age were all ones I might have chosen anyway, even if my stepfather weren't pressuring me to have sex with as many of them as possible. I can't say whether I would have come out earlier if I hadn't been raped by my stepfather during my adolescence. I can't say whether I would have come out at all. I can't know *anything* about how or where my life, that other existence in which I was not abused by that man, would have gone.

Identity, though, wasn't the issue so much as this longing for something I had never had the chance to put a name to before my stepfather reached his hands into my developing erotic life and unclaimed me from myself. I wonder if you can see his hands penetrate my chest cavity, see him fumble around, see his two enormous, full-fingered hands stain the quiet cardboard dollhouse room of what was my incipient desire, knock over all the furniture, throw the little people around, tear the curtains from the windows—he doesn't want to hurt anyone, he says. He just wants it all for himself. He pushes his hands through the walls, and the shredded fabric blows in the new and chilly breeze. He pulls his hands away after the room has been mined. He only likes beautiful things he can break apart. This is the inside sex of me, a place of ruin and damage and tear. I knew how to live fragmented, parceled, all particle and loss, all sever and compartmentalization. I was already a world of secrets when she met me, and then she gave me another room to add to my collection of selves, another self to tack onto my extremities.

There at that table in that college diner, I drank my extra-sweet coffee, the smell of this woman still clinging to my hands. I ate my waffles with strawberries just like I had the last time I ordered them, before I'd gone to bed with a woman, and now I didn't know if everything was different. She had done this before. She was already out, did not have these inside complications upending what had been a stunningly beautiful morning together.

We sat in that cafe booth and unravelled. There was a low, narrow mirror that ran around the perimeter of the room, just at eye level when I was seated. The booths sat perpendicular to the wall, and I glanced into the mirror surreptitiously (or thought I did), wanting to see who was looking at us, what they were saying. Wanting to see if I looked any different. I was used to monitoring and interrogating my sex on my stepfather's behalf. This would be a secret I'd keep from him. I was twenty years old. He'd first put his hands on me when I was twelve or thirteen, first put his penis into my body when I was fifteen or sixteen, he had pushed his fingers into me earlier than that. I had no one to talk to about what had cracked open when this woman told me the night before, while she gave me a massage: *You let me know if I do anything that makes you feel uncomfortable*—and how no one had ever said anything like that to me before. Who gave me that kind of respect? How could I not fall in love with her?

I ate my breakfast and understood that this would be taken from me. Already I could hear my stepfather's voice, degrading my desire for this woman.

I told her she couldn't tell anyone, and she agreed to keep us a secret from the people she lived with and who loved her. And then I would sneak into her room when no one was looking and scream all night. I made it hard for her to keep secrets, to say the least. She tried anyway.

•§•

What are the stories that have been living in my body for these forty years, but most especially over the last about-twenty years—since I both broke contact with my stepfather and came out as queer? Because those two lifestory-altering experiences occurred for me during the same time frame, they have been woven into each other, one entirely of and about the other. My queerness is necessarily about my trauma. My experience of incest is entirely queered. I can't tease them apart—and maybe I don't need to. Incest threaded through gender threaded through desire: that story is still true for me. My body is an interweave of difficult and delicious story. Perhaps all of our bodies are.

At just the moment when I was meant to begin to explore my body's stories, gendered and sexual stories, stories of desire and possibility, a man entered my life and, soon, my body, a man who took it upon himself to retrain me into *his* stories. I have been living in and struggling with those stories ever since.

But these days, twenty or so years later, there's a new story rising like bread in me, like candle flame, rising like a skirt over the subway grate, and I don't quite have the language for it yet. Something about the possibilities for and of my body—not just about what my body can do, but about what it can be, what it can mean. I hold in my hands a glimmer of who and how my body could have been, even if he hadn't come into it and tried to blow it apart.

The story of your own becoming

Just for a minute, create a list of your identities. Again, this
doesn't have to be comprehensive. Mine might include queer,
sexual abuse survivor, white, Midwestern, femme-of-center,
college-educated, able-bodied. Is there a part of yourself, one
of these selves, that you don't tell people about or share widely?
Could you write a story about that part of yourself, when
you first discovered/understood that identity, or recognized
something new about yourself? Give yourself ten minutes.
Follow your writing wherever it seems to want you to go.

dolce

voice

who asks you to tell your story?

"What happened to you? What was your childhood like? Want to tell me what brings you in today? How are you doing? Why don't you like me to touch you there? Why are you so quiet/loud/scared/angry/sad all the time? How come you have so much sex? Why don't you like surprises? How come you won't have sex with me? What happened that night? Why don't you want to talk about it? Do you want to tell me what happened to you?"

To be asked to "tell your story," one of your core-being stories, is to be asked for a piece of your heart, a chunk of your Real Self. When someone says to me, *I want to hear your story*, my belly tightens with hope and anxiety. Sharing my history of sexual abuse and how I've lived since is a wildly vulnerable act. *What if they can't take it?* I worry. *What if they can't really hear me?* And, maybe even scarier to consider: *What if they can?*

Who asks to hear traumas stories—I mean, really hear them? And how long does it take to believe that someone really wants to hear us?

Cops ask some of us. Parents ask. Sometimes a friend will ask. Sometimes lovers ask. Therapists, of course. That's not very many people. Most of the people we spend our lives around don't ask and don't want to know. They want a pop song, a poster, a bumper sticker. They don't want the sticky sweet rot of our true details. That messes up the cool ocean breeze and gently swaying grasses of their triumphant sunset cinematic fantasies of Everything Is All Better Now.

This sounds cynical. I understand the triumphant sunset cinematic fantasy, of course I do. I carry it, too. It's a great place to visit, but a hard place to be expected to live.

•§•

Of course, a powerful draw of therapy is that someone to listen to our whole story with compassion and empathy and non-judgment (at least, ideally). The bounds of the therapeutic relationship mean that our telling is contained and confined, which we often need.

Consider what it takes for us to unravel our full story for those who share the rest of our lives. What a risk, to allow ourselves to be more fully beheld.

We believe no one will love us if they know who we really are, what we carry, what we've done, what's been done to us—and the more we don't expose ourselves to those we love, the more certain we are of the old story of our unlovablity.

And then what if they can't hold it? We are afraid that our stories, that we ourselves, are "too much"—and given that our story has probably frightened or overwhelmed friends, that we've had family ignore or discount what we told them, this fear doesn't arise out of nowhere.

The page asks for your story. In writing, we can be free to say just what we want to say, to tell the story however we want to tell it, without editing ourselves based on how our listener reacts. A workshop participant once described to me a difference she appreciated between a traditional support group and the survivors writing group: in the support group, she spent a lot of the session rehearsing what it was she wanted to say, or editing it based on the group's energy, so she couldn't focus well on the folks who shared before her. In our writing group, though, we all wrote together, and when it was time to share, because her story was already crafted, she could give more attention to the other stories being shared in the circle—and trusted that she had the full attention of others in the room as well.

Just because someone has asked for our story doesn't mean we should tell them, doesn't mean they can hold us, doesn't mean they're safe. We listen to our instincts. We know when someone is interested, *really* interested, in hearing more, when someone has shut down or slipped into overwhelm. We expand or pull back in, accordingly. We don't want to slip the sticky heartbeat of our stories into hands that cannot hold them, into ears that have turned to stone—or worse, to negative judgment or disbelief. We employ the skill (likely developed during our abuse) to redirect attention away from ourselves. Sometimes we tell those wrong folks anyway, because we are hopeful and lonely, because we want to believe they're good for us (no matter what our intuition says), and sometimes because we believe or feel like we have no other choice.

I have had ridiculous responses to my stories. Someone once asked, "Did you like what you did with your sister?" Someone else asked, "Do you think about doing it again when you see her now?" Others have believed that now they understood, after having heard some part of my history, why I was queer, or why I was feminist. Some listeners have cut me off with the sincere appellation "brave," when what I wanted was to be understood as so much more complicated than that.

•§•

For me, the ideal environment in which to *tell my story* is an open-ended evening with the lover or friend who has asked. Hopefully, it's someone I won't have to emotionally caretake while I'm describing my history. We have cups of tea, sit together on a couch in a quiet room. I want several hours ahead of us—nothing scheduled, nobody waiting for us, no other plans.

This sort of telling only has happened a few times in my life, and every time the story shifts, grows, because in between tellings, *I* grow and shift; I learn the words for things I hadn't been able to say before, and let other parts slip away.

I ask a great deal of the people in my life who ask to hear this story. I want them empathetic but not flooded. I want them mostly quiet until they ask penetrating and specific questions. I want them sad and angry—so I can see what it looks like to be openly sad and angry for the girl I was—but not so much that I'm not able to continue. My trauma story is long, and I tell it matter-of-factly with little visual emotion, except shame and periodic inappropriate laughter. I ask my listener to hold a lot. I ask them to hear these horrors that I rattle off like the casual descriptions of a school day—because, for me, they were. I ask my listener to come into my world, to meet me where I live, which is the place where sexual violence is routine and matter-of-course. If that's not where my listener usually lives, it's a hard door to walk through. No one listens perfectly, but there are people in our lives who can hold our stories, and us, with grace and generosity.

What I want to tell is the truth, to burst the bubble of that sunset fantasy. What I want is to download it all so that I don't have to tell it again, even though I will never stop telling it. What I want is to get it right so that you can see the land I live in and what I look like inside, so that I don't have to be alone there anymore.

The gift of your voice

Is there a story or an experience or even a secret you would offer up if you knew the person you were speaking to could hold your words with empathy and grace? You might begin with the phrase, "What I always wanted to tell you was..." (Change those pronouns however you want to!) Give yourself ten minutes, and see where the writing takes you.

disembodied story

When talking about our body's stories, we must also consider our disembodied stories. I'm talking about the fragments of memory or possibility that float within us, untethered from the timeline to which we're able to root most of our memory and sense of self. I'm talking about the stories that are bloodless, have no musculature or veins, are all structure but no bone or emotion or voice. I mean stories that we only stay on the surface of, stories that are porcelain masks, shiny and clean and glaze, with no heartbeat, no mess, no breath.

Much of our early writing will be disembodied. If you grew up in the USA and went to public schools, you were probably trained to take yourself and your body out of your writing. You were trained to keep an "objective" distance from your subject; you were taught that *you* are not an appropriate subject for intellectual or creative inquiry. You were taught to keep a thick pane of glass between your words and your reactions, emotions, thoughts, and feelings about a subject. You were taught to stick to the facts. You were taught to write in a way that was grammatically correct, technically accurate, clean, clear, concise, dead, dry and boring. Maybe you weren't able to learn how to do this. Maybe you got so bored, or your assignments were returned to you so bloodied with red pen, that you stopped writing altogether.

Many of us who are trauma survivors write disembodied-ly for another reason— we are detached from this body, this thing that carts our brain around, because we don't want to have to fully inhabit this crime scene we wear every day. We became so overwhelmed by the cognitive dissonance of having to live in the skin that betrayed us that we found it easier to step outside the confines of this fraught playground, this embattled tangle of cells and neurons and chemical/electrical reactions and sensory input, and just live as much as possible in our heads.

Some of us call this state of being *dissociation*: we lose time; other selves make time in our bodies when we are no longer present; we are able to see our bodies acting or being acted upon while we feel like we are outside of our own skin. For many of us, the experience of dissociation or disembodiment is less extreme: we are simply not aware of our bodies. We treat our body like an animal we have been given leave to neglect. We don't sleep enough or we sleep too much; we overfill our bellies; we try not to feel when we're having sex; we refuse to go to the doctor; we push ourselves hard and harder at the gym or around the track; we try to live on coffee and ramen noodles and bottles of red wine. We abuse what someone else taught us only exists to be abused—the tender eloquence of our very soma.

•§•

For the first years of my writing practice, I stayed with my ritual and routine story: this is what he did to me, these are the details, these are the facts. I was crafting a testimony, something for use in court. Ask me how I *felt*, though, when he had his mouth on me or held an object in his hand that he pushed into me, and all my inside lights turned off. I could almost hear the fuse exploding. The way I survived, like so many of us, was *not* to feel, *not* to be present. During his assaults, I developed the ability to create fantasies that I could almost physically climb into, walking around inside somebody else's sexual landscape while, somewhere else, a forty-something-year-old man, sweaty and pale and coated with stringy gray hair, heaved on top of me.

The story of my sex became a disembodied story. The story of my orgasm became a disembodied story. Orgasm without a body is orgasm without words, unlanguagable. Just contraction, contradictions, exhaustion. You can't even call it release. It's simply mechanics, the body keeping its contract with itself, and then the rape is over.

How do you tell a bodiless body story—especially if the teller prefers not to *have* a body?

You do it slowly. With patience. And compassion. And humor. And help.

When we are disembodied, we want to skim over the surface of things. We don't want to use embodied and sensory detail. We don't want to waste time saying how something *feels*, smells, tastes; maybe we can give you how something looks, maybe what it sounds like—those senses allow us to keep our physicality at a distance. We don't have to drop in. We can't—because to drop in means we'd have to feel it in our own bodies, first, before describing the feeling in our characters' bodies. And we've spent so many years training ourselves not to feel. Why would we want to start now?

Our trauma stories are often our most disembodied stories. They are the stories that we most often can't find welcome for in everyday society, the stories that are most often unwelcome at the dinner table. These are the stories that our communities tell us—directly and indirectly—to shut up about, the stories that make other people uncomfortable, these stories of the complicated realities of our living in the aftermath of trauma in a body that remembers and won't let us forget.

When our body stories are without language, we feel trapped inside our skin with no way out. We feel unfinished, nonsensical. Monstrous. We feel we are without a mouth, without a throat. Yet, we keep trying to find words for the story the way a child nudges open the door to the basement and calls down after a noise she heard—even if she is terrified, she prefers the known terror to the unknown, the unseen, the unsayable.

Sometimes the only words we can put to a trauma story, a body story, are fragments, the words of confusion and uncertainty. Sometimes all we can do is define what the story *isn't*, describe a silhouette, trace out a possibility in negative space—it wasn't this *or* this, it wasn't *that*. We can get closer to who we are, were, by finding and claiming the words for what we weren't. We use the words of shadow, we use the words of *No*.

When we are mute, it's not as though our stories, or our bodies, fall silent. Instead we are screaming without sound. Memory churns its sadness under the surface of our skin, but we don't know how to describe it. We feel what wants speaking and we open our mouths and nothing comes out but a cough, or a report of yesterday's weather, or other bald banalities to which we affix our tongues. For a time, those safeties are the only places our words know to go.

Sometimes the page has to come before the throat—that has been my way. I needed the shout of ink crushing plain paper before I could lift the story into the fragile architecture of my throat and break that seal, speak the truth.

The stories that fragment the body without words sometimes want to testify, sometimes skid away from the pen like mercury. Not every story wants to be told. Not everything will have words, and not all the words we have will be written.

The unwritten body is a scattered craft table, a drift of clouds. All those sewn-shut mouths. It's not that the body is not speaking if we don't write it, it's that those stories are untranslated from skin's mother tongue. When you are translating the body's knowing into a spoken language, you can't rely on the old forms. You can't just let them go, either. You need everything at your disposal: fragment, seesaw, winter breeze, rain shower, metaphor, irony, voice tone, point of view, sestina, morning glory, tea kettle, wine bottle, dialogue, fiction, nonsense—you will need all the texts you have ever known in order to decipher the truth of your body. You listen closely, and write the stories over and over again. You write in the voices of each of our multiple selves, let each alter who wants to hold the pen for awhile write their own part of the story—we do not have to be a singular "I" on the page. You pair this one with strawberry jam, this one with crochet, this one with a baseball flying through a window, this one with a fist to the face. You take all the sensations, all the speakings. You filter them through your own body's songs, and you find out what it was that your body has wanted you to know or say.

Sometimes you listen to others' body songs. You gather with other people learning to speak their body's stories, and this gives you more language for your own. When we write together, we learn how other people say it, learn new melodies for these aching songs. We try those words in our own mouths, use what fits, leave the rest.

The body is a deep pool, an ocean, the body is all metaphor and peculiar specificity. We can dip our toes in, we can swim in the shallow end of our skins. I can describe a little bit of what he smelled like when he would put his face close to mine—and when the world starts to go numb or I freeze, *I stop writing that story*. I turn to other topics. Forcing myself back into these embodied memories is simply re-victimization, and that's not what I'm after.

Instead, we're teaching our creative selves, our reembodying selves, that we will show up for what they have to tell (through) us, and that we can be trusted with the words given to us to put on the page. We learn to listen to our instinct, that thin fibrous voice that persists in us even after we have had to spend years not listening to her wisdom. We learn to find the physical, embodied language of our disembodiment. And as we do so, we thread these experiences, gently and powerfully, into the narrative of ourselves; we come to know and tell ourselves differently.

These days I can tell I'm disembodied when I sit down to write and the words come stuttery, stopping and starting, too much on the surface, not in flow—when I'm trying to control the writing rather than allowing my body to be a conduit for the words. I reembody through timed writes, describing my physical surroundings, taking the writing slow, dropping down into specific physical and sensory description: I tell you my character is angry but I'm not letting you see her face, feel what that rage is like in her skin, behind her eyes, what her mouth tastes like, how her jaw is tightened, how every muscle in her back and arms have gone tight again. Describing it means having to feel it: *getting* to feel it.

When we learn to hear the language of all our body's stories, we can hear what our younger self wanted, needed, anyone to hear. We don't pretend it didn't happen, we don't pretend our bodies are mute. We honor the wisdom of disembodiment, and we show up more consistently, with curiosity and a moving pen, bearing authentic wit(h)ness to our own truth.

Body of voice / Voice of body

Write a love letter to your body—either to your body as a whole, or to a specific part or parts. Remember that love letters can take lots of different tones: appreciative, tender, curious, apologetic, longing. Give yourself ten minutes. "Dear Body..." What do you want to say?

Consider the idea of a body-less body story: write your body as a constellation of objects. This exercise is similar to the one we did at the end of "the page has room for my incomprehensibility" (p. 22). Number 1-10 on your page, and draw two vertical lines down the page, creating three columns. In the first column, write ten parts of your body. Cover that list (with your hand or a piece of paper), and in the third column, write ten common, everyday objects (like branch, typewriter, barbell, light switch... you see what I mean?). In the middle column, write the word "is" – you'll end up with ten metaphors, along the lines of: *the arm is a branch, the head is an anvil.* Let one of these lines choose you, and write. Give yourself ten minutes, and follow your writing wherever it seems to want you to go.

articulate fear: writing what scares us

Last night's Write Whole workshop left me emptied out and full, all at the same time. We wrote about fear, using Joy Harjo's "Fear Poem, or I Give You Back" as our prompt. We wrote about apologizing for things that weren't our fault. We wrote about the many fears that weigh down our shoulders every day:

I'm afraid if I write it, it will be true. I'm afraid I'm making it up. I'm afraid someone will contradict me, call me a liar, tell me I'm not making sense, call me crazy, use all of my words against me. I'm afraid I won't be able to write it down right, that I won't have the right words, that I can never describe it the way it really happened. I'm afraid of how I will feel when I'm writing what it was like that first day he took me into the basement. I'm afraid of the power of what I have to say; maybe someone will believe me if I write it down...

It's not unusual to be frightened to enter into this process, to write freely, tell the full and true stories of our bodies, to transcribe exactly what our soul asks us put down in black and white. And understandably so. We were trained by abusers to keep our mouths shut or people we love will get hurt. We were trained by our teachers to make an outline, not to write a word until we know exactly what we want to say. We were trained to hold ourselves together, not to reveal the places in us that are cracked or uncertain, stippled with fissures of vulnerability.

We're afraid that others will misunderstand us, or that we'll be ostracized or teased. We are afraid of being shamed. We're afraid that we'll say it right, that people *will* understand, and the secret will finally be revealed. We are afraid that once we let the memories out of their little boxes, our history will overwhelm us and we will not be able to do anything but cry or rage. We're afraid of the righteous power of our rage, the deep ravine of our sorrow. We are afraid to be exposed. We are afraid of retribution. We are afraid of being hurt, hurting others close to us, hurting other writers in the room.

I often feel fear when I'm writing. I may be afraid of feeling nauseous or triggered after writing. I may be afraid I'm not competent enough a writer to do justice to the story I want to tell. Or I may be writing something I was never supposed to speak of—there may be a psychic response rising up in me, protective ghosts trying to move my pen off the page: *don't say that; you'll get us hurt if you say that.* I'm still afraid he'll come after me if I tell.

If I'm afraid as I write, I can stop writing if I choose to. But being afraid doesn't mean I *have* to stop writing.

Security specialist and author Gavin de Becker, in his book *Gift of Fear*, writes, "Real fear is a signal intended to be very brief, a nerve servant of intuition ... [Fear] is not an emotion like sadness or happiness, either of which might last a long while. It is a state, like anxiety. True fear is a survival signal that sounds only in the presence of danger..." Elsewhere, he writes, "The very fact that you fear something is *solid evidence that it is not happening.*"

Just because I'm afraid doesn't mean I have to stop writing.

•§•

In her interview for Elizabeth Benedict's *The Joy of Writing Sex*, Dorothy Allison said, "I believe that fear is useful … What you are most afraid of is where the energy will flow the strongest, and for a writer, if you write in that direction, toward where the fear is, it's like a homing signal for what you need to do."

Folks come to a survivors writing group both wanting to write their trauma stories and afraid to be asked to do so. Toward the end of a group, I'll ask participants to think back to our first meeting: what were the stories or situations they were afraid they might be asked to write about? Then I invite them to go ahead and write one of those. The stories we're afraid of are stories we protect, and stories that we protect are powerful stories. These stories, the ones that live beneath the stories we tell more often, are rough around the edges, have more squirm in them. Allison reminds new writers that we keep a lot of energy bundled up around what we fear. Listening to and writing with fear is a powerful practice of writing with instinct, listening to what wants to get written.

We have good reasons to be afraid of writing about our experiences of violence or trauma. We have compartmentalized the grief or torment that arises when we visit those stories, and we don't want to be flooded with feeling. We are afraid that even if we write it clearly and in detail, the people we share it with still won't *really* understand what it was like for us. Whatever we were threatened with if we ever told what was being done to us: we are afraid, even now, that the perpetrators will make good on those threats. We want to keep the trauma locked up in a ward behind our eyes. We think we are safer that way, silent. But maybe you already know what Audre Lorde, in her book Sister/Outsider, said about safety and silence: "I was going to die, if not sooner then later, whether or not I had ever spoken myself. My silences had not protected me. Your silence will not protect you."

My beloved, a day or two after we'd just met, offered me this writing prompt: *What would you write on a piece of paper that you were going to burn immediately after writing?*

There are pieces of my own story that I haven't yet tried to write. They sit, still and bulbous, inside me, and I'm afraid of what will happen when I attempt to find language for them.

What do we do with the stories that we both want and don't want, with the stories that we need and that we don't want to commit to the page?

We pay attention to what we're afraid of, don't we? I can tell you how my stepfather's face looked when he was getting angry, when he was shifting from Fine to Fucked Up. I remember the nuances of the dining room table, the one I stared at during the hours and hours we had to sit there and confess all of our psychological workings, every thought and fantasy. I remember my sister's face, I remember how the overhead light hung shadows around the living room, I remember the qualities of silence around my stepfather's voice, how his house seemed to swallow us, the way he wanted to. Those details, when I can get into them, are important—they allow the reader to be there with my narrator, exactly in the situation with her.

Of course, this doesn't just apply to writing that's drawn closely from life. There're fictional stories that scare us, too. What happens when you meet a telling, a character, who both draws you in and repels you? What happens when you let yourself all the way into her, anyway, even though you find her disturbing, even though you question what it means about you that you can imagine her so clearly? I think it can be useful not to analyze too much, but just to write it—don't worry about where she comes from. We all have plenty of models of terrible behavior to draw from. Use your fear of her to reveal her vividly for the reader.

There's power in the material we're afraid of, and we can make it ours, we can take it back. All those stories we fear: I say write them, even if you need to tear out the pages after you're done writing and shove them into the back of a drawer.

•§•

When there's something I'm afraid to write about, very often it's something I'm ashamed of. In conversation with Krista Tippett, social scientist Brené Brown said that "shame drives two primary tapes: *not good enough*, and *who do you think you are?* So to me, it's a very formidable emotion. Its survival is based on us not talking about it, so it's done everything it can do to make it unspeakable." Shame takes an enormous toll on our sense of ourselves, on our self-confidence. It uses so much energy that could be better spent elsewhere—falling in love, playing with the dog, developing a skill or passion, walking by the ocean, finding a more interesting job.

When I think about the stories I've been ashamed of, I think about the stories that, once someone hears them, will keep them from fully buying my shiny surface pretense that I am and always have been fine, that I can take care of everything by myself, that I've got It All Under Control. I get ashamed of needing, of wanting, of being sad and lost, of not being a better adult with a balanced checkbook and house and obvious career path. I have been ashamed of things I did during the abuse to survive and things I did afterward to cope. In his book, *Healing the Shame that Binds You*, educator and counselor John Bradshaw writes that, although shame itself is a "healthy human emotion," "toxic shame is unbearable and always necessitates a cover-up, a false self... Once one becomes a false self, one ceases to exist, psychologically." Shame is an extraordinary tool of control: anywhere that shame has laced its tendrils, we will feel tugged toward silence.

The shaming voices tell me my writing is stupid and worthless. They tell me no one cares. They tell me that everyone will hate me or think I'm weak or unprofessional if I write that, or that I'll lose my family or friends, or that I'll get hurt—finally, he'll come after me if I tell *that* part.

One reason that Dorothy Allison directs to write right into our fear, I think, is to help us get around the roadblocks around our writing, these inner censors that stop up our flow. Fear says, *You can write this far, but no further—you know what happens if you step over this line.* But we *don't* know, because we haven't tried. And sometimes (maybe even often), when we step over that line, what happens is we gain more control over our history and memories, and we make poetry of our truth and struggle, we say what we were never supposed to say—and we do not die.

Natalie Goldberg, in *Writing Down the Bones*, invites her writers to "go for the jugular"—that is, write directly into those things we're not supposed to say. Write it all down. Write about the fear, the shame, itself. Write about being afraid to write, if you can't write the thing itself yet. We learn to listen intently to the internal conversation between the part of our psyche desperate to disgorge all the shame and rage we've held in our guts out onto the page and the *other* part of our psyche that's been protecting us by insisting that we keep these stories silent. We learn to *write it slant*, as Emily Dickinson told us to—we use metaphor, poetic language, imagery, and fiction to release the truths we were never supposed to find words for.

All through this process, though, keep listening to your body, your gut. When we're writing about trauma, it's a kindness to ourselves to go slow. I've had writers come into a writing group with the intention of getting everything down, one memory after another, no stopping, no break—and then on the other side of those eight weeks, the memories would be purged and they would be healed. They didn't want to listen to me when I encouraged them to slow down and take care of themselves. Understandably, they just wanted it all *out*. They wanted to tell it, wanted to get the hard part over with. Some of these writers stopped attending, though, part way through a workshop series; they got overwhelmed with feeling, felt so bad after writing, and didn't know how to contain it. The writing no longer felt like an inviting practice anymore—there was nothing enjoyable or positive about the writing anymore. It became a place they associated only with nakedness, shame, and horror.

Toni Morrison said, "When I sit down in order to write, sometimes it's there; sometimes it's not. But that doesn't bother me anymore. I tell my students there is such a thing as 'writer's block,' and they should respect it. You shouldn't write through it. It's blocked because it ought to be blocked, because you haven't got it right now." It's ok not to push ourselves to write it all out *now*. This isn't about getting to a finish line. This is about learning a new way of being with our words and our creative selves, reconnecting with our creative intuition. This is ongoing practice, a new way of being. Theodore Roethke, in his poem "The Waking," writes, "I wake to sleep, and take my waking slow. / I learn by going where I have to go."

Listen to yourself when something inside you says, *No, I'm not ready to write that now.* That same inside something will let you know when it's ready to release those words.

That inside protective part isn't ever going to jump up and down and clap its hands and say, *Hooray! Today, we get to write about the scariest thing that happened to us!* This instinct is doing its job by urging us away from the parts of our trauma memory that it has worked so hard to keep locked up. What we want to do, slowly and surely, is let this protective part of ourselves feel that when we write into our fear, we will not die. We might feel sorrow, or loss, or shame after doing these writes. Usually, these rueful feelings abate after a day or so, and writers find that something in them has strengthened; they return to the writing group after a week ready to write more, and maybe write harder.

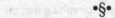

When I was writing the essays for my MA thesis, I had to write a section about the way my stepfather "talked me into" certain things, which meant having to go back to that time and remember clearly what had happened, and when, and how. I wanted the sensory detail—the smells, and textures. I wanted the tone of his voice, and the way he used voice modulation as a form of control. After some stops and starts, finally I hit a vein of memory, and for an hour or more, I sat on Church St. in San Francisco at a little table outside of Muddy Waters cafe and wrote, trying to record exactly what it felt like as a teenager to realize that I was utterly under someone else's control. I cried as I wrote. I drank cup after cup of coffee, trying to swallow away the nausea that rose as I wrote. I was afraid to stop, afraid that if I did, I wouldn't be able to get to this place of flow again, at least not with this particular memory. I wanted to stay with it for as long as my energy would hold out, and I pushed myself hard.

Afterward, I was emptied, depleted. I dropped into a depression, and spent several days recovering. I couldn't write, went to work, pretended everything was fine. But I wasn't fine. I was lost in the body memory of those old days, the ones I had been writing about. It would have been kinder to myself—and better for my writing—if I had trusted myself as a writer, gone slower with that memory, and taken care of myself well in the aftermath of such exertion.

•§•

Athletes attend to their bodies before and after a marathon. They prepare for such an expenditure of energy—they run sprints, build their stamina and muscles, feed themselves well, and take care of themselves after. We writers can forget that we are athletes, that we are capable of feats of strength and effort, and that we both require and deserve the same sort of routine maintenance and care. As poet and essayist Mary Oliver writes, "Athletes take care of their bodies. Writers must similarly take care of the sensibility that houses the possibility of poems."

After writing something that frightens us, something that brings up shame or sorrow or fear, I encourage us to do something kind for ourselves. (Revisit that list at the end of the introduction for some self-care ideas.) In so doing, we are telling our inside selves that we understand that we deserve care, that this practice doesn't have to retraumatize us. We may feel some of the same emotions we felt when we first experienced the trauma, but *in writing it, we are not re-experiencing the trauma itself.* We are re-collecting it. We remember, contextualize, shape it. We find language for its—for our—nuances and contours. We allow our silenced voices to speak. We tell our intuition that we'll listen now, we can pay attention to its guidance when it offers the stories that it believes we are ready for.

We're strong enough to write what scares us. We're brave enough to share those stories if we choose. And we're wise enough to take care of ourselves as we do so. Writing your fear doesn't mean disregarding your emotional needs, doesn't mean bulldozing over your creative instinct, doesn't mean writing everything you've been terrified for decades to say (or even know) all at one time. It means slowly walking into the fertile cavern of loss, carrying a candle and a pen, remembering all the time that you can walk yourself back out again when you're ready.

The voice of our fear

Read that Joy Harjo piece, "Fear Poem, or I Give You Back" (check in the endnotes to find out where it's published, or search for it online). Read it aloud, if you're in a place where you can do so. Then give yourself ten or fifteen minutes, and write exactly as you're drawn to write in response. Copy down phrases or words from the poem that jump out at you, and begin with those. Write a letter to fear, or allow fear to write a letter to you! As always, follow your writing wherever it seems to want you to go.

---

when we write desire we re-enter our skin: restorying our erotic selves

The definition of *restore* is to reinstate; to return (a thing or person) to a former condition, location, or situation; to repair or renovate; to give (something previously stolen, taken away, or lost) back.

Think of *restory*, then, as reinstating, repairing, or renovating through story.

Restorying our sexuality allows us to come back *here*, into our bodies, the space behind our eyes, the site of violence against us. Restorying or rewriting our desire—our history and our present longing—can re-embody us. Writing is a way to settle into ourselves, slowly, back inside our skin. Not the only way. One way.

When we write sexual desire—any desire: fantasy or fiction or how our sweetheart touched us just yesterday—when we experience the want, feel its flesh and tingle, and, too, struggle and ache, we sneak a little more into our skin. We can write, and so we can *imagine*, a body free of flashbacks, for example. Because we are intimately familiar with an erotic desire riddled with holes and loss, we can describe that, too, in aching detail.

We who are sexual trauma survivors know how to embody other people's desires, because that was our job. What erotic writing can allow us to do is come into ourselves, our own wonders and imaginings—allows us to smell and taste ourselves again, or for the first time.

In writing about sexual trauma, we can forget—maybe we *want* to forget—about the weight of erotic desire. We may want to wipe sex from our skin because the very thought sends blood pulsing through the body that was raped, makes flush that landscape of loss and terror.

But we can't ever fully vacate this place, this body, not while we're living, and an embodied erotics, a deeply creative lust for the world, is meant to be ours. We deserve, if and when we choose it, to settle fully into our bodies again. One way I've inched up to the edges of my skin again is through writing it.

Through writing, we can claim the heavy trail of longing, bent or shaped by our survival. We can write exactly the sex we want and deserve, and when we write it, we embody it, and when we embody it, that's a reclamation. That's a restorying. That's a restoration. What was slashed and burned can take new life again, given time and space.

•§•

A few years ago, I was visiting my mom at the end of a Body Heat Femme Porn Tour. While my tour-mates slept in my mom's tiny, sacred-space living room, my mom and I sat in her kitchen sipping coffee, and she asked me why I write about sex: did it still have a connection to my stepfather? She knew part of the story. She knew that he'd asked me to write sex stories for him when I was in college. I'd been a nineteen-year-old young woman sending stories on demand to a rapist. I started writing my *desire* sometime after that. The stories for my stepfather were a peculiar sort of pornography. He'd asked for them maybe in an attempt to colonize what he was beginning to recognize might be a place of interest or safety or escape for me—writing. In the stories I sent him, I'd written about things I actually cared about. I had not learned to fake it. I wrote stories about young women curious about other women's bodies. When he wanted two men and one woman, I wrote a story about a young woman who happened to be friends with a gay male couple who welcome her into their bed for a night, rather than the stereotypical two straight guys bonding over the shared body of a woman. I don't remember what he said about them. I don't want to tell you about the story he sent me. It ought to have been entered into evidence when we filed charges against him.

This is what I want to tell you: writing these stories opened something up in me, something he could not touch nor take away. I made the story a stand-in for my body, created something that could replace me, for a little while, at least.

I tried to explain this to my mother. I said, "Writing the story was easier, was preferable, to masturbating over the phone." (How can a statement that *wrong* look so calm, sitting there on the page?) My mother started to cry. Her thin body got all wobbly. We sat in her white-painted kitchen with tchotkes adorning every surface, though part of me had slipped back into the apartment I'd rented as a college student, that attic room paneled in rough-hewn boards where I'd written those first sex stories.

In that moment, I became aware of the physical work that those stories had done for me.

It feels like a kind of violence now, how I saved myself at the expense of these characters, how I learned to turn story under story, take space back through words, let these things under my pen and fingers do the labor that my body had just grown too damn weary for.

I used my stepfather's demand for stories and his attempts to pervert my creativity as a way back into my oldest longing. I got my hands on myself, on that desire. He could not break that off in me, and by the time I was away at school, it was too late for him to take it over. I could have felt ashamed about the sex I wrote, but it was honest and real and mine.

It didn't take long for me to write sex that I didn't share with him. I believe that writing my desire led me back to my love of words, led me to the journaling, led some part of me to safety, completely out of his reach. Writing about sex was the doorway through which I got free. I can't put too much finer a point on it than that.

At that same time, when I was having physical sex with my then-boyfriend, I was mostly not in my body. My fantasies were occupied by all kinds of terrible, violent images. Even having sex alone I had to remind myself where I was, who I was, that the fingers on my body were mine. Sex simply wasn't a place to be safe.

Writing, though—when I was able to write about sex, I was able to be in my body. I could feel turned on and curious, powerful and vulnerable. In order to describe what my characters felt in their bodies, I had to reach around inside my own physical knowing. I had to imagine feeling those things myself so that I could describe them for another.

This wasn't any intentional healing practice. This was horniness, sorrow, trauma aftermath, closetedness, and coming out. But it worked, just the same. I sat in that small college-town cafe and felt extremely dangerous and brave, writing all of these things.

There's a Dorothy Allison quote that I like to hand out to new erotic writers (and not only erotic writers!); here, Allison vividly describes the importance of learning to write sex:

> If I hadn't learned to write about sex, and particularly to write about my own sexual desires, I don't think I would have survived. I think the guilt, the terror I grew up with was so extraordinarily powerful that if I had not written my way out of it, I'd be dead...And I think it's vital [to write about], aside from whether it ever becomes good fiction, particularly for women with transgressive sexuality...[or] people who in any way feel their sexuality cannot be expressed. Writing can be a way to find a way to be real and sane in the world, even if it feels a little crazy while you're doing it.

My desire to live outside of my stepfather's control was a fundamentally erotic desire—it was a desire for *life*, for living, for freedom. The sex my stepfather demanded and forced on me was not erotic—there was nothing alive in it.

Before I could live the life I wanted I had to be able to imagine it. Writing offered me space to imagine an existence that didn't have death and fear at its core. And I got *there* by first writing about sex, because sex was the easiest and most obvious doorway into desire, into longing and dream. I didn't know, when I started writing about sex, that *through* sex I would explore so many other hungers and curiosities. I had been trained to sexualize everyone and everything, every relationship and every thought. I was twenty-one years old and in love with a woman I couldn't have and still being sexually abused by my stepfather: sex was what came out on the page very, *very* often. It took many years of writing to unthread my hungers from each other, to unbraid trauma from eros, brainwashing from bodily integrity.

If we use the same words as our perpetrators but we mean different things by them, have the words themselves raped or desecrated our mouths? Can we take the ways we were bent and use that curvature for our own ends? When does it unbelong to the men, the women, the people who warped us? When is it no longer the ghost of their hand over or under our own, telling us what to do, how to do it, forcing us to let them see?

Our embodiment gets twisted by and during sexual trauma. Writing is a way to untangle ourselves, our selfness, a way to right ourselves, a way to see and understand our wholeness.

The voice of our longing

I call this, unsurprisingly, "Firsts." Make a list of ten different "first times" that someone might experience in their sexual life (such as, first kiss, first physical arousal, first time making out in a movie theater, first one-night stand). For this exercise, I'll encourage you to think about *consensual* first times. Feel welcome to include first times you haven't actually experienced! Look over your list, and notice which of these firsts is most calling your writer's attention at the moment, and let that be where your writing begins. Don't worry; you can come back and write about the others later. Follow your writing wherever it seems to want you to go. Note: This is a great one to do as a group—create the list of "firsts" together on a whiteboard/flip chart, and then write from one of your own or another's first.

witness

what writing can do
for survivors

This is what I believe: Give us safe space, a "room" of our own and we will create change in our lives. We learn what it means to lie and truth our way to safety, to lie our way home. We must take what we need to continue the process of survival, which is ultimately a process of resistance: the pen the paper the time the space the cafe or bedroom or kitchen table the 3 a.m. living room the subway train the cemetery the laundromat the whatever it is we need.

Take me backward into your dreams and let me watch you stumble. Your language is yours alone, the sounds of your body the stretch and wrinkle of your face the wrinkled words and nods, shrugs and shivers and shifts of eyeballs. You know your own way and I cannot tell it for you. I can hold your hand, though, and promise to listen while you float in your own waters, while you choke down the nausea of history in your instance to see the clownfish and schools of yellowtail floating around the coral of yourself. (2003)

In the years I've written with groups of sexual trauma survivors, I've become convinced that every person has artistic brilliance in them. There hasn't been a single person in any writing group I've ever facilitated who hasn't generated work that surprises them and astonishes listeners. Not one. And this isn't because I'm some kind of genius facilitator—this is about what happens when survivors gather to share their stories through poetry and metaphor, song and testimony.

Pat Schneider says in her book, *Writing Alone and With Others*, "What I believe is not what everyone believes. It is this: There is no place for hierarchies in the heart, and the making of art is a matter of the heart. Art is the creative expression of the human spirit." Together, we who participate in these writing groups engage in the co-creation of a space that allows for risk, performance, and play. We who have been denied hearings by those in power can assist and heal ourselves and each other. There is powerful pleasure, connection, and transformation possible through the sharing of ourselves through story, and deep change occurs when we have the audacity to articulate the truths of our lives.

When we come together this way, assiduously working to remain aware and respectful of the differences among us, and share our words, we get to acknowledge our ability to create beauty—both because we listen to our own poetic phrasing and descriptions, and because others tell us what is beautiful and strong for them in the writings we offer. We hear, witness, and open (to) the beauty in ourselves and in others; we "seek[] a language that allows [us] to imagine a new world without forgetting the tragedies of the past," as theologian Sharon Welch wrote. It's a revolution when we, who have spent years reiterating to ourselves the lessons of ugliness learned at our abusers' hips, are able to acknowledge splendor in ourselves.

One Monday night, several years ago, a group of writers gathered in my living room for the fourth of eight meetings of a survivors writing group. Three walked in together, laughing, having met at the front door of my apartment building. One was already here, and the others arrived soon after. My homely little living room with its tangerine-orange walls was full of conversation as the writers made their tea and gathered up plates of snacks: nuts, strawberries, baby carrots, potato chips, and dark chocolate. The tenderness, delight, and anticipation was palpable. If not for their readiness to claim *trauma survivor* openly, the writers would not have found themselves in this room, thrumming with the heartbeat of creative connection.

This deep connectedness doesn't emerge in every single group—sometimes folks don't click quite as completely; that's a possibility for any group of people. Still, it's not uncommon for the writers, two or three weeks in, to find their hearts broken open to one another. We find we care about each other as people. We care about each other's histories, but even more, we care about one another's *now*. Folks exchange phone numbers, offer rides to and from the subway, email each other during the week. We begin to allow ourselves to connect.

At the beginning of an eight-week session, people enter the room with some wariness, even if they have been through one of my survivors writing groups before: *Who will be there this time? Will they be able to hear me, to hold my words? What will I be have to write about?* The energy in the room is tight, contracted—as trauma survivors, we all know how to keep our hearts protected. And we all know how to take enormous risk. In the beginning, we only know that we share these truths: all of us have had experiences that we were taught not to talk about, and all of us want to write. Connection and connectedness flourishes within the group through the stories and creative risks we're willing to take.

On this Monday evening, these writers, most of whom had been strangers to each other only a month before, held each other in deep regard. They talked before and after the group and during breaks, about important issues in their lives: dealing with death, the realities of long-term grief, struggles with aging parents, laughing as one shared a story about getting lost while driving someplace she knew well. Some were quieter, mostly listening; others were gregarious. And then, during the writing time, one of the women broke out of a style that had been linear and concrete into a new sort of writing filled with extended metaphor and surprising imagery. One of her peer writers told her, *You're on fire tonight!* We all knew we were witnessing something majestic, a writer exploring and sharing a new facet of her writing voice.

The group laughs during the breaks between writing, ready for some release. During the timed writes, they are intent on their pages, pens flying, scratching, pausing briefly then pushing forward. It's very simple, what we do in here, in this room together: we find words for one part of a difficult-to-tell story; we find language for something that has up until this moment been broken away in our psyches, silenced. We write, and then we read aloud; we move these unspeakables into voice, into our own voice. Then we are *witnessed*—peer writers we admire and appreciate listen to us. In this room, we get to openly admire, wildly appreciate, one another.

For those who have been shamed, called stupid or dull, for those taught that kindness is weakness or weapon (and what American has not been taught this?), for those who believed no one would listen, for those whose voices went dormant, for those silenced or terrorized, the steps we take together when we write, read, and respond allow us to organically unlearn old lessons, and allow our psyches to gently internalize something new, something that was always true: we have a necessary story to tell and we are enough for that telling; we deserve (and deserved) to be listened to; we have something to share; the story of our survival helps others heal and grow. Our words are necessary sustenance for ourselves, yes, and for others in our communities, too.

There is magic that happens for a survivor who sits down and writes herself to the page in stunning visions, who sits down with other survivors and reads her real self: her surviving, wondering, hungry, difficult, fragmented, gorgeous self. The writing opens up the tight fist of power and control and drops us out—the writing opens up a chasm, the writing throws over a bridge, the writing topples buildings and walls, boulders fall, steam rises, the room opens. We don't do anything when we hear each other except bear witness, and maybe that's all that matters. *Yes, we hear and, yes, we speak our listening and, yes, we say this is where I swell when your words touch me. Yes, we listen hear want desire imagine. The pen is a vision is a dream shimmering, the oil slick silvery rainbow over the deep well of tide pool we will eventually dive into.*

Writing makes a difference. Visualizing and hoping makes a difference. When we write this way, we risk becoming aware of ourselves differently. We can take the lessons we were taught, the rules and regulations of our traumatized selves, and walk through them like a ruined house of mirrors. We don't have to be who they—the abusers, the school teachers, the boys on the bus—told us we were.

What I have learned deeply, what I have internalized through this transformative writing practice, is that there's no such thing as "doing it right" when it comes to writing and when it comes to sex and when it comes to living in the aftermath of sexual trauma. We are infinite in our abilities, in our possibilities.

•§•

Someone said, if we don't tell our stories, others will tell them for us, and they will get them wrong. The stories that the others tell about you will be used to build policy and pathology, will be used to build boxes to hide you in, used to build walls to close around you, used against you. If we do not tell our stories, the stories told about us will be used to our detriment.

We are a nation of subjected and silenced people. We are a nation of people trained into the difference of others as reason enough to kill them. We are a nation raised on our supremacy—*America is the greatest country in the world!*—and we believe it even as we see our leaders stripping away our bedsheets and clothes, snatching the food from our and our children's mouths, tearing down our homes, thieving the books from our children's hands and tossing it all on the bonfires of their war, tossing it all into their own furnaces, selling our labor on the open market to the highest or most connected bidder and pocketing the money themselves.

Still: We have our bodies. We have our hands and feet thighs legs arms eyes noses breasts mouths bellies chests butts foreheads fingers lips toes and yes genitals yes cunts and cocks yes, and we have our voices. We can use them to our own ends, and in service of those we love and all we believe in, rather than allowing ourselves to be deployed in service of those in power through our silence. Through this writing practice, I open to the world around me. I walk around heavily awake, I smile more amply, I touch the cats on the ledge with my eyes. I am present. I am seen and I see. I am heard. This is the opposite of dissociation. This is the practice of embodiment, the practice of resistance, the practice of freedom. Offer your witness to those who need it.

Give yourself ten minutes for some letter writing:

What would you want to be able to say to a "new" survivor (someone recently assaulted, or someone just remembering violence they'd repressed, or someone just recognizing that what was done to them was, in fact, sexual assault)? What would you want to be able to say to a younger you?

being and bearing witness

Last night at our Write Whole meeting, the writers were talking about the difference between positive and negative responses when they share the stories of the violences done to them. They described friends who weren't able to really hear them, family members who denied their truths or told them to get over it. One woman said she was told, after telling a friend about an experience of workplace harassment, *Oh*, the woman laughed, *I thought it was so much worse! You always made such a big deal out of it.*

Who says things like this?

Now, certainly there are times when I don't know the right thing to say to a friend who's hurting, but some version of "is that all?" almost never makes people feel better. A cathartic writing exercise I've used in groups involves creating a list of all the ridiculous or hurtful things people have said to us when they thought they were being "helpful." We create a communal poem on a big sheet of paper, then write from that poem as a prompt. Also, I like to share Catherine Tufariello's powerful poem, "Useful Advice." In the voice of a woman in her late thirties who is trying to get pregnant, the poem describes the advice folks have to offer her. The final line: "Why are you crying?"

The way we are received matters—it informs what we say, how we will say it, whether we will feel encouraged to tell more or tell less. I believe most people want us to tell less; they don't want to have to hear the details—they are uncomfortable hearing about a situation that they can't take some action to fix or somehow make better by *doing* something.

One of the women at the group last night said, *What's great is getting to come here and not having to hear any of that stuff.*

She is part of an especially strong and connected group of folks who are deep in their healing and paying strong and close attention to one another. We are all doing a good job of holding the space together. Certainly, there have been groups in which people have been wildly insensitive with each other, unwilling to hold to our agreed-upon practices, asked frustrating or insensitive questions, read aloud writing that was racist or classist, clashed around politics, come into the space inebriated or altered, responded even to positive feedback from an extremely defensive position. People in my workshops have made unchecked assumptions about each other, haven't paid attention to requested pronouns; we've thought we know best and *still* sometimes offer unsolicited and unhelpful advice to one another. Everyone comes with their own stuff, and just because we are a group of survivors doesn't mean we are always more sensitive to one another than non-survivors can be. We don't usually act or speak thoughtlessly with one another because we're mean or wish to do intentional harm; rather, we hurt one another because we've got blinders on, or we're hurting, or we've made assumptions out of privilege or ignorance—sometimes just because we're human, and humans stumble into each other hard sometimes.

Listening often feels like not doing anything, doesn't it? Even for those of us who *know* how powerful it is when someone sits with us and truly listens to what we are feeling. I don't know about you, but even knowing that, even after all this time, I *still* tense up when someone I love tells me about things going "wrong" in their life. *Oh no,* I think. *What can I say to them that will be helpful? How can I make it better?*

(That is, in my head, I make it all about me.)

I have more than a few friends with chronic illnesses. When I first heard their stories of deep bodily suffering—and the ineptitude, hostility or indifference of Western medical response to fibromyalgia and or Lyme or chronic fatigue—I listened as they told me about the unhelpful advice they received over and over (and over: "Yes, I've tried Chinese herbs, yes, I've tried yoga, thanks"). And though I wasn't suffering or living with chronic fatigue, I could relate to unhelpful, unsolicited advice, and the way that such advice often felt like a closed door in my face, a way of distancing, of foreclosing on the conversation. And so I took deep breaths, struggled with the longing to fix it for them, commiserated and kept listening.

We know the labor involved in being present with someone in trouble, in sorrow, in despair, even in big and powerful joy. We know how it is to express ourselves fully to and with someone who loves us, who is not compelled to fix us (and who, in not trying to fix, also isn't communicating to us that we are in *need* of fixing), who can hold our stories and in so holding tells us: *you are not too much—I can love you when you are struggling just as I can love you when you are joyful.*

•§•

Survivors' writing groups are about story and about voice, and they are about wit(h)ness. A sharing of our inside realities. A *not* having to hold all of it on our own anymore. A learning that we are not now nor have we ever been all alone in our experience of trauma—what we have been through resonates with others, even if they look different from us (that is, in spite of the assumptions we make about who can and can't understand our lives). This is why I like groups that are mixed—folks of different races, classes, sexualities writing together; people whose experience of trauma is different; or people of different genders writing together. I have been especially moved by men and women writing together about sexual violence.

Our society teaches us that because we look different from each other or are from different backgrounds, we cannot comprehend and open to each other. Our society also teaches us the inverse: because we look alike or experienced something similar, we *must* be able to understand each other. But we know, through lived experience, that this is not true. A roomful of sameness will not save us or guarantee our safety.

We in these groups of gathered sexual trauma survivors don't automatically understand everything about one another. Our experiences of violence and trauma are unique, inflected by our age, our gender, our sexuality, our race, our class, our nationality, our belief systems, our politics, our communities, how or whether we've found healing, who has supported or not supported us, what our relationships with our families have been like—*everything* we are or are perceived to be comes with us into a writing group.

The structure that we use for the writing helps us to maneuver around these human tendencies, helps us to refrain from saying thoughtless things to each other. The structure helps us to actively listen to each other. In active listening, we're asked to reflect back to a speaker exactly what we've heard them say—so that they know we're actually paying attention. As a writer (and as a *person*), I have felt the power of the feedback we give each other in the writing groups; when someone repeats back to me a line of my own writing, I feel successful as a writer, and I feel seen: those words mattered, someone heard them. I was able to communicate effectively across every social and human distance placed between me and that other person. Something connected. My words made a difference, are no longer alone.

Writing about unhelpful witness

Read Catherine Tufariello's poem "Useful Advice" (see the endnotes for publication information). Read it aloud if you're in a place where you feel comfortable doing so. Give yourself ten minutes: What "useful" advice have people given you? What would you say back to them, if you could? What do you wish they'd said instead?

---

sharing our healing

There is a hierarchy of healing in our country: those with money can afford well-trained therapists with experience and skill, while those with fewer resources maybe get a few sessions at a clinic, many of us not even that. We are isolated while we are abused and then, after, we can be isolated further in a therapist's office. We learn that *this* information belongs in *that* room: our friends and families don't know how to hold our hurt, and when we cry or rage, are overwhelmed or triggered or scared, our need for support is deflected to the professionals. "Have you talked to someone about that?" they ask us when we come to them for support. *Wait*, we think, *I thought I was talking to you.* We may learn that we are too much, that we are too needy, that we can't be held and met by others in our community—we need a specialist. We're sent outside the circle of our community to be made well, and are supposed to come back whole, less discomfiting, less noisy and sad and angry, able to fit smoothly into the gears of society again.

Of course, I believe in the positive healing power of a good one-with-one therapeutic relationship. What I want to think about is what happens when we support one another, directly, in our healing. What if the community recognized that each individual's healing is *all* of our healing?

Consider what we offer each other when we are whole and real and complicated and broken and perfectly imperfect together, when we can share freely our experience and creative resilience with one another. Folks who have found home in 12-step meetings can speak to the power of this sort of community acceptance, wit(h)ness, and support: a place where people of shared commitment and struggle can gather to say and hear that folks in wider society seem not to be able to hear and/or hold. I have heard folks say, after writing group meetings *and* after 12-step meetings, how astonishing it is to get together with strangers and be *real* like that, so open and honest and vulnerable. We've been trained to have our barriers up, keep our masks on, not get messy where other people can see us: we're supposed to play the pretend game of Being An Adult—*Everything's ok. Everything's under control. I am perfectly fine. I've got ahold of my bootstraps and I am taking care of business. I'm fine. I don't need any taking care of or support. Really, I'm fine.*

Some of us who are survivors lean hard into this game of pretend. We want it to be true. We want to show those who abused us, and those who didn't protect us, that we made it through. We understand that living well is the best revenge. We pretend nothing happened, and maybe for awhile, we are able to move forward with this charade. And then, one night over drinks with a good friend, the truth in us breaks through—*we* thought we were portraying someone together and perfect; they were seeing someone they loved who was acting a part and was obviously hurting and not able to ask for help.

Perfect is a pretense. *Everything's fine* is a pretense. Writing groups of the sort we're talking about here and 12-step meetings and some therapy groups and other intimate group experiences have taught me that all of us are struggling with feelings of inadequacy and fear and deep loss and sorrow, all of us are supremely triumphant over something inside every day that wants to kill us, all of us want to and deserve to be celebrated not necessarily for the big achievements but for the small majesties: *Hey, you got up and made your bed! Right on! You brushed your teeth today even when no one told you you had to. You had enough food in your fridge to feed yourself and your kids, and even though you are fucking exhausted and scared, you got up and made breakfast for them and yourself. You ate today. You stopped eating when you were full.* You get the idea. Sometimes I want a brass band behind me when I return an email I've been putting off for a month—*You did it! Hooray!* We all still have that small one inside that wants to be seen and acknowledged with acceptance and non-judgment.

Folks have internalized this idea that we can't do healing work alone *or* in community without a trained professional either ahead of us, guiding us along, or behind us, overseeing everything—*just in case.* Because we might get hurt. Because we need protecting. Because we cannot take care of ourselves or one another.

What I'm saying is that this is another way, an additional tool for your toolbox, another possible path to walk during the travels you take through your healing. Radical self-care can take many forms—tending the body, the soul, the psyche, the heart, the mind; the self in solitude and the self in togetherness.

I'm sitting on a back deck on a sunny Tuesday morning in Oakland, California. The dog holds the ball in her mouth, barking around the orange plastic at people coming by to search for recyclable bottles in the trash cans. Someone across the block is mowing a lawn. The kids at the nearby middle school shout and scream-sing along with their exercises during gym period. Through all this noise I can still hear birds, the bees investigating the jasmine thatch that clings heavy to one wall of the back yard fence. My sweetheart is inside, on the phone with a friend who has called with sympathies—my beloved's best friend has recently died. In the midst of all of this, I steep in a well-developed and familiar sense of loneliness and isolation, a sort of suffering I've experienced all my life: my chest heavy, the sad wells up in my throat, and I sit in a corner, alone, sure that everyone else in the world knows some secret to friendship or connection that I never learned.

Most of us feel this way sometimes, I think—that we're alone, left out, not keeping up, not part of the in-crowd or the right group, will be found out for the frauds we are and locked out of the clubs that we built our identities on. All of us know what it means to feel abandoned, left alone, left out, just plain *left*. Yet, the terrible thing about isolation is that it shrouds us from the fact that this is a shared human experience. We listen instead to the voice inside that tells us we're the only one going through this, that no one else will understand, that no one else wants to hear about loneliness, for god's sake.

This is the insidiousness of isolation, its self-perpetuating nature. We are trained to rehearse these messages inside ourselves long after the people who may have first taught us to believe that we were all alone in our experience of abuse or rape or incest or violation are gone. My stepfather has been in prison for almost twenty years and still I hear him telling me that we're not like other people, that we have to keep this to ourselves, that nobody else will ever really understand me, that no one else can be trusted.

Under these circumstances, we learn, don't we, to keep to ourselves. We pull all our tendrils in. We breathe shallowly. We hold our arms close to our bellies.

We who were trained young to mistrust human affection, we who had words of appreciation used against us as weapons, we who were shaped under the too-watchful eye of a controlling or wrongly-admiring parent or caregiver: we, in order to find some place of safety, teach ourselves to isolate. I've found this to be among the hardest lessons to unlearn. At some point in our lives, all of us have to go into the cave alone, to tend to our wounds and keen and heal. But I've spent the better part of two decades psychically in that cave, and in the last several years I have begun to explore the possibilities of healing within community.

Maybe you are like me, most comfortable alone, reading and writing or walking or coding or tending the yard or cooking or painting. Some of this is the artist's lot. Some of this may be an innate and beautiful introversion. But some of it is self-protection. If I don't put myself into other's hands and hearts, they can't harm me, and they can't be taken away from me. In this way, I don't have to battle my stepfather's old messages that still rage inside my head: *That person is dangerous, they can't be trusted, they're only out for themselves, and if they find out the truth about what I'm doing to you, I'm going to hurt them and then hurt you more.*

How do we disentangle from the deeply held certainty that we are alone? I have studied the tactics of abusers for many years, have sat with hundreds of other survivors of domestic, intimate, and sexual violence, and listened to this theme emerge again and again: *I am all alone. No one knows what I'm going through.*

When we write about this in writing groups, the sense of shared experience is palpable—*me, too, me, too, me, too* resonates all through the room. The other writers listen and nod in recognition as someone reads of their loneliness. *Me, too—I feel isolated, too!*

We need that *Me, too.* We need it over and over, until it can begin to touch the places in us that believe we will always be alone.

One of the things we get to do in a peer survivors writing group is to offer one another back into a home in community, and we do it in an old way. We say, *Bring your songs here, and we will listen to you sing them, we will sing them with you. Come and listen to our songs and take what you need from them.* We get to show the naked skin of our fear, our panic, our loss, our sorrow, our fury, and someone else in the room will nod: *Me, too.*

We can gather in a room, spend an hour or two writing about pets or the shape of our childhood beds or our invisible scars, and get to meet, while listening to one another's responses, just how much we have in common, how much we are not different or bad, how much we are not alone in our experience. We will use different words, there will be different details, nuance, and yet at the heart we will hear something that resonates with us in nearly each person's writing. We will surprise each other. We will see each other, and we will be less alone.

Of course, sometimes there are personality conflicts and struggle among group members that impacts the whole group. But that is part of being human in community, too. We can learn that conflict isn't necessarily cataclysmic. We can learn that sometimes someone takes care of themselves by leaving a group or community—that we get to take care of ourselves the best ways we know how. We can learn to apologize, own the ways we hurt others, tell the truth, navigate conflict, and still love one another. "Creative power, the power of love and the power of the web of life, can never guarantee the results of its oppression. When freed to be creative, people's responses can delight or dismay, but they always escape our control," writes feminist theologian and author Sharon Welch.

In his groundbreaking book, *The Theory and Practice of Group Psychotherapy*, psychotherapist Irvin Yalom relates the Hasidic tale of a rabbi talking with the Lord about Heaven and Hell. The Lord shows the rabbi Hell: a room in which a group of people sit around a table at the center of which is a pot of delicious-smelling stew. Each person holds an extremely long spoon, with which they can just barely reach into the stewpot, but the spoons are too long for the people to bring the stew back to their own mouths, and so they are hungry and suffering. Then the Lord shows the rabbi Heaven. The rabbi sees the same room, the same group of people with the same long spoons around the same table at the center of which is the same pot of delicious stew. But in this room, the people were happy, full, laughing. "At first the rabbi could not understand," writes Yalom. "'It is simple, but it requires a certain skill,' said the Lord. 'You see, they have learned to feed each other.'"

We can share the load, these burdens of history, these shards that live in our skin and bone. We offer an affirmation that looks like artistry. We say: *Yes, you are not too much, your words are not too much, your naming is not too much.* We receive that *yes* back for ourselves. We give ourselves a structure, a framework, a scaffolding for this work. We agree to the tenets of generosity and kindness and confidentiality. We understand that we are receiving stories and not being tasked with fixing anyone. It is ourselves we fix when we listen and offer and open. It is a gift we give ourselves when we sit in the circle and take in others' stories, offering our own in return, when we step into the fire of "not good enough" and read aloud anyway, when we are afraid that the inside flame of our very being isn't ok and then we get to hear someone else we admire very much sharing that they have the same fear and we can *see* their light and their genius and we both wonder at and understand how they could possibly feel unworthy or that their writing was stupid. Over time, that wonder and appreciation begins to reflect back into our own hearts. We feed one another and are fed in so doing.

This is not an instant or even comfortable undertaking, because we are writing into our sorest spots. This is a human effort, one with teeth and bone and blood and sweat and labor and laughter in it. It is an undertaking not of ease but discomfort and risk, with new breath all along its edges. We don't have to be alone in the stories we carry within and along the surface frame of our skin. We can allow our community to hold it with us, to hold *us*, to hear the who and harm of who we are and still love us, still welcome us, still find us worth sitting next to in the circle, still worth admiring, worth a generous kindness.

A roomful of people speaking the so-called unspeakable—this is joy, even if we leave feeling heavy. Of course we are heavy: the murk of our waters has been churned up. We are afraid we've betrayed the mantle of silence that saved us. We weep in the car or on the walk home. We feel thick and scared the next morning. The lightness creeps in slowly, later—something releases within us. How to explain the invisible, inexorable process of transformation that is healing from and through trauma, except to say that by the following week we are ready to sing again, we come to group with our pens uncapped and something inside us more open and alive and ready to be seen.

We can shape a community that can hold us when we are struggling. We can (re)learn to allow ourselves to be held, (re)learn to believe that we deserve such a reception.

Our fears about offering and accepting wit(h)ness

For two minutes each, write about the following:

- when being alone feels good

- when being alone hurts

- what scares you about being alone

- what scares you about being with others

Then pause, breathe, and write for seven more minutes, about anything that came up for you during those four writes. Follow your writing wherever it seems to want to go.

how to hold kindness

For a long time, I didn't believe I deserved kindness. I'd done terrible things under my stepfather's command and control, and as a result, I felt outside of the human bond. I didn't know how to talk about my experiences. Authentic connection was foreign to me—I felt plastic in my skin, inhuman in my blood. I'd been turned out of my family for saying no to my stepfather's abuse: being turned away from the clan, no matter how damaged and damaging that clan, still tears something primal in us, for we are pack animals. We learn the power of the harsh word, self-protectiveness, keeping your cards close to your chest.

Kindness requires vulnerability; it requires the open hand of a *yes*. We who are surviving trauma often don't believe we deserve that yes. We know how much more deeply we can be hurt when we are kind to someone and they're mean to us in return, or when we are kind to a pet (or a pet is kind to us) and that pet is hurt or taken away. We know how it feels to have our expressions of joy or curiosity made fun of, shamed, or demeaned.

Most of us in our American culture are discouraged from offering generous kindness to others. We're more likely to be viewed with doubt or mistrust, or treated as someone weak or childish, when we approach the world with kindness. Our thoughtful acts are assumed to arise from a selfish place in us. No good deed goes unpunished, the saying goes. In our families or communities, we may have been shamed for our acts of generosity or empathy, may have been treated like someone naïve, someone who didn't know how the world worked.

Nice guys finish last, we're told?

In writing classes, we may have been taught that being nice to each other would just weaken each other's work—if no one pointed out the flaws, the artist could never improve. Instructors create cultures in which students battle each other to find the most problems in each other's writing; we get approval by cutting one another down. We learn that saying what we like about someone's writing is useless—*great, now tell us what you* really *think.*

To be *kind* is to be affectionate, loving; the adjective comes from an Old English word meaning natural, native and innate. *Nice,* on the other hand, derives from an Old French word meaning careless, clumsy, needy, and foolish, from a Latin root, that means literally, not knowing. *Nice* and *kind* are rooted in completely different places in human consciousness—to be *nice* is to dither stupidly; to be *kind* is to offer compassion and well-meaning out of an innate, natural drive.

To be kind is to be human.

It's kindness to witness another person's growth. It is kindness to listen to another person's story. It is kindness to allow others to offer these things to us a well.

And that—receiving another person's kindness—is often the hardest part of the writing group for us, whether we are trauma survivors or not. It's easy for us to share what we like about our groupmates' writing—they're such good writers. But we *know* that our own writing is crap. We *know* it's weak, incomplete, ineffective. We *know* the difference between what we intended to write and what actually made it onto the page. So we give disclaimers before we read—*this really sucks, this isn't done, I can't believe I have to follow that amazing piece of writing, I'll just read it and be done with it, this isn't anything, this is just journaling, nothing good*—and then we read our words and we shrug and roll our eyes, doing our best to diminish the words physically. Even after fifteen years in groups as a facilitator, I still often disclaim my own new writing; more often, I dismiss the work after I've finished reading—I shrug or grimace: *Pretty bad, right?* This is my writer's self-protection, drawing myself back in after exposure.

As survivors, we are good girls (no matter our sex or gender). We know how not to be too proud of ourselves. We know not to get too big for our britches. We know it hurts less if we knock ourselves down first than if we stand up proud and true and sure and then someone we like and admire comes along to shove us off our high horse. We all learned the self-protective value of keeping ourselves small. And this is why I don't ban apologies or apron-wringing or disclaimers before folks read their new writing—sometimes those disclaimers are what the work needs in order to be able to come into the world. The writer, otherwise, would keep the words on the page. The disclaimer is a way of warding off the evil eye—*kina hora, kina hora*—it's protecting this tender, newborn thing we are about to offer out into the hands and ears of others.

Often, the most forceful disclaimers precede some of the most powerful, risky, intimate, strong words shared in the group. Our disclaimers can be kindnesses we give our still-tender writing selves—and don't let anyone fool you: our writing selves are always tender, no matter how long we've been at this work with words. We may have published widely, written for years, and still we show up empty and afraid at the page every day, hoping for something to happen. I have found that the most blustery writers—the ones who walk in and demand a *real critique*, the ones who ask for their work to be torn apart—are often among the most vulnerable: their bluster is a powerful defense. It's not uncommon, in my experience, for these writers to get defensive when peers give even the most effusive praise—they question our feedback, worry at what we didn't comment on, take everything very personally. *Come on*, they say. *Tell me the truth.*

Kindness isn't a lie. Kindness isn't Polyanna-ing anything. Kindness is offering a counterweight to the screams of the inner critics, who are telling each of us, in great detail, what specifically is wrong with this piece of shit we just driveled onto the page. Our feedback to one another during writing groups recognizes that there's already an unbalanced response to this piece of writing underway: the inner critic was tearing it up before we even finished writing it. Our saying what we like and what's strong about a new piece of writing can sometimes feel like telling an abused child specifically what's beautiful and brilliant about her, when her parents have been telling her for years, her whole life, that she's stupid and ugly and bad. They have been specific in their criticisms, which is why we must be specific in our naming what's powerful and strong. That abused child may have to hear the same things from us over and over before he will even entertain the possibility of believing us.

In the writing group, we regenerate our capacity for kindness. We strengthen that muscle so devalued in our society.

I take this issue of kindness and generosity in the writing groups very seriously. Where else are we going to learn a new way of interacting with our loved ones and greater community? Some of us learned kindness at home or from a trusted adult or from pets. Many, many others of us were born into unkind homes or had homes that turned unkind at some point in our lives. We were trained away from a child's natural capacity for goodness. We modeled at school, some of us, what was modeled for us at home—we learned that the mean girls and the mean boys have power. And even as adults, this seems to be true: bullies get their way, leaving the rest of us wary, thin in our skin, less interested in exercising the muscle of kindness, which requires the strength of our vulnerability.

Maybe you grew up in a country that modeled kindness with the buttering of the morning's bread. Maybe you not only heard the Golden Rule but watched your family live it. Maybe you came from a place where kind men weren't called pussies or sissies, and kind women weren't derided as doormats. Maybe you don't come from an America where the most popular TV shows portray contestants tearing each other down, families calling each other the worst possible names, groups of people conspiring and lying in order to survive, to win. Maybe you come from a country where children are treated with respect and care, where partners consistently treat each other with a deep generosity and adoration, where people don't deride one another, relentlessly, on every social media site that exists.

Maybe you come from a kinder country than I do.

I come from a country that is schizophrenic in its kindnesses—it claims to put children and families first and then turns its back while children are tortured and neglected, and money and resources for social services are siphoned off to feed a war machine that is determined to decimate anyone who doesn't agree with its doctrines. I come from a country where there are kind *people*, some of whom will serve me a meal when I have nothing, and still go to the ballot box and vote against my human rights as a queer person or as a woman, and will see no contradiction. I come from a country whose primary religion—a religion whose core message is *kindness*—has been used to enslave, torture, and kill. We are taught to be nice to our sister or brother, but have to stand silent while Dad calls Mom names and Mom calls us stupid or bad. We come from a country where the individual is first above all other clan or creed or community, and so communal connection has deteriorated.

Is it any surprise we may view an invitation to kindness with a wary eye?

Kindness can be a tonic, a strengthener for our creative work; both writers *and* writing can flourish in an environment of focused attention and generous reflection, in which each of us is met as a "real writer." No matter that we don't feel that way at first, or maybe even by the end of our group; others treat us as such anyway. Slowly, gradually, beneath the protective shell we had to build in order to navigate our home life or school, the work of kindness tends to the creative seeds in us. In the writing groups, kindness is our base camp, our bedrock, the air we breathe. And because we've come into the room from a poisoned environment, it takes time for us to trust the atmosphere enough to take off our gas masks and deeply inhale.

Witness (in) kindness

Take five to seven minutes, and write about why you don't deserve kindness.

Then pause. Take a deep breath.

Then write for five to seven more minutes, and tell me why you *do* deserve kindness.

(Sometimes this exercise is easier to write in the third person—
write about why she/he/they deserves kindness—to give
yourself a little distance, a wider lens.)

competitiveness and jealousy

She has failed to grow up and become a success.
Every month she gets a magazine in the mail. It comes from the alumni
association of her undergraduate college. Against everything she knows
is good for her, she brings this magazine into her house, sits down with
it, flips it open to look at the faces of alumni who are achieving. Making
names for themselves. Successful. Here are the politicians, the scientists,
the social entrepreneurs, the designers, the computer programmers, the
movie and television producers, the hedge fund managers, the actors.
The writers. Every month she scans the list of books published recently
by other alumni. She hopes not to see the name of someone she knows.
She hopes none of these now-published writers graduated after her. If
they are older than she is, she's a little easier on herself: she still has
time. She scans the personal essay section, to which she has once again
failed to submit her own piece, the story she's imagined sending to them
for five years, eight. Every month she undertakes this self-flagellation,
looking at the faces of former classmates who now head law firms, run
major organizations, made millions of dollars selling their ideas to Silicon
Valley. She tortures herself with the faces of the just-graduated, the
young-and-up-&-coming who already warrant press coverage for their
achievements. Every month she reminds herself that she is a failure.
No matter that she has made a life with art and creation at its center. No

matter that she has a life full of color and laughter, morning sunlight, a cat who curls next to her on the couch and purrs while she writes in her journal. No matter she knows—somewhere inside—that she has enough, so much more than many: a safe home, a full refrigerator, lights and water and heat that turn on when she wants them to. She has a small garden plot in the community garden down the road where she can dig her fingers in soil, where she tends the fat hands of chard, tall cosmos and hollyhocks and borage and lavender and salvia, tends tomato and broccolini and a small thicket of herbs. Never mind the pots of basil and feverfew on her windowsill, the chickadees and nuthatches and goldfinches that visit the bird feeder she's hung from the bottlebrush tree just outside the window near her kitchen table (which is also her office, also her desk).

They never tell her own particular kind of success story in the alumni magazine, or write about the thousands of students who left the college grounds and did not become standouts in their fields, at least not in the headshot-press release-TED talk-thought leader kind of way. Instead, some of those folks went out to craft small and beautiful lives that tendrilled through the communities in which they settled, made home and family, or didn't, figured out how to survive during the days or months or years when getting out of bed took all the energy they had to spare. They grew to know themselves well, if they succeeded at staying alive, and learned to listen to different forms of success: the kind that goes unreported except in poems, in novels, in glances with strangers across the subway on a chilly February morning. (2015)

What happens when despair rises, when we are overwhelmed, when we have negative feelings about one another, when we are floundering or jealous or envious and can't bear to hear about one more writer's success, even (especially) if that writer is someone we adore, because it just reminds us what failures we are?

These are wounds that don't soothe easy and are rooted in our deeply-ingrained sense of worthlessness and scarcity: that we, ourselves, are not enough. If someone else achieves, there will be less left for us. Our families may have set us up to compete with our siblings. We may have been taught that we had to be better than everyone around us—in sports, in school—in order to be worthy of our parents' or community's approval or love.

Does this feel familiar to you?

My stepfather taught me that if I wasn't the best (according to his definition of "best"), I wasn't working hard enough. I went through high school jealous of the kids who were more successful than I was. When I got out from under my stepfather, I was cut off financially and had to withdraw from college and get a job. At the same time, I stepped out of all competitions that I'd grown the most embedded in and accustomed to: competing for grades, competing with other women for men's sexual attention, competing with other women to be the best and most right *kind* of woman. I took my ball and left the field. I hadn't made it, and I was tired of trying—I wasn't going to play anymore.

•§•

I always get jealousy and envy confused, so I looked up their definitions. *Jealousy* is a fear of loss, a fear that someone will take what you have. *Envy* is a feeling of inferiority, and wanting what someone else has.

These are normal, natural, and healthy emotions, and ones we're taught that we're not supposed to feel if we are self-confident, self-assured, self-contained. If we don't need nobody for nothin', that is.

Sometimes when I am steeped in envy or jealousy, I write about it. Sometimes I don't—sometimes I don't want to put a thing into words. Sometimes I just want to get through the day without specifying for myself how green-eyed envious I am that everyone else (I imagine) had a better childhood, had supportive family or at least a strong and encouraging community of mentors and friends, and isn't battling the old voices of brainwash and terror every time they try something new. Sometimes I can avoid the self-pity; sometimes I just let self-pity clot up all over the page. Self-pity needs a voice, just like all the rest of our feelings do.

My initial inclination is to try and foreclose on shameful feelings like envy, self-pity, jealousy—those greasy, gross little gremlins of feeling that make my skin tacky, make my stomach hurt, make me feel small and stupid and vulnerable. I believe, when I am inside the envy, that everyone else will achieve more than me, that I am going to fail because I am worthless. Then I look and realize that I am still writing. That's the goal: to keep writing.

There's tremendous energy and power in anything repressed. Writing fully into our difficult emotions means tapping into powerful material and energy once in awhile. Read it aloud in workshop from that shaking silo that self-pity shoves you into—I mean read it even though you *know* you are the only one who has ever felt or been this awful, and find yourself met with a roomful of nods and grateful exhales, relieved laughter: thank god *she* had the nerve to write that, we are all thinking; she's given us permission to be more nervy and honest in our own writing next time.

Sometimes the envy or jealousy are about grief. My adored writer friend and colleague Renee Garcia speaks of writer's grief. She says that no one talks about what our writing selves mourn: the writing we haven't done, all that we haven't dedicated ourselves to, all the time and words and poems that we've lost.

When in 2012 I was preparing to leave my day job as a data analyst to focus all of my attention on writing and the writing groups, I got completely tangled up with panic, frustration, and much self-recrimination. The voices inside said, *Why haven't you already done this? You are forty years old and you still don't know what you're going to do with your life? Look at everyone in your circle, the professors and computer professionals and therapists, all the people with their shit together, Jen. Why can't you get your life together? You've said you*

were going to write books since you were six years old and here you are—still
playing around.

Now, if any friend or writer in group came to me with this sort of narrative, I'd
encourage them to write it, to be gentle with themselves, to start again anyway, to
use it as material until it got boring and then let their writing lead them into the
next possibility for their work.

Isn't it always easier to advise someone else to do exactly the thing you ought to
be doing?

I understand the struggle around allowing these voices out in their fullness, I
understand the struggle around setting them free—I get caught in their tethers,
their sticky tendrils, their emaciated need. These voices want me to be safe, and
are more comfortable when I keep myself small instead of when I risk following
big dreams or try something new.

So this is the grief. Yes, I've spent hours upon hours pressed down into my
notebooks, scrawling the saving words that will never see the light of day. It's not
fair to have needed so much time just to convince myself that I deserved to be
alive. It's not fair that so much was taken from me just during that early moment
of adolescence, so that it would take me twenty years to find the capacity for
stability, to believe that I am capable of standing still and easy on these feet that
have carried me, running, all this time. This is my writer's tantrum today. *It's not*
fair to have to take time to survive. It's not fair it's not fair it's not fair.

It's ok to notice these places of loss and sorrow, to write what's not there, to feel
the ache when I read about one more twenty-something who's had her first
book published to wild acclaim—who maybe is a survivor herself and who still
managed to get herself together to sit down at the computer and put one word
after the other and then send it all out to an agent.

(Then I remind myself that Theodore Roosevelt is supposed to have said, "Comparison is the thief of joy." Then I watch a couple hours of *Scrubs* reruns. Then I get back to work.)

The mourning doesn't end, maybe won't end—but it abates when I'm doing my work. The voices get louder, the grief and self-pity increase, when I am not writing; and then I can feel as though it's impossible to cross the field of wailing to get back into writing anything at all: won't the critics be too loud? But just sit down. Just write it. Just put it on the page and let the next things come. Those old voices begin to slip into a background place, and I can focus on this *now*.

Trauma doesn't want us in the *now*, and of course, for so many of us and for so many years, the *now* was an awful place to inhabit. We can move slow, we can invite a word at a time and build a stable ground for this work that has been our lifetime ambition. We are mourning and we live with loss and we write anyway.

Because I write so often with trauma survivors, I get to witness trauma's response to a survivor's decision to commit themselves to a creative life, or to write the stories that have been silenced, or to write the book they have always wanted to write or the poems that sing behind their closed morning eyes or create the stage production that has been longing to emerge for years. I get to bear witness to the backlash, to hear writers give voice to the inner critics feeding them depression and sitcom television and salty food, the inside talk that sounds like, "Honey, no one cares if you write that book—it's not like it actually *matters*. What difference could it make for you to write that stuff now? It's not like it's paying your rent? Why don't you get a *job*?"

This is where a creative community can be transformative. When I am filled with self-defeat, when the trauma aftermath has straitjacketed me in its soft talk and old abuser's voice, if I can bring myself to enter (just as I am) into the room with those who love me and (in those moments, maybe more importantly) love my writing, I can receive a counterbalance to those voices and find the strength to try again.

I'm not going to pretend it isn't still hard to do this.

When we are not writing, when we are overwhelmed with work and life, when know for sure that we will never write anything of worth or measure, when we are sick and scared—this is exactly the time to have available to us a community of peers who adore us. Yet, this is also exactly the time when we who have survived trauma will often turn away from that community. (Is it like that for you? It is for me.)

When the writing is flowing well, when we're strong in our work, when that submission was accepted or we finished a poem or we got the residency or an editor responded positively to our writing—those are easy times to connect with our friends. We can be worthy of celebrating. We've got a fantastic Facebook post. We can be worth the space we take up in a room.

But when we are struggling with our work, when the words are stuck to the insides of our fingers and will not emerge no matter how many freewrites we do, when the book mocks us from the computer screen, when the day job asks for more of our time and we can't even get to our twenty-minutes-a-day, when we are sick with fear or loss or sorrow or flashback or chronic trauma aftermath— how can we ask our writing beloveds to hold us then? Why would we *inflict* ourselves upon them? Especially because we *know* that they are doing better in their own work. We *know* that everything comes easy for them. We *know* that *they* sent out their submissions or got paid for a piece of writing or have all the time in the world to write or don't ever have to deal with flashbacks when they just wanted to write for twenty minutes about the birds at the bird feeder in the early evening light.

These certainties are rarely accurate, of course, at least in my experience. They're whispered to us by those inside voices that will do whatever is necessary to keep us from undoing what they have worked so hard to create: a system that keeps to itself, doesn't tell the secrets, holds everything together, tight and impenetrable.

Our creative communities can love us when we're at our "lowest," when we're scraping the bottom of our creative barrels, when we're scared and hurt and certain that the words will never come again. They *want* to love us in those moments because, first, they want to love us in all the moments; second, they believe in us and our writing; and third, *they themselves* need that exact sort of love and support when the clamor of their inside voices gets loud.

We who were convinced that we were unloveable, that we were not worthy of care and attention until and unless we were perfect, we can find this hard to believe (to put it mildly).

•§•

I've learned to pay close attention when I am feeling either envious or jealous — when I want what someone else has or when I am afraid someone's going to take what I have. (Not that I have much of a choice; I get so puckered up with Grinch-like sour grapes that I can hardly move.) These feelings squeeze me tight, making it harder for me to move and breathe. I don't work as well when I'm clenched and not breathing. Our writing comes out stilted and sore when we try to keep the naughty, knotty emotions out of it, when we play like we're prefect pretty princes, when we pretend to be the good kids with calm faces who sit still in our chairs and write, *I had a good summer it was fine* when what we really want to say is *My best friend got to go away to camp and now she won't stop talking about it even though my dad lost his job so I couldn't go and I had to stay here and watch my little sister all summer and it was stupid and boring.*

Some days our writing is going to offer us something full and strong, a feeling of powerful sexual desire or a meaty, dense, certain anger. These are muscular feelings: we flesh out into them as we write. Other days, the writing takes us somewhere else — into shame or vulnerability, say. We can turn away from the writing on these days: that's entirely our choice. I still get afraid of loosing viscid, uncomfortable feelings like shame, greed, envy, disappointment, or embarrassment onto the page. Maybe if I don't write about them they'll go away—even after all this time, I can still make this bargain with myself. And though it's true that they're just feelings, that, given time, they'll shift away from what's making me ill at ease—what I'm left with, in the aftermath of this kind of avoidance, is the sense that the notebook is not actually a safe place for *all* my feelings, especially the ickiest ones.

After years, sometimes decades, of stuffing ourselves down, of pretending like we were fine all the time, sometimes we'll pretend even in our own writing, when we're alone with our pen and our thoughts. But self-deception, at least for me, is the worst kind of poison. It continues to be big work to go ahead and freewrite those (at least) three morning pages when I'm feeling at my most terrible. Afterwards, though, I always feel lighter, more free. That's the gift of practice. Then I can close the notebook, leave the gnarl and oog on the page, and, if need be, treat myself to some fingers-full of vanilla frosting anyway.

Wit(h)ness that's messy and real

Give yourself ten minutes, and write an ode to jealousy. Get all the way into it. Write a love song to envy, a paean to covetousness, an alleluia for the green-eyed monster. And then, yes, follow your writing wherever it seems to want you to go.

safety and survivors writing

Safety is a big issue when working with folks who've experienced sexual or other abuse. I've thought quite a bit about what's involved in creating a "safe" space. What does *safe* mean for us? There's physical safety, and then there's emotional or psychic safety. If I live in a safe home or safe neighborhood, I can trust that I'm unlikely to get beat up when I walk out the door of my house, nor when I walk back in. If I live outside of a war zone, I am safe in knowing (with enormous gratitude) that there aren't bombs falling from the sky when I walk to the bus. In the years since I broke away from my stepfather, I have been safe from his physical violence: there've been no assaults in the night, no agents sent to harm me or those I love, both of which I absolutely feared. There's safety in knowing there's a roof over the place I sleep, that I have stability with that place, that there's food in my cupboard and refrigerator, there's a bed and a door that locks—these are all markers for me of physical safety.

(Just the ability to step back and be *aware* of my general physical safety points to vast amounts of privilege, of course.)

The sort of safety I tend more to be concerned with in writing groups is of the verbal, emotional, or psychic sort, having to do with triggers and rememberings, having to do with communication: what we say and how we say it.

I live and work within a subculture of folks whose art and labor center around healing and creating radical change in society. People in this community talk openly about trauma and about sexuality, about radical self-care, about taking care of our bodies, about how creativity can and has healed us. We talk about consent and resilience like we talk about breakfast cereal—it's a part of our normal, everyday conversation. We are cautious about our speech: we don't want to say anything that will trigger anyone. We ask for permission before hugging someone. We are careful to acknowledge our privilege when/where we are aware of it and may apologize for privileged behavior we were not aware of until someone called it out. We step up and step back, making room for the voices of those around us with less mainstream societal privilege. We are aware of -isms, we clarify caveats, we understand that words are political, that grammar has power, and we work to hold space for many different ways of verbally engaging with and in the world. We give trigger or content warnings whenever we are going so speak explicitly about sexual violence, because we understand what it feels like to be in the middle of a book or a movie or a TV show or a simple conversation that we were just relaxing into and then *BAM!*, a rape scene wads us into a small ball, leaving us sick and angry and down for the count.

We place trigger warnings in front of our stories, our poems, our blog posts, Facebook notes, tweets. We put a warning sign in our mouths and point to the side door: *Hey, you can go out and have a smoke right now, buddy, if you don't want to hear about my rape.*

We want to be careful, conscientious, responsible. We are all about consent.

As childhood trauma survivors, we're worried about hurting other people. We've had instilled in us the idea that our very being, our healthy behaviors (resistance, for example), hurt other people—the perpetrator *hurts* when we say no, or our mother/father/caregiver will be *hurt* if we tell them explicitly what's being done to us. We were trained to believe we're responsible for others' feelings and reactions.

We come to believe that others' reactions to our words are our fault or responsibility.

•§•

What does safety mean in the context of a survivors writing group? Is safety the same thing as comfort?

When I say "safe space," with respect to these writing groups, I mean a space, both in the psychic and physical sense, in which folks can feel/be unmolested by others' judgments, bodily encroachments, or misdirected emotion, in which participants won't be called upon to defend or explain themselves or their writing, and can expect to be welcomed with kindness and enthusiastic support.

Still, in these spaces, none of us can afford to make assumptions about others. We are all afraid, we are all in need, and all have untold stories within us, carry great lusts and desires that are unmet and scare us. We must be safe enough to take the risk to speak ourselves to each other without fear of re-silencing. Novelist Dorothy Allison speaks about her desire to hold on to the fantasy that there was safety within the shared feminist community of which she was a part. However, she had to acknowledge that she had never really felt safe in that community: "I have never been safe and that is only partly because everyone else is just as fearful as I am. None of us is safe, because we have never made each other safe."

While safety is an important factor, we must be willing to risk walking on the outside of what we know as comfortable. That walk will be easier for some folks than others. I do not, in these groups, commit to keeping everyone comfortable; this is discomforting work, actually, and there are those for whom the discomfort is too much. *Discomfort* is not a failure of the group, however. As survivors and writers gathered together, our responsibility to each other is to write authentically and honestly, to listen intently to one another, to trust our creative instincts.

Writing about trauma isn't always comfortable. Choosing to enter this writing means we've decided to open a wider space for our creative voices and that means we are ready to stretch and build some new muscle.

•§•

As survivors, we have been working for years to be worthy of the very air we breathe, and this means undertaking a great deal of self-censorship: of our speech, desire, feeling, movement. We censor ourselves all the time, everywhere, in everyday conversation, with those we know just in passing and those who are our nearest and dearest. Many of us have trained ourselves to live in very small boxes so that we don't offend anyone and will be allowed to exist. We may even censor our private thoughts and journals: maybe our notebooks were never safe, we know someone could read them at any time, so we are careful with what we write or say. Maybe we are afraid of unleashing our true self *anywhere*, certain that if we give our real feelings any free rein, even in private, they will take over.

I encourage writers, as much as they can, not to censor themselves in their writing, and, at least in survivors workshops, I don't expect people to give trigger warnings before reading their work aloud.

In entering a workshop for survivors of sexual trauma, I remind writers that they can expect, every week, to write and listen to writing that has to do with sexual violence. I tell them that they can trust that, from the first meeting on, some of the writing—either their own or others'—will trigger big or difficult memories or feelings, and that they can be proactive in thinking about how they want to take care of themselves.

Trigger warnings in a space dedicated to survivor voices feels both redundant and unnecessarily protective, even parochial. It's an apology: *I have written something that uses precise language to describe what I or my character experienced, and now I'm going to share it with you—I'm sorry about that.*

We get a space, *one place*, where we don't have to apologize for our stories or our lives.

When it helps, writers can consider a safety plan for themselves—what are you going to do to take care of yourself during this time of powerful writing? Your toolbox of self-care might include good friends, therapy, personal journaling, meditation practice, chocolate, music you love, runs on the beach, time in nature, dancing, exercise, time with pets, room to cry, room to scream and shout, cooking, baking, building, singing, swimming, playing ball, building sandcastles, swinging on a swing set—the possibilities are endless. The point is to have some ideas already in mind for how you will hold and honor your strong feelings and reactions and be gentle and kind with yourself through this powerful work.

•§•

The word *safe* means, variously, *not in danger or likely to be harmed; not dangerous or likely to cause harm; not harmed or damaged; something that does not involve any risk.*

Do I really want a life that doesn't involve any risk? What if I'm ok even if I'm not completely safe—that is, even if I'm taking risks and I can't know or control the outcome?

Girls are supposed to be safe: not dangerous or likely to cause harm. Quiet. Passive. Sugar and spice and everything nice, all that. What happens when we shove back at that idea, crumble it, take back our dangerousness? What if I don't want my writing, especially, to be safe for everyone reading?

"Safe" can be a trap, for me. Safe, too, can be a way that I control others: *What you're doing/saying makes me feel unsafe.* How often have white women used that to turn a dialogue away from conversations about the impacts of racism, for example?

My notebooks are dangerous places, because they're where I navigate the maze that is my real heart and mind—filled as they are with much triggering material as well as the *occasional* offensive, mean, un-PC, judgmental, catty, incautious thought.

We're not living if we're spending all of our energy trying to be perfect. Being the perfect survivor takes so much effort, effort that could be better spent laughing with friends or going for a long walk or creating a new art installation or going back to school or undoing patriarchy.

As much as possible, don't censor yourself in your writing. We gather together in these rooms to move away from the pressure to censor. We come together as survivors and writers to stretch our resilient, creative selves, to build writing muscle and to build community. We are not there to feed each other pablum, or to tell all the safe stories. We are there, like novelist Sapphire said, to *push*.

Let your wit(h)ness be risky

What's one thing you would write if you didn't have to censor yourself or apologize to anyone after writing it? Anything. Remember that prompt I mentioned in "articulate fear: writing what scares us": *What would you write on a piece of paper that you were going to burn immediately after writing?* Write that. Take ten minutes, and write those words down, however they want to come. Let this be a private write, just in your notebook—you don't ever have to show it to anyone.

What if your words didn't have to be *safe* for other people?

---

diy wit(h)ness: ideas for gathering your own group

While it's fantastic to find a welcoming space to write that's facilitated and run by someone else, a writing group you can settle into and will invite you to discover the words for your stories, I am interested here in describing/discovering a way for groups of sexual abuse survivors to gather as peer writers. We have the capacity to co-create and hold this sort of space, for one another. We don't have to wait for someone else to decide to start a survivors writing group. If we know that this is something we want for ourselves, we can do it: we can put the word out in our communities, and invite others to co-create with us a circle of creative support, in which each individual is participant and co-facilitator.

The core groundrules for Writing Ourselves Whole writing groups, based on the Amherst Writers & Artists method, are as follows:

- keep confidential all writing shared in group

- exercises are suggestions (folks are welcome to write about anything they want, even if it has nothing to do with the prompt given)

- everyone writes (including the facilitator)

- sharing is always optional (no one ever has to read aloud)

- if folks do decide to share, we respond to all writing as though it's fiction, and we tell each writer what we liked and found strong about the piece they read

The Writing Ourselves Whole workshops that I facilitate often end up, for many (but not all, by any means) participants, being "life writing" workshops, where the writing is a telling of our own stories, getting into that thick truth of the everyday stories we exist within. As a facilitator (and as a writer), I am interested in opportunities for us to tell the whole truth(s): you get to write whatever you want here because we keep it all confidential; you get to respond to the prompt or write about something else—you can even write about how much you hate the exercise; you can read aloud or not, and if you do decide to read aloud, we only say what we like and what's strong; and because I draw upon the AWA method, we talk about all the writing as though it were fiction (rather than saying "you" to indicate that the writer and the one written about is necessarily the same), unless explicitly instructed otherwise by the writer.

How we talk about something matters. We offer each other risky stories in these groups, so we need to be tender with each other in response. Talking about the new writing as fiction objectifies the work in the best way, highlights it as an artistic creation rather than a confession, and allows us as writers and as listeners to experience the distance between who we are and how we tell our story. This part of the structure also holds line for us between writing group and therapy group. These writing groups are not therapy groups, nor are they intended to be. We create art while putting words to stories we were never supposed to tell.

What happens in that in-between space, the transformation of memory and fantasy into words and onto paper, is sacred, and talking about a work as though it's fiction protects and honors that risk and sacred space.

•§•

Before I was certified as a writing group facilitator, I had training as a peer, crisis, and support group counselor from queer youth service organizations and domestic violence agencies, had participated in anti-racism trainings, and I'd been writing alone for eight years and had begun to be published. All of these skills came in handy (to say the very least) during the writing groups I've facilitated. I understood that, often, the most helpful thing you can do for another person is to listen to them, attentively and devotedly. The trainings I'd gone through helped me learn how to sit with big, difficult emotions. If you or others in your groups have these skills, you may want to bring them to bear—but I don't believe they're required before a group of writers can create and sustain a sexual trauma survivors writing group.

In a writing group, one thing (among others) folks seem to seek and deserve, as survivors and particularly as writers, is a hearing, a witnessing, in a safer and confidential space. Read about different group formats and styles. Get a hold of Pat Schneider's book, *Writing Alone and With Others*—it's an invaluable resource. Lauren Miller and the Blueprint Collective wrote a book about June Jordan's revolutionary *Poetry for the People* program, which includes ideas for forming groups as well as fantastic prompts. Julia Cameron's *The Artist's Way* has a section toward the end about peer support groups that will also be a big help to those seeking to gather and sustain their own survivors writing communities. Maybe you don't want to offer the writing any feedback at all, as in Natalie Goldberg's classes—you simply want to write, and read, then write some more. Choose together what will work best for your group.

I have a lot of ideas about what sexual trauma survivors writing groups should look like—take them as suggestions, as sparks for your collective imagination. So, without further ado, and not in any particular order, some thoughts about running and sustaining a writing group for sexual trauma survivors:

- Congratulations and hooray! The group you're about to form will benefit not just you and the other writers, but each of your relationships, families, workplaces, and wider communities. It's beautiful work you're getting ready to do. Thank you.

- The group should meet in a public space, like a library or community room at a college or mosque/synagogue/church or meditation center. The space should be private (with a door that can close) and secure, for confidentiality's sake. Ideally, it's also easy to get to by car (with good parking options) and public transportation, and wheelchair-accessible. If there's a rental fee or donation requested, the group can decide how it wants to deal with that: all contribute every time, different people cover the cost each week, etc. Maybe a public space is not an option, or the group prefers to meet in a private home. In that case, think about how to share responsibility for set up, food preparation, clean up, etc., so that it doesn't all fall on the shoulders of one person.

- I believe there should always be snacks, both healthy and unhealthy, and responsibility for providing snacks should be shared. I have, at all of my groups, carrots, fruit in season (usually either grapes or strawberries), potato chips, chocolate, and nuts. Sometimes I also offer freshly baked banana bread or sweet potato scones. Maybe you'll want a full, potluck meal at each meeting (I've found that many writers really love to cook!). You'll figure out what your group prefers.

- One person should be the facilitator each week—this person will be responsible for bringing the prompts and readings, keeping time and "holding" the space. (Or you could have two folks co-facilitate each week—in any case, it makes sense to me to have responsibility for facilitation rotate, so as not to land too consistently on one person's shoulders.) Every person will facilitate differently—that's not only ok, that's good! Take cues and ideas from one another, share ideas for prompts, and hold to whatever structure you've decided upon.

(I offer these three ideas first because I believe that any practices you can build in that will help diffuse resentment from the outset can only help the longevity of the group.)

- Think about how long you want your meetings to last. I like a two-and-a-half hour group if we're meeting weekly. Sometimes an hour or ninety minutes is perfect. Discuss among yourselves what will work best for everyone.

- Folks should each have strong support networks and self-care practices outside of the group. There should be tools/resources that each person can lean on when they have an emotional response to the writing (their own or others'). Support networks often include a therapist or counselor, but don't have to. I invite folks to consider letting friends or other supportive folks know that they're going to be joining a survivors writing group, just so those friends have a heads-up that the writer might be calling them to touch base for some support. I ask them to think, too, about self-care during or after your writing time: what can you do to create some good space for yourself? How can you be kind/gentle with yourself during this time? Consider making some mental plans for that. (Revisit the list at the end of the introduction for some ideas.)

- Don't be surprised if you feel more vulnerable after leaving a writing group in which you've shared something exposing about yourself than you did when you were in the circle; after you leave the group space, your internal censors and protective psyche kicks in, worrying that you said too much and everyone now thinks you are ridiculous. This is a very common experience. This psychic freakout comes from a protective place—your internal structures simply want to keep on keeping you safe by keeping you isolated; that's what worked for years, and these bits of protective architecture don't yet know or trust that the abuse is over and you are safe now. Writing in community about your experience of trauma (and about other things, too!) can be a part of retraining your psychic self, teaching those inner protectors that they can relax a bit, that you are safe in telling the truth, that you're not going to be hurt or suffer retribution from abusers.

- Stay focused on the writing during writing time. If someone goes off-track while giving feedback, for instance, and starts talking about how the writing reminds her of *that time she went to her grandmother's and you remember her grandmother, right? How she smoked all the time, even in the kitchen while making dinner, and the ashes used to fall into whatever she was cooking, and*—you just want to gently ask that person to finish her story at the break, and refocus on what folks liked about the *writing* that was just shared.

- Only respond positively to brand-new work.

- Remember: There are support and therapy groups for trauma survivors—this writing group is something different: a space in which each group member is a writer/creator/artist, first and foremost.

- Consider ahead of time how the group wants to deal with conflict between members.

- Be easy with yourself and one another if something goes "wrong" in a meeting. Talk with others in the group or trusted folks outside the group (without violating the group's confidentiality) about what happened, and how you wish things had gone differently. Try not to keep your worry inside, or beat yourself up, or tell yourself to "just get over it." Apologize, if that's appropriate and helpful given the situation. Write about it, if only to discharge any shame, guilt, or triggeredness that lingers. Let yourself move on. Keep breathing.

- It's ok if someone brings a prompt that doesn't resonate for you—write anyway. Write about not liking the prompt, even. Remember that it's always ok to ignore the prompt!

- Similarly, if someone's writing doesn't ring all your bells, there will still be *something* about that piece of writing that you can authentically admire, or that stays with you. Practice truly attentive and loving listening and witnessing practices.

- I will repeat that: Practice truly attentive and loving listening practices.

- Be consistent in your meeting/writing schedule. Choose members who can commit to six or eight weeks or three months or some set time frame, after which time you can evaluate how the group is going.

- Bring a diversity of voices in the room—in writing style, background, education, writing experience, and in other ways as well.

- I sincerely encourage you not to engage when someone says, "I want you guys to really tear this up—it's the only way I'm going to get better." We don't offer critical (that is, negatively judgmental) feedback to just-born work. Period. It's absolutely possible for someone's writing to improve through consistent and clear positive feedback.

- Know that sometimes someone will start writing with your trauma survivors writing group with full intention to continue for the allotted time frame and then will find that it's not right for them to continue. Sometimes folks are able to process a decision to leave with the group, and sometimes they're not. It can be difficult, as a group, not to take this personally—we worry that there was something we wrote or said that drove the person away. I encourage the group to briefly acknowledge the person's decision to discontinue the process, and to hold gratitude for that person's commitment to taking care of themselves.

These groups are about many things, including: finding language for what has been unspeakable or unhearable/unwitnessed; generating rich and varied survivor writing; breaking isolation; building a strong, empowered, and vocal survivor community; and learning to listen to our instincts and intuition, both on and off the page. Our intuition offers us subjects and phrases for our writing, and also lets us know when a situation is right or not right for us. We can miss someone's presence and writing and communicate that to them, while also offering deep support to them as they make the choice that's best for them.

- We can set intentions/groundrules/practices that the group will commit to. These might look like Amherst Writers & Artists practices, Natalie Goldberg's freewriting guidelines, Julia Cameron's ground rules for an *Artist's Way* group, June Jordan's *Poetry to the People*'s principles, Writing Ourselves Whole's practices, consciousness raising group guidelines, other support or community group guidelines—or some personalized amalgam of these and others. In my groups, while I draw heavily on the Amherst Writes & Artists method, I also tap into my training as a domestic violence advocate, queer youth peer support advocate, and psychoeducational group facilitator. I draw on Natalie Goldberg's description of freewriting, Anne Lamott's invitation into short assignments and shitty first drafts. Both Peter Elbow and Julia Cameron invite groups to come together to support one another's writing, creative, and artistic efforts without teachers or other leaders. There are many powerful models available. Let the group you're co-creating decide what structure will work best, and every so often, revisit that structure. As a group, decide what's working, what could be shifted, and allow for trial and error, growth and change.

- Give folks room for emotions—tears, anger, joy. Try not to interrupt someone when they're crying. Make tissues available in the room so that folks can grab one as needed. Also, there's no need to apologize for crying. If you tend to worry about this, remember: you are not taking up more than your fair share of space. You are just right. If you cry in the middle of reading your piece aloud, feel welcome to pause and weep, and then continue reading—if you don't feel you can continue reading, someone else might offer to read for you. You can say yes or no to this, and it's *always* ok to pass/not read, or to choose to read only a section of what you write.

- I encourage writers not to censor themselves in their writing, to remind themselves that, 1) it's ok not to read what they've just written, and 2) each writer in the room is a *survivor*, with well-developed self-care practices, and that even if we hear something painful, difficult, or that triggers a memory of our own traumas, we know how to take care of ourselves. Survivors are often worried about this issue: *should I avoid writing about certain things?*

What if someone gets hurt by what I write? We can't know what everyone in the room's triggers are, though; if we try to protect others as we write, we will end up writing very little, and what we do write will have no energy, no bite. I invite us not to censor ourselves anymore. We have been censoring ourselves, many of us, for years. It's a new practice, in fact, *not* to censor. In uncensoring our and our characters' true thoughts and feelings, our writing will have greater power, potency, energy and depth.

- The group can decide for itself whether or not to offer trigger warnings before folks read their work. Because, as I say above, I don't know what each writer's triggers are, I tend to fall on the side of inviting writers to take care of themselves and not give trigger warnings, *especially* in a trauma survivors writing group. What if we offered our words and experiences without apology? Do what's right for your group, though. Sometimes it feels best to say something like, *Hey, there's explicit description of sexual violence in here, you guys...* or, *Listen, there's explicit sex in this piece, just a head's up.*

- Make a firm and clear commitment to confidentiality, especially if folks in the group share a larger community or friendship network. Do not tell others outside the group about things you learn (or think you learn) through someone's writing. Do not discuss what someone has written when you see them at a party or rally or even at a trauma survivors support or therapy group—let each writer decide how and when to disclose their stories, and allow/expect others to offer you the same respect. Do not write about content shared in group—with the exception of your own writing, of course—on any social networking site or blog. Be strict about this. Err on the side of being too cautious. If one of your co-writers says, *You know about this; I wrote about it last week,* then just nod and keep listening. Say, *I didn't want to assume.* Let them guide what you do with information that has been met and responded to as fiction. Do not gossip with group members about other group members—that will kill a group.

- Build and keep one another's trust by holding to the practices to which you've committed, remaining kind with one another, assuming positive intent, *openly* and egregiously delighting in one another's work and writing voices, and keeping confidences.

- Hold open space for writers to write in whatever language they choose. Bilingual (or more-lingual) writers might not always want to write in English. Writers can choose to translate what they've written or not; I like to invite writers to read the piece aloud as written so that the group can comment on the music of the words, even if we don't all understand the meaning.

- Be generously kind with one another. Practice and foster a deep kindness. Learn to expect to be treated and met with kindness and a generosity of spirit.

- Share books you've discovered, workshops/classes, calls for submissions, residency and fellowship information, award details and other opportunities with one another. Undermine the culture of competitiveness and scarcity with abundant generosity.

- Be in each other's corners (as my friend Renee Garcia would say). Become cheering squad and biggest fans for each writer in your group. Remember what it takes to put pen to paper, at any time: deep courage and conviction. Make room for one another's disappointments and frustrations—listen without succumbing to the urge to fix it. Offer brainstorming/ideas if the speaker wants that sort of thing, and be willing to hold one another's pain without trying to make it better or make it go away. Cultivate the ability to ask for advice or suggestions when that's what you want, and to ask "just" to be heard when that's what you need. Remember how much work and what a gift it is to deeply listen, what a kindness it is to be willing and able to carry someone's burden with them.

- Resist the skid into what I call the "trauma olympics"! Some support groups devolve into an attempt to tell the worst story, to "one up" the previous teller, to prove that we deserve to be in the room by describing all of our horror stories—not because we are using that material toward strong creative ends but because the culture of the room is such that only the horror stories are rewarded. Understand that everyone's story will be different, everyone has experienced horror, and no two stories will be alike.

- Resist the urge to offer therapy, especially if you are a therapist or there are therapists participating. Folks don't come to a writing group for therapy—they go to a therapist for therapy. Folks come to a writing group to write.

- Be willing to break the frame when necessary—listen to your intuition. If someone is in a big cry or a big emotional response, be willing to press pause and really be present for those feelings. Do something playful as a group sometimes—go out for ice cream or karaoke or to a public garden. Cultivate a structure that is resilient: strong and flexible.

- Decide whether it's ok if folks drink alcohol during your group and make that clear—some groups are ok with wine at group potluck meals, for instance, and others aren't. Decide and communicate whether other forms of inebriation are welcome at your group.

- Vary your writing prompts and exercises. I very rarely use exercises that are specifically related to sexual violence—my prompts are open-ended (objects, lists, visualizations, poems, sentence fragments, images, songs, videos) intended to spark an emotional, sensory, or memory response, and it is often the context of the group that determines what's written—I can offer the same prompt at a trauma survivors group and at an erotic writing group and, because of the context, the writing in the first group will tend to skew toward relating to trauma or recovery, and the writing in the second group will skew toward the erotic, sensual or sexual. There are many resources for writing prompts; I've shared some of my favorites in the bibliography.

- Consider some signal to call the group to order: a bell, singing bowl, word or phrase. After a time, hearing this sound or phrase will bring our creative voice to attention.

- Have a conversation ahead of time about group members flirting or dating. In my groups, I'm fine with light or friendly flirtation, but encourage folks to be tremendously respectful of one another's boundaries, and to avoid hooking up until the group is over—I've had fighting couples in my writing group, who've used the writing as ammunition and the group as battleground, and it isn't pretty.

- Be consistently mindful and attentive to one another's environmental sensitives, allergies, and accessibility needs.

- Turn off or silence cellphones during group meetings. Unless it's an extreme emergency, don't text or email while someone is reading/sharing!

- Decide how to deal with laptops in the group—some people have a hard time writing longhand when another writer is tapping away at a keyboard. I myself am fine with folks using laptops in groups, though I ask them to stop typing when we are reading/sharing.

- On a similar (if more prosaic) note, decide what to do about eating during writing time. For instance, I ask folks not to eat crunchy things during writing/sharing; it's too distracting for me!

- Think about how you want to respond to writing that is offensive to folks in the room. Remember that we invite one another not to censor ourselves, and we respond to all writing as fiction. We might say, for example, how worried we feel for a character, or how angry we felt (and how well the writer crafted a character who could piss us off so intensely). We can talk about our individual feelings and responses to a piece of writing without blame, shame, or guilt.

Your group might meet for eight weeks or might be ongoing for many years— over time, you will shift and grow together, and your group culture and practices will shift as well. Keep writing, take risks, try new things, build community, fail, succeed, and—all the way through—be easy with one another, and be easy with yourselves.

Creating space for survivor witness

Give yourself ten or twenty minutes, and write out your vision
for a survivors writing group. How would you like such a group
to come together and sustain itself? How do you want to feel
when you walk into the room to write with this group? How
do you want to feel when you leave? What energies would you
like to have in the room? Write into your hopes and dreams for
such a space, big and small.

See the Appendix for many more writing exercises, as well
as ideas for where to get more prompts, and how to create
your own!

self-care

self-care

this is a ceremony

Listening to the inside languages that only your body knows is an act of intimacy with the self. Finding words for the unspeakable, and then sharing those words with others, moving one more story out of isolation and back into a circle of supportive, kindred spirits is one of the most powerful healing ceremonies I've ever experienced.

We were already without ceremony before we were violated. We were already without magical words, without the teas or tinctures or potions that our great-great-great-grandmothers made in the old countries (or in this country, before the occupation), without the dances and prayers that shifted with the season or the tides or the moon. We were without the foods that our bones were bred from, we were without the stories. Even before we were abused, even before that wretched substitute language was lifted from our mouths and replaced with a harsh cottony silence, even before he or she or they put their bodies against our bodies and said *Stay* and said *Open,* said *Break* and said *Silence,* we did not have the ceremonies to retrieve our lost selves, and no one else did, either. So we watered stuffed animals, we pounded our heels on pavement or dirt, we forced honesty out of metaphor in the lined pages of old notebooks, we opened our mouths in the new churches, but it didn't save us.

We found new ceremony to fill the places where we were stripped, where we were clearcut, where we were starched and bleached and boiled.

Some of us raised our screams in gatherings that spilled into streets, we chanted, we banged spoons against pots, we wore denim and leather (materials just too thick to penetrate easy). This was a ceremony.

We opened our bodies and let sex drive sensation in. This was a ceremony.

We opened books filled with the words of other initiates who had relinquished their silence, who had dug hands into their throats and clawed out the cotton, who had found words for what was wordless. We brought their language onto our tongues, into our bellies and lungs, against the bald sides of our eyes. This was a ceremony.

We ran for miles and didn't eat. This was a ceremony.

We drove steel into our forearms. This was a ceremony.

All these ways we worked to find ourselves again, because there was no one left to tell us the old ways. We wanted to make the right magic so our souls would finally come back and wear our skins again, move our mouths and limbs with joy, re-endow us with the capacity to taste, to sing, to stumble and bleed and get up and keep going.

We stood with others whose ceremonies had been stripped the way ours were, with those whose ceremonies lay long buried in the middle passage and burnt in Virginia or swung from elms, with those whose ceremonies were burnt at the stake or drowned in the river, were driven into railroad tracks, whose ceremonies were marched over trails of tears, people whose ceremonies had gone dormant because the languages to express them had been jailed and outlawed and beaten. People who had been told they didn't need ceremony anyway—weren't they men, after all? We stood and stumbled together. We were not enough and we were everything. We stood together like we weren't supposed to. Every time we touched hands, touched one another, shared one more true story, we breathed in a little better. *We* were ceremony.

Maybe you come from a culture or a community that taught you how we are to hold one another after an experience of trauma: after sexual abuse or the death of someone you love, after deployment to a war zone or rape or being beaten by a lover or emotionally terrorized, after a natural disaster or life-altering illness or another form of trauma. Maybe you came from people who know how to listen and be deeply present with those afflicted and victimized, these veterans of the wars of life. Maybe you come from people who have learned how devastating it is to be separated from community by virtue of the trauma itself. Maybe you come from people who understand that if we want a community of wholeness, we must be willing to be present with one another's wounds and pain. In listening to each other, in welcoming the truth of the harms we have suffered—or the harms we have inflicted—our communities could let us know that they see who we are, that we are still a part of the human family.

Trauma puts us out of the house of the community, even though many—even most—of us will experience something both traumatic and too taboo to talk about around the water cooler: miscarriage, abortion, cancer, gender nonconformity, sexual harassment, racist violence, casual misogyny, molestation, rape—so much more do we navigate everyday without being invited into the language we need to understand and save ourselves, the language we need to share our reality with those we love. In our isolation, it's easier to believe that we are aberrant, that something about ourselves brought on what happened to us, that we are in fact somehow to blame for our suffering, as our perpetrators, our communities, or our religion might tell us.

The mainstream American culture I'm familiar with has few rituals. We gather for sports games, we mark the passing of another year with drunken birthday celebrations, some of us carry forth and build new traditions at the holidays that are important to us. Some cultural communities mark rites of passage in a person's life—coming into the world, coming into adulthood, passage into and out of parenthood, having a love partnership, making the transition into death. But many of us don't participate in such rituals. We question the use of these old beliefs in our modern age. Who needs ritual? Isn't it just representative of some old, repressive, and likely patriarchal cultural construct, meant to tether us psychically to a tradition that values conformity over individual expression and development? Many of us walked away from those rituals and traditions in order to find our own voice and fullness. And yet the human desire is for some sense of deep connection. Even those of us who are introverted do not wish to be fully outside the human community (we just don't understand why they have to be talking to us all the time).

I have this vision (maybe fantasy) of a ritual for survivors of sexual violence that would incorporate the survivor fully "back" into their community/-ies important to them. In this circle would be friends and non-perpetrating family members, community elders and young ones, survivor's advocates, and representatives from institutions important to the survivor: school, police, government, mosque/temple/synagogue/sangha/church. In a comfortable room this group gathers to share good food. There is music and embracing. Then the group sits in some semblance of a circle, on a mismatch of couches and overstuffed chairs. There is a moment or two of silence, and then the survivor begins to speak. They tell their whole story—as much as they wish to share.

The survivor is uninterrupted in this telling, though their community may make sounds of acknowledgement, sorrow, understanding, indignation. The circle listens closely even though these are terribly difficult details to hear—they listen because they understand that *this burden is not only the survivor's to carry alone*; the violence was done to the whole community, and the whole community has the responsibility to know and help carry the story. The telling might take a half hour, it might take several hours. Maybe there are brief breaks. During the breaks, people move around and stretch but they do not make small talk or otherwise distract themselves from the process underway—this is difficult and sacred labor.

When the survivor reaches a point of completion, there is a moment of silence, and then another. The eldest person in the room thanks the survivor for their generosity, their willingness to allow the community to share this burden and intimacy with them. Each of the people in the room reflects back something that they heard or something that stays with them, to offer tangible witness and *withness* to the survivor. The eldest person in the room tells the survivor that they are welcome in the family and heart of this community, expresses sorrow for any feelings of loneliness and isolation, and reminds the survivor that they are not alone. The survivor receives the message that they belong and are seen.

And then the people eat and drink and dance. They bring their whole hearts and whole bodies into the room, and the survivor understands that they belong, even after telling the stories that they were ashamed and terrified to speak aloud. They dance in life and community even though they were told that telling would mean isolation and shame and death. No one pretends that the work is done—the celebration is a part of the labor of living and being in community. Holding each of our neighbors' and loved ones' real stories is a part of the work of living and being in community.

We don't have this kind of ritual in the writing groups, of course. But we do offer each other authentic witnessing: we listen with our whole selves, with no attempt to fix the pain being shared, and we respond with our appreciation for the writer's artistry and creativity, and we tell the writer some of what we heard—their story now lives in our ears and hearts and mouths as well as in their own. They no longer have to carry that story alone. One more small piece of that great wall of isolation has been dissolved.

The ceremony of self-care

One of my favorite prompts is to read aloud a page from the
novel Ceremony, by Leslie Marmon Silko, which begins:
"Ceremony // I will tell you something about stories, / [he
said] /They aren't just entertainment. / Don't be fooled. /
They are all we have, you see. / All we have to fight off / illness
and death. // You don't have anything / if you don't have
the stories."

Give yourself ten minutes, and let this section of the poem be
your prompt.

What would a community accountability ceremony look
like for you? Who would be there? Who would not? Where
would it be held? What would you want to say? Follow your
words wherever they want to take you on the page, and into
this vision.

what writing can't do

Writing, alone and/or in a group, can do big work. It can introduce us to the inner workings, the inner contours, of our minds. It can give us new language for, and understanding of, our experiences. It can help us to feel our skin again. Writing practice can reconnect us with our instinctual self, with our intuition. Writing about our most difficult experiences can have positive health effects—physically and psychologically. Writing with others, especially other intimate trauma survivors, encourages us, emboldens us; we find ourselves more willing to take risks in our writing, whether or not we ever read aloud. We speak what we were taught to leave unspoken. We speak the words of violence and trauma and resistance aloud when we read our writing in our group, making it more possible for us to speak the words of violence and trauma and resistance when we are confronted with hostility or abuse in our lives. Receiving positive feedback from others can, over time, teach us that our words have impact, that our creativity is strong and fierce, that, yes, in fact, *we can write*, no matter what our third-grade teacher told us. Writing can be a lifeline, a trusted witness, a safe ear, a means of meditation and grounding, a way to discover what we really think and feel, a way to record our lives and dreams. Writing can lead us into new forms of understanding. Writing and sharing in community can leave us feeling that the ones who experienced all of that trauma are now less alone: we are telling their stories, we are standing with them in that alone room, we are holding their hands—those younger selves are no longer all alone. Their stories are being told.

So, yes, there is a lot that writing can do.

And there are things that writing can't do.

Writing can't make the trauma not have happened. Writing can't magically heal us. Writing by itself won't change our relationships with other people—we still have to take action to alter those relationships. Writing repeatedly with complaints about a difficult relationship, job, or other situation without taking any action to effect change off the page will not change our situation for us. Writing can be therapeutic, but it's not therapy.

Simply writing with others won't fully upend a well-developed tendency toward isolating; many of us know that it's perfectly possible to be alone and lonely when spending time with others. We still have to make a decision to connect. We still have to allow ourselves to be connected with. Reading aloud, giving others the opportunity to hear our brand-new writing, can create tiny fissures in the walls we have built around ourselves. The walls don't crumble after one writing session, after one writing group. Please don't expect that.

We can lie to ourselves in our notebooks. Picking up the pen is a powerful action, *and* just because we pick up the pen doesn't mean we immediately undo all our denial, partial truths, codependency, and other adaptive, self-protective behaviors. Writing practice can be a tool of transformation, and it can also be one more coping mechanism. Notwithstanding my belief in all that a writing practice can do for survivors of sexual violence, it's not a magic wand. Writing won't fix anything all by itself. (And I really wanted it to, for years.) Sometimes we still have to put the pen down, look up from the page, and engage in our real lives.

I don't know about you, but I have a well-developed capacity for magical thinking. I spent several years writing, over and over and *over*, about my frustrations with a relationship that wasn't working. Something in me imagined, I think, that if I just wrote my feelings *right* enough, then the situation would change.

I wrote the same stories repeatedly. I discovered patterns and figured out what I needed to do for the situation to change—and then I hit repeat: write the stories, look at the patterns, see through the words what I need to do to change, but I didn't take any action. Instead I just kept writing. And the writing began to hurt. Never mind that the writing (along with other voices) was pointing me toward a solution—I wasn't ready to act yet.

I stopped writing in my morning notebook for awhile, and removed myself from what has been, for me, the safest and most consistent place of meditation, discovery, and support. Radical self-care can look like not forcing yourself to hear something you're not ready to hear—and, of course, there are times when that's just denial. For me, this was a major red flag, but I wasn't willing to look at that for a couple more years.

•§•

Sometimes the writing leads me to things I don't want to know. Sometimes when I follow the threads of my writing when I'm working on my novel, something happens for my characters that I didn't want to have happen to them. I want them to just be all right, to be safe, to be well-loved: haven't they suffered enough? But the writing tugs at me, it says: *No, it happened this way*—and if I'm really listening, I take a deep breath and turn away from the brightly lit street into the alley that's all overgrown with weeds and strewn with broken glass and overturned garbage cans. I understand that the characters are going that way, and if I really want to be true to the story, I better not be afraid to follow.

When it happens in a freewrite that I stumble upon some uncomfortable truths about myself, that can be a bit harder. Sometimes I want to quit—I think I should just turn on the television and forget all about this dumb writing thing. I try to write my way out of it, write my excuses and self-blame. Sometimes the writing can take the blinders off—and I'm not always ready to be in that bright sunlight.

Still, even when it's embarrassing or hurts, I'm grateful when my morning pages or personal writing leads me into this sort of discovery place; it means I'm letting myself be present to the process. Yes, there are days when I don't want to open the notebook, when I don't remember why it matters, when I feel too sticky and gross inside to let anything out through the pen. Sometimes, on those days, I won't write in the notebook. And sometimes I'll "force" myself—which means I take a deep breath, stamp my feet, grumble out loud, get the tea and the candle and open the notebook and write anyway.

I don't know that it ever gets easier to drop down into the notebook during times of difficulty—no matter how many times I've been reminded that the writing always leaves me better than it found me; I walk away from the notebook, even after the most difficult writes, feeling that something in me is lighter, ready to be free.

Care for the places writing can't heal

Give yourself ten minutes and write: what do you wish writing could do that it cannot do?

writing practice for humans

How do I write about embodiment or embodying writing when I am so removed from my own skin, when the words can't find a frame to fall into or away from? How do I write about the body when I'm busy trying not to have one? The body is a human experience, and it's when I don't want to be human anymore, or when I don't feel worthy of my humanity, or when I want to dissociate myself from what humans are capable of, that the writing is hardest for me. Those days, when all that seems to live beneath my skin is the aftermath of trauma, those days, I tend to release my hold on what grounds me—physical exercise and words—and I slip back into the practices that will get me out of my body quick: I eat too much, too fast and carelessly; I watch too much TV; I work more thoughtlessly; I isolate from people who love me; I listen to the voices in me that believe I am worthless. I take my pen off of the page.

The difficulty erupts in a moment of overwhelm, big sorrow, or loss, and suddenly there's no time to write but plenty of time to stream bad sitcoms for hours. Of course, guilting myself about not doing what I know I should be doing is also an addiction, a form of self-abuse, never something that actually helps me back into healthy or healing practice.

I remember when I learned I was human.

I was thirty-three years old and I lived alone in San Francisco. I had just split from my ex-wife, was already in a new relationship, had left my most recent job working as a domestic violence advocate, and was so raw and skinless and frantic with guilt that I often felt unable to get enough air in my lungs.

The last straw for me as an advocate had been a meeting in a community center that had as much industrial comfort that a pre-fab building in a strip mall can have: soft, fluorescent lighting, beige-mauve carpets, windowless meeting rooms with cheap plastic chairs and one heavy wood table, floral print paintings, boxes of bulk tissue next to baskets of fake pastel flowers, and a wall, in the foyer, papered with bright flyers from service providers around the area. In one of those windowless meeting rooms gathered a group of seven women, survivors of domestic violence, for the psychoeducational support group I led. My job was to share a lesson of some kind—information about self-esteem or dynamics abusers use or the cycle of violence—and then open the floor for the women to talk about their relationships and learn new ways of dealing with things so that they were less likely to find themselves in abusive relationships again.

At that fateful meeting, one of the women I'd counseled often—a short, round woman with blonde hair she wore long, who had a manic way of speaking, like she'd been raised by auctioneers—described being angry with her teenage daughter for flirting with the child's father, the same man who had sexually abused this girl. The woman in my group was blaming her daughter for her ex-husband's violence. All I could hear was the mother saying that her daughter had asked for the abuse, and something inside me broke apart. As the advocate, it was my job to hold allegiance with the women who came to our agency for support and information; I was resolutely meant to be on the side of the mother.

But in that moment I was so angry that I wasn't able to speak for some time, and my head raced: *she blamed the victim for the violence? After all these months in group? What was I doing here if someone could still say such a thing?* While the group continued and other women shared, it gradually dawned on me that I *was not* a formerly battered woman—I was a formerly battered *child* who had gone into the work hoping that other mothers would have the resources, information, and self-esteem necessary in order to make different decisions from the ones my own mother had made. I was furious at this woman for blaming her own child for that child's molestation, and in a flash, I understood, finally, that I was also furious at my own mother. I could hardly hold it together, though I pinched my lips tight, gripped the armrests on my chair, and pretended to be a functional facilitator: "Does Jane's experience resonate with any of the rest of you? Dionne, do you want to say more?"

But inside I was spinning. None of these women's decisions would impact my mother's; I could not save my own mother through the bodies of these other adults. She was always going to have done what she'd done, and my sister and I were going to suffer the consequences. I left that job just a month or so later, in December.

So it was that the next month, at the beginning of the new year, I wasn't working a day job, and felt guilty about almost every single thing I was doing or had ever done. I'd failed as an activist. I'd left my partner of nearly ten years for one of her co-workers. I was navigating femininity again, after a decade walking in the world behind the safety of butch drag (and deeply ashamed of having failed as a butch dyke, as a "real" queer). I'd abandoned nearly all my close friends when I left my wife, believing they wouldn't want to have anything to do with me.

Beneath all that was the nausea and loss I still carried from my childhood, the bloated distance between my sister and myself, how I could barely speak with either of my parents without feeling the desire to vomit great sobs of rage over the phone lines.

One weekday morning, I climbed aboard a 5-Fulton MUNI bus, which ran directly past my apartment in the Western Addition, and rode straight west out to Ocean Beach. It was a sunny day in San Francisco, blue skies and a softness like something friendly in the air. The beach was quiet when I walked down the dunes, just a few joggers and tourists sharing the sand with me. I took off my shoes (in January: amazing!) and walked barefoot in the low tide surf.

I sang to myself one of the songs I'd learned at Glide, a big, social-justice-centered Methodist church in the middle of San Francisco's Tenderloin district—"Pass me not, oh gentle Savior/hear my humble cry." Even though I didn't feel worthy of the air I was breathing, sometimes the songs helped me slide underneath that feeling of shame to something—*gentler.*

I sang quietly and walked along the grey-sand beach, raw with new infatuation, devastated over my breakup, ashamed of my mother and ashamed of myself. I began to cry. I wondered what gave me the right to enjoy that sun, that beach, that surf, as fucked up as I was. I wondered who I thought I was to think I deserved any joy at all. The power of that hostile voice inside was vicious, persistent, and so very familiar.

And the thought came to me suddenly—with my feet in the cool foamy water, the day opening itself around me, seagulls and sandpipers digging for mole crabs in the wet sand, and me trying to avoid stepping on the tiny translucent jellyfish that washed up with each shallow wave—that I might not be perfect *or* monstrous. It occurred to me that in fact it just might be the case that I was *both* flawed *and* just fine.

The water washed its chilly salt across my toes, swept away my footprints. The sun reflected in a blur on the wet sand. I thought, *Maybe that's what it is to be human.*

Maybe I don't have to be a monster. I don't have to be the worst ever, just because I'm not and can't be perfect. I can *just be human.* I can be deeply flawed and still a good person, still ok, still acceptable, still someone worthy of love.

This was an entirely new idea to me and I hated it.

I cried harder while I continued walking along the beach. I didn't *want* to be flawed like a regular old human. I didn't want my friends to look at me and know things about me that I thought I was successfully hiding. I didn't want blind spots and tendencies to repeat all the same stories and behaviors—sure, I did those things, but I didn't want anyone to *know* about it. I came to understand that I'd never been as masked as I'd believed I'd been. I felt overly exposed and utterly ridiculous. I kept on singing to myself, choking up in the sweet, briny air.

Have you seen a Möbius strip? It's one of those things kids get shown when adults want to demonstrate the concept of infinity, and paradox. They take a long strip of construction paper between two hands, twist it with one hand, and then tape the ends of the paper together so that you have a loop with a flip in it. Then they say, *Now look: if you drop your pen at any point and start making a line along the length of the paper, you'll end up drawing on both sides of the strip without lifting your pen—how is that possible?*

I remember being delighted by Möbius strips when I first discovered them, and made bunches of them, amazed every time that the strip of recycled paper from my dad's old dot matrix printer had a line that traversed the whole surface of the paper; I never had to pick up the pen to get to the other side—this two-sided piece of paper had turned into a loop that appeared to only have one side. *How was that possible?*

Sometimes our new topologies just don't make logical sense to our old eyes, our old ways of thinking. We have to meet the paradox of ourselves with curiosity. Wonder and delight aren't always easy when the boundaries appear to have moved indefinitely and I'm walking and walking on this new path with no end in sight, and those footprints next to me on the sand look an awful lot like my own. Haven't I been here before, in this place of confusion and loss? Will anything ever make sense again?

•§•

I didn't lose all my self-hatred in that moment of revelation on the beach. Still, I breathed into this complicated new idea: I could be imperfect and still worthy of life, of joy and growth and pleasure. I believe this is about the time when I became aware of the possibility of *life itself* as a practice.

The word *practice* comes from a Greek word for practical (as opposed to theoretical); doing rather than *thinking about* doing. At the time, the only thing I did with enough regularity to be thought of as a practice was write—besides drink cheap red wine, watch bad movies and remind myself how terrible I was, I mean. I had no spiritual practice and no physical practice or exercise habits besides wandering the hills of the city to and from the cafes where I wrote.

As I walked on that morning city beach, avoiding the glistening balls of tiny beached jellyfish and on the lookout for intact sand dollars, I felt how hard it was for me to accept the idea that I was human, that maybe I wasn't any more terrible (*or* altruistic and good) than anyone else. (I wondered whether my ex-wife would agree with me, or think I was just letting myself off the hook with some new survivor philosophy that gave me license to shit all over the people who loved me.) Like many survivors (and many writers and other artists, too), I had bought into the idea that I was, alternately, truly more evolved than and superior to those around me (able to see all of their issues, with vivid, insightful clarity) and wholly despicable (capable of deeply bad behavior in order to survive my stepfather's violence, and not worth pushing to get out of bed in the morning since all I was going to do was end up drunk on the couch at midnight, hating myself for watching reruns of *Friends* instead of writing).

Who was I if I wasn't wholly good or wholly bad, if I wasn't perfect or evil? What if I was a regular old person, who did some good in the world and who was also capable of inflicting deep pain on those I loved? Who was I if I was worth loving even with blind spots and unacknowledged prejudices, even though I wasn't going to save the world or all battered women or just my mother, even though I wasn't perfectly selfless, even if my masks hadn't actually worked as well as I'd convinced myself that they had?

In those moments on that beach, I sang as I walked on and I sang as I washed over with shame and embarrassment at being a regular old human being. I couldn't make eye contact with anyone. Then I laughed in delight—maybe I was having a small breakdown. I filled suddenly with joy that I *got* to be human, that I *was* part of the human race, that what my stepfather had done to me, and what I'd had to do to survive it, hadn't made me an abomination.

I saw that this idea would take some getting used to, would take some practicing—and then I understood that there wasn't any part of life that wasn't, that didn't take practice.

•§•

Ten or so years later I am still practicing. I still struggle with those old, embedded (and common) ideas that I have to be either perfect or perfectly awful. I succumb to the crazy-making story that our sinner-or-saint mentality trains us into, and it takes deep breathing and a recommitment to practice to remember that I get to be neither of these things, that I get to be both imperfect and ok/good enough/human.

Someone explained to me, years ago, that flying an airplane is mostly course correction. The pilot decides where she wants to go, and starts heading in that direction. But then an unexpected wind blows the plane off course, and she has to adjust the instruments to come back to the original trajectory. Then she's got to veer around a storm; the pilot doesn't beat herself up for not being able to just fly straight through thunderheads—she just gently steers her plane back toward her final destination. Hit a bump in the Gulf Stream? No problem—she rides out the turbulence, then sets her vessel back on course. Start out heading forward, veer left, come back, veer right, come back, stop and stare out into space, come back. Weave, notice, redirect.

For me, the practice of retraining myself to believe or even allow the idea that I'm neither a selfless angel nor self-centered monster looks a lot like course correction. I'm going along pretty well for awhile, but then I hit a bump in the road: I get triggered during a conversation with my lover, I get a hostile catcall while walking up 14th St., a therapy session touches on an especially ugly memory.

Suddenly I find I haven't moved my body in a week (unless you count walking from the couch to the kitchen cabinet for more chocolate), nor have I consumed a green vegetable, nor have I made time for that call to my best friend in Atlanta (though I've surely made time to flop back on the couch for reruns of *Law and Order: SVU*).

At this point, the most familiar and comfortable thing for me to do is to shame myself for this backsliding. It doesn't take much; all I have to do is tune into that flow of vitriol that the censor/perpetrator in my head is constantly pumping out.

Course correction gives me a different option. Rather than beating myself up, I could take a step back, figuratively speaking, and notice what I've been doing, give myself a break, and tap myself gently back in the direction I'd rather be heading.

Course correction, in this case, looks like harm reduction, small steps rather than broad pronouncements and overhauls. Maybe I don't have to turn off the TV immediately, but maybe I could take a break after this episode is over; I don't have to change everything about how I'm feeding myself, maybe I could see if my body might be hungry for something other than Top Ramen and dry boxed cereal; I don't have to start writing for eight hours a day, but maybe I could write a few pages.

This is real work, and it's slow. I hate that it's slow. It looks like a shabbily-made patchwork quilt, which isn't much for anyone else to look at, but has within it bits of all the selves I've ever been, plus bits of wisdom and care from those beloveds who've chosen to walk with me for any length of time on this path—and, if I let it, it sure does keep me warm.

Self-care as human nature

What does it mean to you to be human? What if you are neither an angelic victim nor a monster? What if you are fucked up (in that human way we all are) and still worthy of life and love and joy? What would that mean? Take ten minutes, and drop into this wondering on the page. Follow those words wherever they take you—and be sweet to yourself after, ok?

trust the process

I have begun to forgive myself for being human, which includes forgiving myself for—or else just acknowledging—that I couldn't do anything differently from how I did it. I don't know about you, but I am so prone to magical thinking and fantasy that it's a major growth step when I can just meet things as they are, when I can meet my history as it is, without getting lost in everything I should have done, should have said, should have been.

 I couldn't stop my stepfather from abusing me, my sister, or my mother. I couldn't heal faster. I couldn't be someone else. I have been as present as I could be in these last twenty years, and writing has been at the heart of that effort to presence. I have written what I saw when I could see it, in myself and in relationships—at least most of the time.

This realization emerged, at least in part, out of my writing practice. The work to accept it, to actually and finally forgive myself (is that ever done?) for being no more and no less than I am, is work I take to the notebook as well. I've come to trust what writing practice can do in my life, even though I can't control it, even though I don't know where it will lead me.

You've heard the phrase *Trust the process*. What does it mean for you?

I've heard it in social change organizations' volunteer orientations and anti-racism trainings; over and over during grad school; at 12-step meetings. Group leaders tend to ask or invite the people they're working with to "trust the process" when they're accustomed to meeting resistance, when they expect someone in the room to demand proof, to ask for data, to explain what's going to happen and how it's going to work. But when it comes to questioning or shifting aspects of ourselves that we're invested in and protective of, whether we know it or not (say, white privilege), rational explanation isn't going to ease the fears of those about to undergo this training, and demand for such detailed explication, in fact, tends to (is *intended* to) derail the process entirely. Those who have developed those training or transformational systems know this; they've experienced the change themselves, have been broken open, have been vulnerable and angry and scared, and have come out the other side a little softer, open-hearted, and fiercely protective advocates of the process. They ask you to trust the process you're about to undergo. They serve you by not answering all of your nitpicky questions or capitulating to your diversionary tactics. They're going to give you the gift of discomfort that comes with breaking open, the gift of joy on the other side of that suffering. Birth always hurts, and is itself a process that is best trusted rather than controlled.

•§•

For me, when it comes to this transformative writing practice, *Trust the process* means opening the notebook, setting the timer for twenty minutes, and dropping in, following whatever twists and turns the writing throws at me or invites me to follow. It means writing the sentence that looks like a lie, writing the nonsense word, writing into that dream that I wanted to forget, or playing with spiders on the page. It means suddenly finding myself writing about the kitchen of the third house I lived in, the one in town, after the one in the country, the one I lived in when I first walked to school by myself, that had a tiny backyard lined on one side with tiger lilies, with violets on another, and a rusting swing set in the middle. I write about the back staircase that led to the backyard, but then I can't quite remember the kitchen—when I go in there, up those stairs, I always end up in the apartment in Omaha that my mom moved to when she was finally done with school and Lincoln and my dad. I just keep going. Maybe I had the idea that I'd write some simple and pretty blog post and instead, writing nudges me down a shady acorn side street, shows me antique stores, old broken-down furniture, the back side of my dad's office downtown, the one filled with smoke where all the Lincoln Public School administrators worked and my dad took notes on memos with a red felt-tipped pen; maybe I use all the old words, the ones I never heard anyone say but Grandma, and that was only when she was talking on the phone to her best friend who lived a couple of farms away.

Trust the process is another way of saying *Trust yourself,* but someone somewhere figured out that we're more likely to trust something external rather than ourselves, and so we tell ourselves to trust the *process:* that thing acting on or through us from out there somewhere.

Trust the process means we push into writing about that afternoon in the garage when we were six—and when we feel ready to stop writing about it, we stop. Stopping when we need to stop is part of trusting the process, too.

Trust the process means listening to the calculus of our instincts and our desires, that interweave of push and pull, the psyche that wants to protect us and the life that wants to burst us open and free. One day we'll choose to write about the dog we loved with all our heart and was taken away from us, and we will have fat tears and throaty sobs on the page (right in the middle of the neighborhood cafe, if you're like me), because it's finally our turn to mourn. The next day we will write about an irritation with a coworker—we'll think we're staying closer to the surface, but both writes take us under our skin and reveal the flank and tendon and tenor of who we are.

Trust the process means you try to get the ego/editor out of writing's way. You step over and write through the roadblocks that say *you can't write that:* someone might get mad, or hurt, or will tell you it didn't go like that or demand to know how you can write what you don't even remember or will want to know who you think you are to call yourself a writer? Trust the process means listening to your instinct, your curiosity. Who can say why a particular image arose for you this morning or in response to a prompt? Your job is not to analyze or dissect or *vet* the image—your job is to write it down and then follow where it leads.

Trust the process means understanding that there are good writing days and hard writing days and writing on the hard writing days anyway, even when the writing feels like it goes through molasses and sandpaper before reaching the page. Even on the days when all the joy is leached from your heart, you set your timer for twenty minutes and go, rewarding yourself after with music you can sing along to in the shower or on your way to work.

Trust the process means not trying to tell writing where it has to go or how it has to get there. Maybe you are clear about a subject—you've got an article or an essay or a poem due and you've got this *thing* to write about, but it's not your job to shape the writing while it's emerging. Instead, you get to start writing about *X* and then follow writing wherever it wants to lead you on the topic of *X*. This might look like a stream-of-consciousness journal entry or a poem, a brainstorm/mindmap or an exchange you overheard at yesterday's staff meeting. There are innumerable associative twists and turns down the neuronal forestry inside our creative selves; you could write about the same subject five days in a row and come up with five entirely different pieces.

Trust the process means practice. Means keep the pen moving. Means don't judge or edit, just write. Means do it again tomorrow and the tomorrow after that. Means look on your creative brilliance with appreciation, curiosity, wonder. Means understand you are meeting the layers of your inside self and they are all worthy of praise. Means keep trying, keep going, begin again, begin again.

Trust your process of self-care

What would it mean to trust yourself as a survivor, to trust exactly the process by which you've survived, by which you are surviving still—your instincts, your intuition, your coping mechanisms, the precise calculus of your recovery? What if you are worth trusting? Give yourself ten minutes to dive into this possibility.

conclusions

begin again

It's not too late.

Begin again. There is still time to do so much of what we wanted from this life.

It feels this simple: Today I don't mourn all the time I haven't spent writing, the books I haven't yet written, the fact that I'll never be a famous "younger author," all the years I spent grieving instead of developing my craft and portfolio. Today I hold hands with all the selves I've ever been and I'm grateful we made it this far. I'm grateful we lived long enough to get to *right here*, to get so fully into this body and these words, to get to peel off layers of mask and persona and pretense, to find our way into this place of possibility and healing.

Grateful, goddamnit, to begin again.

This is what I want to say: There's time—there's ten minutes today to write, there's an hour to take out the notebook and draw or play in words or jot down notes for a song. There's a half-hour for a walk, there's a place for your creative experimentation and discovery. Yes, a lot of time has passed. Yes, there are days and years gone. But we still have time.

Some people's journeys went faster than ours; they were able to get to the work of their dreams more quickly. There are people who underwent "worse" experiences than I did who have written their books, painted their paintings, made their work already a reality. Me, I took the time and the path that I took. Today I am sanguine about that. Today I'm not wallowing in regrets. Today I am tender with gratitude: we made it here. Today it's not too late. Today we get to begin again. We get to do what we can today, and then begin again, again, tomorrow.

(Tomorrow I may not be so sanguine. I almost surely won't. We'll have to wait and see.)

Still, you know what a big deal this is, right? To feel hope? To feel peace? I can hear the morning bird outside singing a today song. *We made it. We get this life. We begin.*

•§•

At the open notebook, at the blank page. It's morning again, and we start over, again. Even if we have been writing for years, still: every morning is a beginning again. Every morning we're afraid we might not be able to do it, or we're afraid nothing will come. Every time we're confronted with that space of blankness that opens out behind our fingers, behind our eyes, behind the parts of our physical selves that do the writing, the places from which the writing emerges into and through us.

Some mornings, the writing is a slog. Some days I don't find the flow, the writing never takes off, keeps clay feet stuck to the ground. On those days, doing the writing is just "checking the box," like my beloved says—getting it done to get it done, to keep that promise I made to myself. Afterwards I stand up and stretch and make toast and take the dog out to play with her ball and know I can try again tomorrow.

Some days I feel as crappy after writing as I did before writing. It doesn't happen so often anymore, but when it does, I try not to blame *writing*—or myself. Some days are harder than others. When I started in this practice, I wanted writing always to save me. I dug in, wrote hard, excavated and cried and raged at the page. I wrote all the way out to my edges. I wrote what I was terrified of, felt lost by, abandoned by, and what I desperately desired. My life changed, grew, bettered—and still I struggled with addiction, depression, PTSD, difficult relationships, loneliness and isolation and lots and lots of magical thinking. Writing practice wasn't a fix-all elixir. Writing practice helped me immeasurably— and I've needed other self-care methods, too, while learning how to be in my body, how to do relationships, how to trust.

If the writing is hard one day, that's not a failing. Check the box, live your day, write again tomorrow.

•§•

This is where we begin: at the self that's still healing, at the self that still aches for acceptance, at the parts of our own story still being written inside of us.

This is where we begin: at the grieving places, the voices in us that still keen, the small death songs our hands have never been able to sing. We write them down. We write down what we could not mourn when we were younger: lost friendships, stolen dogs, missteps, old wantings, adults who could have helped us but were not allowed to, or couldn't, or wouldn't.

This is where we begin: in the deep joy, in the play, in the silliness, in the desire, in the word wonder that struck us when we first began to move pencil across blue-lined pages. We begin again in that early delight: the fact we can shape out of only *words* a thing that didn't exist before. We begin in wonder, in longing, and with hope.

There is always a beginning. I've facilitated workshops for fifteen years, practiced writing alone for more than twenty, and I still feel like a beginner. I want answers and clarity, and the one thing (possibly the only thing) I'm sure about is this: we have to keep starting over. We have to decide to pick up the pen, again. We have to open the notebook to a blank page or the next empty line, take a deep breath, and write. We have to step into the mystery that is this process, the alchemy of want and haunting, language and upbringing, creative mastery and deep curiosity, healing and play.

I will spend a lifetime seeking the language for what it is that happens when we who have survived a traumatic experience sit ourselves down in a writing place and begin to let our words flow, openly, authentically, and without censorship— when we write whatever wants to be written, however it wants to be written. I keep writing. I step in again, I remove my armor again, I meet the confusion and fear again. I trust that whatever words come will be the right ones for the moment. There is a logic to this practice, this process, and it's a logic born of the underground, the current and network of interconnected pathways and experience that shapes our entire lives. It's a logic we can't see or explicate, a logic that tethers itself to something intricate and unconsciously knowing.

This is how we write what matters, how we drop in deeper and deeper until we find language for the thing that resists, that squirms away from the pen. This is how we stay with the writing anyway. What matters most is writing into the scene and feeling a memory or idea that has risen up for you to follow with your words, is putting it down as exactly as it comes to you, which may not be what you thought you were supposed to be writing about. What matters most is the relationship between you and your writer's instinct—telling that inside voice we call muse or creative drive that you will show up for it, you will follow where it leads, even if you are frightened or angry or certain that what you're writing is shit *and* will make everyone you love hate you. What matters most is writing it anyway, is writing back into a relationship with your intuition, your erotic and poetic instincts, the place of love in you that is and always has been about *yes* and life and wonder. That voice in you that never abandoned or betrayed you, and couldn't. That sense not of self-preservation but of self-implosion. The deeply creative and organic instinct.

The creative process requires trust and a capacity to get lost in something both inside and outside our sense of self. We unbecome when we are writing well, when we are *in flow* (as social psychologist Mihaly Csikszentmihalyi calls it)—we are the story, we are the poem, we are the memory, we are the words emerging onto the page or screen.

This sort of unbecoming is almost impossible when we busy surviving violence, when we are still undergoing trauma, when we have to work so hard to hold on to any sense of self, when we can't imagine being something other than what and who the abuser demands of us.

What matters most is returning to the heart of the story, beginning again to see who we are and could be, allowing the story to redefine us repeatedly, releasing old narrative when it no longer serves us. What a transformative writing practice can show us is how to implode into our own joy and possibility and multiplicity, how to be all the words and metaphors, how to constellate and particulate, how to emerge from broken both very small and very, very large.

Dancer and choreographer Martha Graham said, "There is a vitality, a life force, an energy, a quickening that is translated through you into action. And because there is only one you in all time, this expression is unique. And if you block it, it will never exist through any other medium. The world will not have it. It is not your business to determine how good it is, nor how valuable, nor how it compares with other expressions. It is your business to keep it yours clearly and directly, to keep the channel open." You say to yourself, *I'm not creative, I'm not a writer*, but the truth is that you are a generative *universe* and we need your description of your experience of this lifetime—of trauma and loss, of desire and healing, of resilience and resistance, of joy and poetry and freedom—if the quilt of our human knowing is to be whole. No one can write your life but you.

In trusting that the words will come, we are trusting ourselves, and we are trusting something other: whatever it is that delivers us the words. I don't have a language for that other; let's stay with mystery, or intuition, or human resilience— regardless, whenever we sit down to write our stories or our poems or our journal entries or our fiction, we invite ourselves into or alongside that other. We knock on the door and we hope again that we will be admitted. Sitting down is the knocking. Lifting the pen is the knocking. Writing even though we don't know what we're going to say, or how we're going to say it, is the knocking. This is how we gain admittance into that place of other, that deepness in ourselves: we begin again today.

Start over: Begin again

Take twenty minutes. Begin writing from the phrase "This is what I believe..." (and change that *I* as you wish: This is what she believes, what they believe, what we—whatever works best in the moment). Write for three minutes. Then begin again, from the same phrase, "This is what I believe..." Do that twice more, so that you have four beginnings. Pause, take a breath, and then write whatever has come up for you in the process of these starting-overs, or about beginning again, or whatever else comes for you.

conclusion: something in you is opening

All I remember is the time we first gathered around this fire, snuck our way through the worry and possibility into new words and voices, when we stepped across our tightropes of fear and walked straight into an empty rent-by-the-hour room in the new gay center downtown. We pulled our chairs in a circle and hadn't yet spilled our hunger all down the fronts of our shirts for everyone else to see. We were risking more than we were aware of in that moment, when we pulled a pen out of our back pockets or dug one out of our bags or snuck one off the table and we set it to the blank page and we said, "This is what I think writing about sex can do." All I can think of is the time I first sat in the circle of survivors ready to make something new out of words and longing. We lifted our pens up off the page after seven minutes of scratching and scrawling, just seven minutes and the whole world was changed because these folks had hope enough to write an answer down and then the brazen, flying-fuck kind of faith enough to open their mouths and let those same scrawled words come pushing up through heart and lungs, formed by lips and teeth, into the circle we'd created. We fly into the words, we jump and groan into the flames, we lift our hands back up, sticky and sweaty, and we get to show off yes the magic that we are made of. (2008)

This work of transformation, of healing, takes such a long time. You never know you're succeeding in the moment of change; you just know you want to stay alive. The metamorphosis arises out of subtle shifts that throw us open. How do we track the tiny changes over time, discern the calculus of our healing?

The truth is that the work is both immediate and slow. As soon as you say the words for the first time—*I was raped; I think something happened to me; I never felt right around him*—something changes. We begin to take hold of a new way of being in the world. As soon as you pick up the pen, something changes. It is both a tiny and an enormous change. Someone told you you were not meant to have words but you take your words anyway. You put those words down on the page. Just some. Just a few. Or you fill a notebook the first time out of the gate. It doesn't matter—you take a step.

It may not feel like a step. It may feel like a stumble. It may feel like a fall, a plunge, a drowning. It may be the sort of overwhelm that requires three packages of cookies to assuage. It's still a step. Something in us fissures. We put on our blinker and pull off the main road, the known road—we say *yes* to the invitation into the darkness and wonder. We don't write at first because we think we're going to get better. We write because we think we're *never* going to get better. We write because we hurt. We write because we love story and we want to imagine ourselves somewhere else. We write because we love the feel of the pen, we like the click of one word up right against the next. We write because the journal is the only safe place we know. We write because nothing makes any sense anymore. We write because it's the only place we can have things in order—or the only place where we can be out of order: disordered, broken, confused, out of control.

It comes slowly. The garden metaphor is too apt just to leave alone. You put a seed in the garden and you wait. You tend the place where you think life might be. And the green comes. Whether we do specifically healing-focused work or not, whether we go to therapy or learn to love our violated bodies or find words for what was done to us and what we did to get through it—we still change. We grow. We build a life: we find something that feels like home, we create connection with others or we don't, we find work, we are of service to others, we may over-indulge in our coping mechanisms. We heal in some ways just by virtue of our choosing to live. Healing and transformation are facts of life. We cannot help but change. It takes work *not* to change, though sometimes we try hard, struggling to be the self we were before, not willing to recognize that we have already changed.

American movies, like fairy tales, often end in the immediate aftermath of a mountaintop moment—the confrontation and revelation, the awareness and proclamation of love, or the moment when the main character taps into that hinted-at but heretofore distrusted or ignored capacity to be their full self. We like to witness the revelation. We like the adrenaline rush of a *yes*. This cinematic mythology, though, leads us to believe that transformation actually manifests in this way in our lives. The movies don't show the work of the day *after* the revelation or climax—they don't show us what happily ever after actually looks like. They don't show how we have to wake up every morning and choose again, begin *again*. How those around us struggle when we change, want us to go back to being who we were before. How, for awhile, in the middle of the process, we can feel like we're walking around in someone else's skin, in someone else's life.

The work of choosing to live and thrive in the aftermath of sexual violence is slow and beautiful and often utterly unwitnessed. It's the work of a seed unfurling its breath underground. We're paying attention to the weeds and leaf mould, we're attending to everything broken and bothered above ground and we don't see how all of that stuff nurtures the soil and occupies our attention while the change in us shakes its roots free and risks sending up a new leaf.

The point is that you may write and write and feel like nothing's happening. You may write about trauma in a space of support and caring, feel welcomed and witnessed and heard, and still go home to the same old rooms and the same old bed and the same old fears of the same old life, and wonder why you are still feeling so bad.

Something in you is opening—sort of like that tectonic shift way beneath the earth's crust that we humans on the surface don't notice until the earthquake. We look up one day and find that all the furniture of our lives has shifted, or just doesn't fit anymore, because the center of us has been rearranged. This is the gift of practice, dedication, and attentiveness, when we keep at it even when we don't know why.

This writing practice, above all others I've tried, has most often initiated and nurtured the lasting changes in my life. On the page I can be in unknowing conversation with the thing in me that is waiting to be born, with the site of transformation, with the seed and sprout and soil; I can be rainstorm and earthworm, churning up the compost, finding what can most nourish the deepest layers of myself.

Writing practice can familiarize us with the unknown, remind us that there is still much for us to be surprised by. And it can give us a way to trace the trajectory of our healing and transformation—if we reread what we have written, it's like looking through photographs of a garden site, from pre-planting to full flourish and flower to harvest and fallow and reworking the soil to seeding again. We can read where we have come from, read what's changed. We may feel no different in ourselves, but when we look at what we write, we begin to trace themes, contradictions, subtle shifts, questions and (often unconscious) answers; even in fiction, we can watch this change take place as our characters develop and grow.

Day to day it can feel like nothing happens. Writing can itself be the process we use to observe change and motion over time—with this practice, taken up again daily and consistently, we trace how far we've come, and where it is we would like to go.

Can we use the practice to see what's coming? What I've been able to predict is more surprise, more curiosity, and more openness. What we can predict is both a greater confidence in self and a greater comfort with the unknown. That we can hover steady with the skill of bees—searching, feeding, defending, resting, and beginning, again and again and again. Always in motion and always at the beginning. What a shift.

•§•

William Stafford wrote a poem entitled "For my young friends who are afraid," which I've used many times as a prompt in writing groups.

What I want to say to friends, young and otherwise, who are afraid, is that our writing—and the stories of our trauma, our bodies, our lives, our possibility—will change. The night sweats happen and then they are gone. The same nightmare drags you through your sleep for years and then its terrifying physics and grammar begin to change around the dreaming you: suddenly you can speak, you can move, you can run, you can yell *No!* when before the only sound you could push from your lips was a moaning cry that woke you and your lover at midnight.

You see from those dreamtime changes that you are healing, your seams are coming together. It's an interminable process. It will seem never-ending.

Feel every minute of it, let the loss and terror burn through and be done with you. Someday it will be done with you. Though maybe not in the way that you'd hope.

This is a terrible thing that I'm recommending, I know.

Write it all down, all of it, even the stuff you know can't be testified to in a court of law but that bulges under your tongue: better to spit the lies they fed onto the page you rather than swallow them. Now and again you can flip back through your record, read how you have changed over two weeks, two months, ten years. Build a bridge to your whole unsullied soul, locked safe inside you, with those words. Write out all your complications, the ways you are always in conflict, the jealousies and inconsistencies and fears.

Don't show it to anybody. Not at first.

Be more afraid of finding out what loss looks like from the inside out, be more afraid of losing the ability to write before you have recorded all that you are, than you are of the words themselves. This is you creating your own rabbit trail. Hansel and Gretel aren't throwing down any bread crumbs or stones for us. It's the only lily-pad-hopping way forward I know. Settle into this skin of confusion with your pen in hand. Stitch time out of your day just for your words.

And then feed yourself well. Visit the doctor now and again. Call the good friends, the ones who leave you alone when you're writing, the ones who don't try to fix it when you cry, and see if they want to go to the beach with you. Put down the pen and pack up a lunch, get on the 5-Fulton without a book and watch through the bus's grimy windows as the grey concrete of the city gives way to the contagious riot of green in Golden Gate Park. Get out at the last stop and walk yourself into a thick, salty sea breeze. Feed the tides your bare feet, take your friend's dry, warm hand, hold the seagull's cries in your newfound ears.

appendices

appendices

appendix a: sample syllabus for 8-week survivors writing group

The Writing Ourselves Whole survivors writing group met on Monday nights for many years. We generally had time for two twenty-minute "writes" per evening, except on the first night, when we took some time to get to know one another, then opened with a short, introductory write for seven minutes, followed by a longer (ten-to-twelve minute) write.

In-between writing and feedback time, we break for tea, snacks, and some good conversation. We close every meeting with a poem that we read aloud as a group.

For an eight-week workshop, I generally worked to build us up gently into a place where we know and trust one another's writing voices, diving into deeper and riskier writing each week. This is just one example of the sorts of exercises or themes I've used over an eight-week period:

Week 1. Beginnings: Introducing the method and introducing us to one another: *Sample intro exercise (something gentle): My favorite place to write; a book I loved when I was twelve.*

Week 2. Coming into body: *Sample exercise: Write a love letter to your body, or to a specific part of your body; the tone might be funny, apologetic, serious, adoring, sad, or all of the above and more!*

Week 3. Myths & truths: *Sample exercise: Create a list of myths about survivors. Select one and write about it as though it weren't true, or write about its opposite: "This is what they say about me, but I…"*

Week 4. Fearless words: *Sample exercise: Offer two fragments: "I told you what I'm afraid to tell you…" and "These are the secrets of my body…"*

Week 5. Spirit: *Sample exercise: Create a list of deities or manifestations of Spirit: imagine your narrator engaged in a conversation with one of these manifestations, beginning with the phrase "I always wanted to tell you…"*

Week 6. Root Story: *Sample exercise: Begin with a brief centering/embodying breathing exercise. Then imagine yourself or your character in a time before now, and hear someone speaking on the other side of a closed door. Who is speaking? Where is the narrator? What time of year is it? What happens next?*

Week 7. Role models / Reaching back through the fire: *Sample exercise: Listen to Sweet Honey in the Rock's "Ella's Song" ("We who believe in freedom cannot rest / we who believe in freedom cannot rest until it comes") and write as you are inspired about your own s/heroes, and ways in which you have been s/heroes to others.*

Week 8. Feeding the writer's spirit: *Sample exercise: After a brief centering exercise, write a letter to your artist-selves from your muse.*

appendix b: exercises to spark more writing

How to use this list: Scan through until your eyes catch on a particular prompt. Early in your practice, set a timer for ten minutes; you can increase the time as you get more comfortable letting the words flow. Write exactly as you are drawn to write: try not to stop or censor yourself. Don't worry about whether you "do it right"—if your writing veers away from the original prompt, just let yourself go there! Try to release any blame, shame, or guilt around what you do or don't end up writing. Just write it. Transgress, transgress. Let the words come all the way into and through your body and out onto the page.

Generate lists: With list prompts, you end up generating lots of possible ideas for writing. Choose the list topic and spend a few moments just letting ideas flow onto the page. Then you read over the list and notice which of the items is calling to you—let that be the place where your writing begins. If you get stuck, you can always choose another item on your list and begin again. List-making is one of my favorite types of exercises to do with a group. I suggest a general topic, and group members throw out specific examples of that topic, which we write on a flip chart or whiteboard. We get the creative juices flowing with the creation of the list, and the group has the benefit of everyone's ideas when getting into the writing part of the exercise: folks can either write from an item they suggested, or run with another member's suggestion if that speaks to them more deeply.

Lists can also be written privately in individual notebooks—that way, folks also go home with a whole bunch of prompt ideas they can write about later.

List topics:

- What my body loves / What my body doesn't love

- This is what I remember / This is what I don't remember / This is what I wish I remembered / This is what I wish I didn't remember

- This is what I felt / This is what I didn't feel

- What I learned / What I didn't learn – What they taught us / What they didn't teach us

- Things I miss / Things I don't miss

- Sounds we cannot hear (rain forming, sap rising, eggs hatching, elevator in the next building, etc.)

- Five things I fear / Five things that bring me comfort (two lists)

- List of ten historical characters – put one in dialogue with one of your parents

- List of six remarkable things I've done

- Make a list of the different jobs you've had (paid and unpaid, both). Leave a couple of lines between each job, where you can write something you learned at that job, whether you still use that skill or not. Let yourself choose one of these jobs as your starting point: describe how you came to have that job, what you liked about it, what you hated about it, or anything else.

- Three things I wish people knew about me / Three things I wish people didn't know

- Tastes I love / Tastes I hate

- A different sort of list: Write down seven action verbs with an -ing ending (such as *running, chasing, sitting, breathing*). Then, in front of each word, write the phrase "Safety is like..." or "Healing is like..." Use one of those sentences to begin your writing.

Begin with a sentence fragment: We can "steal" an opening from another writer, and then take our own piece in a completely new direction. The following are phrases I've used often as prompts for my own writing and in group (if they are unattributed, they're phrases that, as far as I can remember, I made up):

- If I told you what I'm afraid to tell you...

- What matters is...

- These are the secrets of my body...

- I'm supposed to want... / I'm not supposed to want...

- What I really wanted to say is...

- I'm not supposed to tell you ...

- No one wants to hear about...

- Have you forgotten me? (her/us)

- Do you have any questions?

- What I never told you was...

- I (she/they) don't believe...

- What kind of times are these when...

- We could have been mistaken for...

- This is what I believe...

- These are the stories inside my skin...

- It was her/his idea...

- Someone ought to write about...

- He looked all right to me...

- My body remembers...

- Who gave you permission to survive?

- That was the year...

- This is what I want my words to do to you (Eve Ensler)

- Tell me, what is it you plan to do/with your one wild and precious life? (Mary Oliver)

- Change, when it comes, cracks everything open (Dorothy Allison)

- The rim of the sky is on fire and the flames are rising (Annie G. Rogers, *A Shining Affliction*)

- On the book of my body lies the dust of... (Lynne Gravestock)

- I came to explore the wreck... (Adrienne Rich)

- Only justice can stop a curse (Alice Walker)

- Creation often needs two hearts (Marilou Awiakta)

- You do not have to be good (Mary Oliver)

- Skin had hope/ that's what skin does (Naomi Shihab Nye)

- Long ago I was wounded (Louise Glück)

- Who are we but the stories we tell ourselves, about ourselves, and believe? (Scott Turow)

- A woman (man/person) who carries a secret is an exhausted woman (man/person) (Clarissa Pinkola Estes, *Women Who Run With the Wolves*)

- You were once wild here. Don't let them tame you (Isadora Duncan)

- There is no greater agony than bearing an untold story inside you (Maya Angelou)

- What are we but our own story? (Terry McCabe)

Other prompts:

What would your body say to you, if it spoke to you?

Write to a younger you. What do you want to tell yourself then? What would you have wanted to know? Or have a younger you write to you now.

If you had only one more day to write, what would you write?

Write about or to a part of your body you are proud of, a part of your body you feel grateful toward, or a part of your body you feel apologetic toward.

Write a time you learned something new about your body.

What self-care practices feel *radical* to you right now? What do you do to take care of yourself today that a younger self would not have been able to imagine?

How would you *like* to be able to care for yourself, if money and time were no object.

Describe a first day at school (elementary, college, training program)—or first day at a new job, or first time riding a bike or first time tasting pickles or... *Firsts* are great to work with.

Write a person explaining to a new (or old) lover how they want to be touched. They may want to focus on one particular part of their body, or one particular sort of touch. Begin with the phrase, "This is how I want you to touch me."

Write a time you got in trouble, and shouldn't have.

Write two lists next to each other: one list of ten adjectives, one list of ten emotions. (After you write the first list, cover it with your hand or a piece of paper). When you're done, choose one of the pairs of words and use them to fill in the phrase, "I'm standing at the corner of ___ and ___"

(*One of mine once read, "I'm standing at the corner of pink and devastating."*)

Begin by writing everything that can be found in one of your character's private spaces: purse/backpack, medicine cabinet, junk drawer, glove compartment.

What are your ten rules for writers?

Write about a time you failed. Write it again as a success.

Write about a place where your body (or his/her/hir/their body) is comfortable: is this place inside or outside? Is this place "real" or fictional? What do you do there? What don't you do there?

Scars: What are our scars? The ones on the body? The ones on our souls? The ones on our spirit? Introduce us to a scar – tell us its story.

Poems to use as prompts (*some of my favorites from the last fifteen years*):

- Useful Advice (Catherine Tufariello)

- Where I'm From (George Ella Lyons)

- Where I'm From (Willie Perdomo)

- Scars (Lucille Clifton)

- Wild Geese (Mary Oliver)

- What I Save (Cheryl Savageau)

- The healing time (Pesha Gertler)

- Inside (Linda Hogan)

- Being a person (William Stafford)

- How to eat a poem (Eve Merriam)

- The Last Time I Slept in This Bed (Sara Peters)

- From out of the cave (Joyce Sutphen)

- Equinox (Joy Harjo)

- Things to Think (Robert Bly)

- If I Sing (Martin Jude Farawell)

- Fairy Tale (Sheila Nickerson)

- Affirmation (Assata Shakur)

- Kindnesses (Naomi Shihab Nye)

- Break the Mirror (Nanao Sakaki)

- Advice (Heather Davis)

- Prayer (Lisa Colt)

- won't you celebrate with me (Lucille Clifton)

- Motherroot (Marilou Awiakta)

- New Bones (Lucille Clifton)

- Two Countries (Naomi Shihab Nye)

- Every Woman Deserves a Poem (River Malcolm)

- I Knew I'd Sing (Heather McHugh)

- Girl (Eve Alexandra)

- Lines Written Before the Day Shift (Michael McGriff)

- First Language (Sharanya Manivannan)

- [asking] (Barbara Jane Reyes)

- You Begin (Margaret Atwood)

- telling our stories (Lucille Clifton)

- Shedding Skin (Harryette Mullen)

- Snowdrops (Louise Gluck)

- Compulsively Allergic to the Truth (Jeffrey McDaniel)

- Peaches (Li-Young Lee)

- No Forgiveness Ode (Dean Young)

- The Word (Tony Hoagland)

(This list, of course, is barely a beginning – bring in your own favorites!)

Exercises for use in groups

Postcards: I place a cloth on the floor, and cover it with images I have gathered over the years: postcards, old photographs, images cut from books and magazines. Let folks choose one and write the story/memory/questions that card inspires. Another option is to ask participants to choose three. After folks have selected their cards, then ask them to give one to the person at their left. (This usually results in a significant amount of groaning.) Writers spend a moment getting a sense of the way in which these new cards came together, and then write the story of these cards: "What's going on among them? Where's the point of electricity at which they seem to meet?"

Objects: Again, I lay a cloth on the floor, but this time I cover it with objects. These include a white camisole, a box of Hungarian cigarettes, a silk scarf, a silver flask, a Zippo lighter, condom, a silk flower, a baseball, an old portable camera, a rattle, a stuffed dog, a book of matches, a sand dollar, ribbons, hoop earrings, hotel-sized bottles of shampoo and conditioner, a prescription bottle, a three-strand pearl necklace, a wooden spoon, an old sewing pattern in its paper envelope, seashells, stones, suspenders, a floppy disc, and many other items. I ask participants to take enough time in considering the items to allow an item to choose them, and then to write the story that item seems to want to tell—maybe about the last time it was used, or what memory or association it brings up for them.

Smells: Bring in small containers containing a scent, like Vicks VapoRub, rosemary, coffee, vanilla extract, cinnamon, and so on. What memory or fantasy springs to mind, or bubbles up through the cracks? *Note: This prompt doesn't work for everyone, especially those who are especially sensitive to smells or have environmental sensitivities—consider using only natural fragrances rather than those created by chemical companies.*

Letters: Love letter to the body. Letter to a deity (or from a deity). Letter to an abuser. Letter to a younger self. Letter to someone who has died, or is no longer in your life. There are so many possibilities with letters. Letter to a place or a time.

Music: You can use all kinds of music as prompts—classical to pop, jazz, children's songs, music in different languages. Let your imagination flow as you listen: what can you see happening with this music? What memories or associations arise for you? What scenario does this music evoke for you? (Another idea: write a scene that seems to contrast with the music.)

Guided visualization: To prepare for this exercise, take some deep breaths, close your eyes (if you want to—closing eyes is not required) and relax. These are very gentle guided visualizations—nothing deep! You might imagine yourself "in a time before now" (as Pat Schneider says when she leads this exercise): in a car; in a bedroom; in a basement; in a garage; on a playground; in a classroom; in a kitchen; in a place of worship; in an attic; in a closet; in a hallway; on a staircase; in a shopping mall or supermarket; on a dirt road or on a highway; walking home from school—there are many other options. Choose only one for any given exercise. Spend a moment with the memory or image: Do you have a sense of how old you were? What time of year it is? Who else is there—and who isn't there? Then, when you're ready, open your eyes and begin to write.

Bookshelf as prompt: Close your eyes and pull a book off your nearest bookshelf. Without opening your eyes, open the book and put your finger down on the page. Take part of a sentence near where your finger has fallen, and use that as a starting place for some new writing. (When I tried it, I pulled down *Voices Under One Sky: Contemporary Native Literature* (Tish Fox Roman, ed.), and opened to a page with just one word on it: "Warriors." How's that for a great starting place?)

Let your day inspire you: If you're feeling especially in a rut, give yourself permission not to write. Take some 3x5 cards or a small notebook and a pen out into your day, and notice the moments when you see or hear something you'd like to write about. Just hold on to those for a few days, and when you're back at your desk, get them out and notice what they spark for you: memory or a new story, maybe? Write exactly as you're inspired to, for twenty minutes.

Developing your own exercises

The best writing exercises, according to Pat Schneider, have specificity—they begin with something concrete. *Remember: any writing prompt is just a door we use to get the pen moving, just a spark for the writer's imagination. Sometimes we stick with the prompt, and sometimes our writing goes in a completely different direction: however the writing emerges is just right! If, while writing, you find yourself getting stuck, try the phrase, "What I really want to say is..." and let yourself write what you really want to write. Follow your writing wherever it seems to want you to go.* Think of a good writing exercise as a starting block: no one runs as well when they're trying to push off from thin air.

Another thing to consider is offering specific suggestions of a direction in which to go with the writing: *Write the story of this object—write where it's been or what it would say if you asked it how it likes to be touched or held. Write what you think this image is trying to tell you, or what happened just before the image was captured on film, or what happened just after.*

Exercises sometimes don't work, and if you can find a way to get feedback from folks, that will help you shape and fix them. But if people find it hard to tell you directly about what worked or what didn't work with a writing prompt, you can still get a lot of helpful information by paying attention to the response your group has to an exercise. In my experience, if writings are vague and sort of wandering, the exercise might benefit from some honing in terms of direction and specificity. Instead of "write about how you feel when this happens," maybe ask folks to make a list of feelings, or physical embodiments of feelings, or start with a list of quotes that offer examples of feelings you want to get to. And remember:

exercises don't always have to be serious! Some of the most successful ones are funny or ridiculous.

There are tons of writing exercises and prompts out there in your neighborhood independent bookstore or nearby newsstand, in writing manuals and magazines, and, of course, online. I got ideas for exercises from writing books like *Writing Down the Bones, The Joy of Writing Sex, Writing Alone and With Others,* or resources like *The Courage to Heal, The Survivor's Guide to Sex,* and *Trauma Stewardship.* I talked with friends about ideas. I thought about particular themes that I wanted us to be able to get to and tried to come up with exercise starting points around that theme. Flip through collections of poems or books of photography, use YouTube videos or toys you found at the Goodwill.

This is just the beginning. Prompts are everywhere— overheard conversation, poems and stories that have inspired you in the past, in images and songs, on street corners, in dreams. Pick a book off the shelf, open to a random page, put your finger down, and then start writing from the word or phrase you fall upon. Everything is a potential spark for your muse.

afterword

afterword

writing our way out of the silences

Dr. Carol Queen

For a decade, at least, I've been lucky enough to work with Jen Cross as we together revived the original-to-Good Vibrations Erotic Reading Circle, a safe space for all kinds of erotic storytelling and imagining. Facilitating that wildly diverse and respectful space with her, sharing work with her, and hearing hers has been one of the purest literary pleasures of my life. And it's a deep honor to have a chance to put a fingerprint onto her opus, her beautiful, fierce, compassionate and so useful book. I know her better for reading it, as is now true of you, and turning its pages has let me look at my own history with fresh illumination.

I've long had my own source of understanding about the price of post-trauma silence, you see. Just as she entered her teen years, my mother was sexually abused by a family member. Raised in a conservative Depression-era Midwestern community, she barely understood what was happening to her, and however its effects shaped her as she grew up, she stayed silent about it for half a century. She didn't tell my father about it until they'd been married for thirty years; the perpetrator had been in their lives the whole time, and as she used to put it, she didn't want to "rock the boat."

She didn't just choose to be silent. She *was silenced*; her community—in fact all of mid-century mainstream American society—not only denied her tools, help, and a voice, but also suppressed her ability to cope with her experience. As Jen notes, "Silencing people in service to this cultural discomfort is an act of re-traumatization," and that was where my mother lived for close to sixty years.

Sexual abuse doesn't just happen to individuals, as this book makes clear, but to families and communities, and I bear my mother's experience in my own DNA. She could never talk about sex, and I have made a life and a career out of saying all the things she could never say... and then some. I do this work for many reasons, but one, inescapably, grows from the magical notion that if I only talk enough about sex, I will give my mother a voice.

Working with Jen in the Circle and knowing something about her work with Writing Ourselves Whole gives me another source of fantasy: If only my mother had picked up a pen and trusted herself to let the maelstrom of her inner emotions out. If only she could time-travel and step into Jen's living room, begin the work of letting her secret self be articulated. She did as much as she could: She got drunk and pounded the piano, externalized what was inside that way. But it didn't let my father understand what was wrong; it did not fully exorcise her pain; it did not leave me with a mother I could turn to for guidance. I raised myself, as she drank wine and created her own discordant soundtrack.

I was the one who picked up the pen. I journaled every day from the age of 12 until I got to college, and any time I needed to talk to myself thereafter, too. I instinctively knew the use of words, the way I could practice breaking silence even when I was too shy, or too weird, to find anyone else to share them with. To break through shyness, to embrace my weird, I had to take my own words, my emerging self, as seriously as I dreamed anyone else might one day take me.

I tell you all this to tell a slant truth. I don't have sexual abuse and trauma in my background in the same way that my mother did, or that Jen or many of her writers have had. But I was born female in the 1950s, began grappling with what sex meant (to me, to my culture, and yes, to my mother) in the 1960s, disposed of my virginity and came out as queer in the 1970s. I have had plenty of pressure toward silence, plenty of sex that was far from full-throatedly consensual, plenty of people who frowned on my sexual journey or presumed to tell me what I had experienced and how it was problematic.

At this point, as my hair starts streaking with silver, these are positives—my bona fides, a source of hard-won credibility. But that isn't how I've been understood the whole time, and my sources of knowledge and perspective have been viewed by some as misadventures at best. Without my notebooks—the one place I could be guaranteed space to document my experience and make sense of myself—I am far from sure I'd have been able to step into my own future. Maybe that's why the Center for Sex & Culture maintains an archive: because I know personally, intimately, how important it is to keep track, to be informed and shaped by our own documentation—both as individuals and within our communities. Every one of us deserves documentation, for we each bring a unique constellation of experience and qualities to the time in which we live our lives. And the only sure way to have this process represent us is to do it ourselves, "bring[ing] forth shards of our as-yet-unarticulated real stories and selves."

I may be making it sound as though I always had access to the words I needed. There was a time I didn't, though, and that story also reinforces what I see as vital in Jen's work. I was a teenager, well aware that my privacy wasn't really mine. Any time my parents wanted to read my journal, they could have—in fact, to this day I'm not sure if they ever did. And I was having a complicatedly consensual relationship with an older man, one that, if it were to be discovered, would put both of us in jeopardy: I'd go to juvie, he'd go to jail. The most precious secret knowledge I had access to, my earliest sexual experiences, couldn't be included in the meticulous record I made of my days. I cooked up a secret code, but marks in the margins weren't, aren't the same as writing out my changing self in longhand. To this day I mourn the absence of any record of those freshly-made memories, the power and detail of which I have just an inkling, 45 years later—almost as long a time as my mother stayed silent about her own formative secrets. "Piece by piece by piece, moment by moment, history reinforces sexual silences: physical silencings, linguistic silences, erasures." And there are still subtle ways I can't fully understand my own history, my sexual fledging, today, because memories don't stay fresh. Just as surely as my mother's trauma and confusion was bottled up, so was my transformative, transgressive sexual development.

My point, I guess, is that *many* of us need the opportunity to write our way out of silences. So many of us are given scant support from others, or have to live parts of our lives in secret so we don't rock some boat or other. "Taking a stand against a cultural meta-narrative is resistance work," says Jen, and there are so many of those narratives to trap us in one or another ill-fitting role, sexual lives that light in us no spark, locked-in selves that never allow us to glimpse the vistas of potential we might access with the right information and support. "Transformative writing is writing that changes the writer in the process of its creation," Jen says, as I instinctively tried to do through years of filling spiral notebooks… and as you, I hope, have also begun to do.

We will never be able to fully understand the impact of all the squandered capacity that trauma leaves in its wake, from the malfeasance of the individual abuser to the systemic crushing of souls and bodies in slavery, war, or their aftermaths. It's just too much to think our way past, which is why we so desperately need DIY strategies by which any persistent one of us can begin to save our singular life, starting right now. "This is you creating your own rabbit trail": You're a flesh and blood creature with an instinct for getting yourself out of the brambles. Do it. Make some tea. Spare a thought for Jen Cross, making space for us all to do this, as the first sliver of the sun shows. As she's lighting her own candle, she's thinking of you.

Then *you* think of you. Write your future self a letter and tell her everything. S/he's waiting to hear from you, you know.

San Francisco, CA
May 2017

notes

p. XI   *Dirt Cowboy Cafe*: The Dirt Cowboy Cafe opened in Hanover, NH, when I was still an undergraduate, and it immediately became my first cafe home-away-from-home. Do you have any of those—cafes where you can settle in and write for hours? Whenever I go back to the place where I went to college, it's always more important to me to make a pilgrimage to the DCC first, to say *hello* to the ghost of the young-writer-me still tucked into a table, bent over a notebook, writing and crying and writing some more.

p. XIII   Stephen King, *On Writing: A Memoir of the Craft*, New York: Pocket Books, 2002.

p. XVI   Writing as a Healing Art Workshop at Dominican University in San Rafael, CA, 2010.

p. XXIV   *Lidia Yuknavitch*: Lidia is a writer, academic, writing teacher, and wicked badass based in the Pacific Northwest. If you haven't yet read her memoir, *The Chronology of Water* (Hawthorne Books, 2010), please remedy that as soon as you can. I got to hear Lidia speak at the 2015 Association of Writers and Writing Programs Annual Conference in Minneapolis, MN. The panel was entitled "Breaking the Body: Women Writers Reconfiguring Creative Nonfiction Forms," and was moderated by (the also amazing) Melissa Febos. Lidia said, early on in her talk, "I'm not here to deliver a paper. I'm here to recruit you."

p. 8   "begin at any time to be free" from Pat Schneider, *Writing Alone and With Others*, Oxford Press, 2003, p. 11.

p. 9   "Tell all the truth but tell it slant – (1263)," *The Poems Of Emily Dickinson: Reading Edition*, ed. R. W. Franklin, Belknap Press, 1998; Ladelle McWhorter, *Bodies and Pleasures: Foucault and the Politics of Sexual Normalization* (see bibliography for details).

p. 10   "This is what I want my words to do" quote inspired by the title of Sade Murphy's poem, https://www.youtube.com/watch?v=it89Q1KrvLs (accessed May 19, 2017)

p. 12   Sweet Honey in the Rock, "Ella's Song" on *Breaths*, Chicago: Flying Fish Records, 1988.

p. 14   Joe Miller, "Goddard's Transformative Language Arts program," *Poets and Writers Magazine*, May/June 2001.

p. 27   Brian Andreas poem from *Story People*, Decorah, IA: Story People, Inc., 1997, http://www.storypeople.com/.

p. 30   "Nulla dies sine linea" attributed to Apelles of Kos, a Greek painter from the fourth century BCE; Toni Morrison, interview by Elissa Schappell with additional material from Claudia Brodsky Lacour, "Toni Morrison, The Art of Fiction, No. 134," Paris Review, Issue 128, Fall 1993.

p. 34   "boston, massachusettes," in Dorothy Allison's collection *Women Who Hate Me* (publication details in bibliography).

p. 39   Audre Lorde quote from *A Burst of Light: Essays*, Firebrand Books, 1988; Jose Ortega y Gasset quote from *Man and Crisis*, trans. Mildred Adams, New York: W. W. Norton & Co., 1962.

p. 58   Dorothy Allison, interview by Ellise Fuchs, "Interview with Dorothy Allison," in *Conversations with Dorothy Allison*, ed. Mae Miller Claxton (University Press of Mississippi, 2012), 144.

p. 60   *when I began to understand that I was an incest survivor.* How could it be that I could spend my adolescence having to have sex with my mother's husband and not understand that I was a victim of incest? It's difficult to understand—or maybe, for some of you reading, it's not. He said he wanted to help me have a healthy sexuality. He said it was for my own good. He said it was the best way for me to evolve. And then, much later, when I asked him to please stop, that I thought my sexuality was working just fine, he said all the same things, but in more violent ways. To live and survive in his house, I had to not just say what he wanted me to say, and do what he wanted me to do, but believe what he wanted me to believe: and so I tried to. It wasn't until I'd been out of his house for almost three years, living almost 1,500 miles away, that there was any room for me to even begin to contemplate a reality other than the one he demanded that I, that our whole family, accept. Little by little, the people I met and new ideas I learned chipped away at the craziness he'd instilled in me—until one day, on the phone with him, he referred to what we were doing as incest, and I had an experience of split consciousness: I understood both that he meant the word positively, as a descriptor of our evolved relationship, and also that he knew that what he'd been doing was criminal, that it was, simply, wrong.

It took another six months or so for me to begin fully breaking away from him—but that day, those fissures all ran together, and a big chunk fell out of the wall he thought he'd trapped me behind.

p. 67   *the Pat Schneider-Natalie Goldberg-Peter Elbow school of thought*: This is a reference to the "Writing Process Movement," first articulated in the 1930's by Dorothea Brande and Brenda Ueland, which entered the academy in the 1970's with the publication of *Writing Without Teachers*, and reaching the public in the 1980's in books by Pat Schneider and Natalie Goldberg. The Movement sought to refocus writing programs away from surface things like grammar, structure, thesis statements, and the like, and attend, instead, to the *process* of writing itself.

p. 68   Jane Hirschfield interview with Voice of America, "Poet Embraces Late in Life Love and Tender Sorrows," http://www.voanews.com/content/poet-embraces-late-in-life-love-tender-sorrows-132785243/162569. html (accessed January 7, 2016); Emily Dickinson quote from *Emily Dickinson: Selected Letters*, ed. Thomas H. Johnson, Belknap Press, 1986.

p. 70   Patrick Califia is a short erotic fiction writer and essayist; in the mid-90s, my dear friend gave me a copy of *Macho Sluts*, which completely upended everything I thought I knew about dirty stories..

p. 73   T.S. Eliot, *Four Quartets (consists of Burnt Norton, East Coker, The Dry Salvages, and Little Gidding)*, Harcourt, 1943.

p. 74   Kitty Tsui quote from the essay "Give Joan Chen My Phone Number Anytime" in *Lesbian Erotics*, Karla Jay, ed. (publication details in bibliography).

p. 85   *shitty first drafts and short assignments* is a reference to writing advice Anne Lamott offers in her accessible and helpful book, *Bird by Bird: Some instructions on writing and life.* New York: Anchor Books, 1995.

p. 101   *Desert Hearts*, directed by Donna Deich, Samuel Goldwyn Company, 1986.

p. 119   Joy Harjo's poem "I give you back" appears in *She Had Some Horses*, Thunder's Mouth Press, 1983.

p. 123   Brené Brown quote from "Brené Brown on Deep Shame and the Courage to be Vulnerable," *On Being* Podcast, https://www.onbeing. org/program/brené-brown-on-deep-shame-and-the-courage-to-be-vulnerable/transcript/6065 (accessed January 7, 2016); John Bradshaw, *Healing the Shame that Binds You*, Deerfield Beach, FL: Health Communications, Inc., 1988.

p. 124   Toni Morrison quote from "Toni Morrison," Claudia Tate, in *Conversations with Toni Morrison*, ed. Danille Taylor-Guthrie (Jackson, MI: University Press of Mississippi, 1994); Theodore Roethke, "The Waking," *Collected Poems of Theodore Roethke*, Knopf Doubleday, 1953.

p. 126   Mary Oliver, *A Poetry Handbook*, Mariner Books, 1994, p. 122.

p. 129   *Body Heat*: The Body Heat Femme Porn Tour is described by my dear friend and Body Heat founder Kathleen Delaney-Adams as "a national touring collective of fierce Queer smut/erotic writers, authors, performers, poets, and dancers. The tour was founded in 2007 with the hope of supporting and promoting Queer Femme visibility and desire through their contributions to erotica, the sex industry, and the sex-positive movement." I had the great pleasure of touring with Body Heat four or five times, each of which was a transformative experience, fabulous and difficult; at the close of every tour I promised myself I'd never do it again (touring can be painful for us introverts, let's just say), and then when the next opportunity came around, I always signed back up enthusiastically. I learned more about queer and femme power, recovery, and survival on those tours than anywhere else in my life, and the femmes I toured with are still my role models today.

p. 131   Dorothy Allison quote in Elizabeth Benedict's *The Joy of Writing Sex* (publication details in bibliography).

p. 141   Catherine Tufariello's powerful poem, "Useful Advice," from *Keeping My Name,* Texas Tech University Press, 2004.

p. 146   *triumphant over something inside every day that wants to kill us:* A reference to the Lucille Clifton poem, "won't you celebrate with me," from *Collected Poems of Lucille Clifton,* BOA Editions, Ltd., 1991.

p. 170   Dorothy Allison quote from her essay "Public Silence, Private Terror" in the collection *Pleasure and Danger: Exploring Female Sexuality* (publication details in bibliography).

p. 173   *push* references the novel *PUSH* by Sapphire (publication details in bibliography).

p. 200   In the section about the psychoeducational group that I facilitated, all names and identifying details have been changed.

p. 219   Mihaly Csikszentmihalyi. *Flow: The Psychology of Optimal Experience,* New York: Harper Perennial Modern Classics, 2008; Agnes de Mille, *Martha: The Life and Work of Martha Graham,* Vintage, 1992.

p. 220   Many thanks to Chris DeLorenzo of Laguna Writers (San Francisco) for introducing me to "begin again" as a prompt when I participated in his writing group back in 2004.

p. 225   Mihaly Csikszentmihalyi. *Flow: The Psychology of Optimal Experience,* New York: Harper Perennial Modern Classics, 2008; Agnes de Mille, *Martha: The Life and Work of Martha Graham,* Vintage, 1992.

p. 225   William Stafford, "For My Young Friends Who Are Afraid," in *The Way It Is: New and Selected Poems,* Graywolf Press, 1998.

bibliography

Allison, Dorothy. *Women Who Hate Me: Poems by Dorothy Allison.* Long Haul Press, 1983.

Allison, Dorothy. "Public Silence, Private Terror." In *Pleasure and Danger: Exploring Female Sexuality,* edited by Carole Vance, 103-114. London: Pandora Press, 1992.

Anzaldúa, Gloria. *Borderlands/La Frontera: The New Mestiza.* San Francisco: Spinsters/Aunt Lute, 1987.

Bass, Ellen, and Laura Davis. *The Courage to Heal: A Guide for Women Survivors of Child Sexual Abuse.* Third Edition. New York: HarperPerennial, 1994.

Benedict, Elizabeth. *The Joy of Writing Sex: A guide for fiction writers.* New York: Henry Holt and Co, 2002.

Cameron, Julia. *The Artist's Way: A Spiritual Path to Higher Creativity.* Tarcher, 1992.

Chapadjiev, Sabrina, ed. *Live Through This: On Creativity and Self Destruction.* New York: Seven Stories Press, 2012.

Cixous, Hélène. "The Laugh of the Medusa." Translated by Keith Cohen and Paula Cohen. *Signs* 1, no. 4 (1976): 875-893.

Csikszentmihalyi, Mihaly. *Flow: the Psychology of Optimal Experience.* New York: Harper Perennial Modern Classics, 2008.

De Becker, Gavin. *The Gift of Fear: And Other Survival Signals that Protect Us from Violence.* New York: Dell Publishing, 1997.

Elbow, Peter. *Writing Without Teachers.* New York: Oxford University Press, 1973.

Goldberg, Natalie. *Writing Down the Bones.* Boston: Shambhala, 1986.

Hanes, Staci. *The Survivor's Guide to Sex: How to have an empowered sex life after child sexual abuse*. San Francisco: Cleis Press, 1999.

Herman, Judith. *Trauma and* Recovery. New York: BasicBooks, 1997.

Heilbrun, Carolyn. *Writing A Woman's Life*. New York: Ballantine Books, 1988.

Richard Hugo. *The Triggering Town: Lectures and Essays on Poetry and Writing*. New York: W. W. Norton and Co., 1992.

King, Thomas. *The Truth About Stories: A Native Narrative*. Minneapolis: University of Minnesota Press, 2003.

Lamott, Anne. *Bird by Bird: Some instructions on writing and life*. New York: Anchor Books, 1995.

Lorde, Audre. *Sister/Outsider*. Trumansburg, NY: The Crossing Press, 1984.

McEwen, Christian. *World Enough & Time: On Creativity and Slowing Down*. Peterborough, NH: Bauhan Publishing, 2011.

McWhorter, Ladelle. *Bodies and Pleasures: Foucault and the Politics of Sexual Normalization*. Bloomington, IN: Indiana University Press, 1999.

Muller, Lauren and The Blueprint Collective. *June Jordan's Poetry for the People: A Revolutionary Blueprint*. New York: Routledge, 1995.

Ostriker, Alicia. "A Meditation on Metaphor." In *By Herself: Women Reclaim Poetry*, edited by Molly McQuade. Saint Paul, MN: Graywolf Press, 2000.

Pennebaker, James. *Opening Up*. New York: Wm. Morrow and Co, 1990.

Pinkola Estés, Clarissa. *Women Who Run with the Wolves: Myths and Stories of the Wild Woman Archetype*. New York: Ballantine Books, 1992.

Pierce-Baker, Charlotte. *Surviving the Silence: Black Women's Stories of Rape.* New York: W.W. Norton & Company, 1998.

Remen, Rachel Naomi. *Kitchen Table Wisdom.* New York: Riverhead Books, 2006.

Rowe, Michael. "Dorothy Allison." In *Writing Below the Belt: Conversations with Erotic Authors.* New York: Masquerade Books, Inc., 1995.

Sapphire. *PUSH.* New York: Vintage Press, 1996.

Schneider, Pat. *Writing Alone and With Others.* New York: Oxford Press, 2003.

Tsui, Kitty. "Give Joan Chen My Phone Number Anytime." In *Lesbian Erotics,* edited by Karla Jay. New York: New York University Press, 1995.

van Dernoot Lipsky, Laura. *Trauma Stewardship: An Everyday Guide to Caring for Self While Caring for Others.* San Francisco: Berrett-Koehler Publishers, 2009.

Welch, Sharon. *A Feminist Ethic of Risk.* Minneapolis: Fortress Press, 1990.

Yalom, Irvin D. *The Theory and Practice of Group Psychotherapy.* Third Edition. New York: BasicBooks, 1985.

acknowledgments

There are so many people who helped move this work and this book into the world.

First, thank you to my editor, Brenda Knight, for believing in this project and for bringing me into the Mango family! Thanks as well to copy editor Sara Giusti, for your close reading and helpful recommendations.

This book would not exist if it were not for the first San Francisco Queer Women's DOE writing group. Renee Garcia, Renee Rivera, Naomi Azriel, Judy G., and Dorian: this is for you.

Molly Eskridge, Kathleen Delaney-Adams, Anna Sofia Jaeger, Juli Hincks, Alex Cafarelli, and Lou Vaile have helped me learn, over and over, what friendship and love can mean.

I've had the amazing fortune to get to be in community with brilliant and inspiring writers. Tara Hardy, Mattilda Bernstein Sycamore, Lidia Yuknavich, Patrick Califia, Dorothy Allison, Daphne Gottlieb, Greta Christina, horehound stillpoint, Simon Shepard, Gina de Vries, Lori Selke, Philip Huang, Meliza Bañales-Van, Veronica C. Combs, Manish Vaidya, Blyth Barnow, seeley quest, Maisha Johnson, J. Mork, Nomy Lamm, Rachel Kramer Bussel, and the Lady Ms. Vagina Jenkins: you each and all inspire me every day to dig deeper, write risker, read louder, laugh harder, get messier.

Some of the pieces here are taken from my master's thesis, *Declaring Our Erotic: Using erotic writing for reclamation and resistance.* Caryn Mirriam-Goldberg and Karen Campbell, my mentors at Goddard College, taught me to question my assumptions and write into the uncomfortable places, thank goodness.

Dr. Carol Queen has been an inspiration since long before I got to sit in a room with her every month and talk with folks about erotic writing, something that astonishes me still today, even though it's been ten years now. Carol and Robert Lawrence have supported Writing Ourselves Whole since the beginning. I don't know where I'd be—or where the Bay Area would be!—without them or Center for Sex and Culture and the space the Center makes for the erotic in all its many forms.

I have to send out big love to Heart Rage, a queer solo-preneur support group, made up of, at various times, Amy Butcher, Zaedryn Meade, Sade Huron, Minna Dubin, and Julia Serano. It was Heart Rage that finally gave me the courage to get a proposal together for this book, who read over my query letters, and pushed me to get it in the mail already, and I am so thankful.

Pat Schneider, the founder of the Amherst Writers & Artists (AWA) Workshop Method, was the first person I ever felt comfortable calling Teacher (with a capital T). She taught me the importance of showing up for writers and writing with a ferocious generosity. I could not be more grateful that her words grace this book. The AWA community in the Bay Area is made up of some of the most kind, generous, and brilliant folks I've met. I am especially grateful to Peggy Simmons, Chris DeLorenzo, John Crandall, Jan Haag, and Rae Gouirand for friendship, support, kibitzing, and, always, inspiration.

Thanks to Rev. Dr. Curran Reichert, who invited me to put my feet flat on the ground, close my eyes, take some deep breaths, and change my life.

Writing Ourselves Whole has been able to partner with amazing nonprofit organizations around the SF Bay Area. I want to call out thanks especially to all the incredible activists at San Francisco Women Against Rape—and in particular, Janelle White, their steadfast Executive Director, and Lisa Thomas-Adayemo, Tabitha Sisson, Zully Batres, the (fierce and deeply-present) SFWAR Directors of Counseling with whom I've been lucky enough to work.

Writing Ourselves Whole has been a fiscally-sponsored project of Intersection for the Arts' Incubator Program since 2010. I am thankful to Intersection, and to Executive Director Randy Rollison, for their support of my work, and of the arts across the San Francisco Bay Area.

Noah and Julian give me hope for the next generation of men.

My mother, Rita Sherman, and my father, Neal Cross, have supported me and this work in more ways than they can know.

My sister, Sarah Cross, is the biggest reason I do anything at all, ever.

Ellen LaPointe makes me laugh, loves with spacious abandon, and meets every day with an open-hearted kindness that I never knew possible. *Those birds are still loving you.*

And, not at all least, I am beyond-words grateful to every single writer with whom I've had the good fortune to write. Thank you, always, for your words.

about Jen Cross

A widely-anthologized writer and performer, Jen Cross has facilitated sexuality and sexual trauma survivors writing workshops for over a decade. Jen has devoted her career and creative life to exploring the power of writing and creative community to catalyze individual development as well as healing.

In 2003, Jen founded Writing Ourselves Whole, an organization that offers Amherst Writers & Artists writing workshops, creating spaces in which the true and complicated stories of the body can emerge. Jen has worked with hundreds of writers, through private workshops and in collaboration with colleges, social change organizations and other institutions throughout the U.S., including at Stanford University, Wesleyan University, the University of California at Davis, Dartmouth College, the University of California at San Francisco, Brown University, Goddard College, the University of Oregon at Eugene, Evergreen State University, Southern Oregon University; the Power of Words/ Transformative Language Arts Network annual conference; the Femme Conference; Survivorship and the Survivorship annual conference; San Francisco Women Against Rape; Bay Area Women Against Rape; Community United Against Violence; and at many other community organizations, bookstores, and schools.

Jen's writing appears in more than fifty publications, including *The Healing Art of Writing, Nobody Passes, Visible: A Femmethology, Best Sex Writing 2008, make/ shift, Sinister Wisdom,* and *Fourteen Hills;* she is also the co-editor of the award-winning *Sex Still Spoken Here* (with Dr. Carol Queen and Amy Butcher). She lives with her beloved and family in Northern California.

Printed in the USA
CPSIA information can be obtained
at www.ICGtesting.com
JSHW031703140824
68134JS00036B/3503